P9-ARJ-722

Contemporary Educational Theory

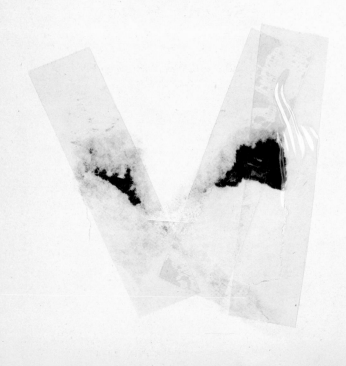

Contemporary Educational Theory

Robert E. Mason

*Southern Illinois University
at Edwardsville*

DAVID McKAY COMPANY, INC.
New York

CARL A. RUDISILL LIBRARY
LENOIR RHYNE COLLEGE

370.973
M38c
85604
Nov. 1923

CONTEMPORARY EDUCATIONAL THEORY

Copyright © 1972 by David McKay Company, Inc.

All rights reserved, including the right to
reproduce this book, or parts thereof, in any
form, except for the inclusion of brief quotations
in a review.

Library of Congress Catalog Card Number: 75–186554

DESIGNED BY JAMES GUTTILLA

Manufactured in the United States of America

Preface

EDUCATIONAL POLICY is expressed through a complicated network of bureaucratic ritual. Even so, its source is in the ideas men have about how their young should be readied for the future. A working assumption of this book is that the proposals which engage wide popular and professional support in a given period gain such support because they express a content, a method, a conception of purpose which large numbers of people consider important. Of course, factors of press agentry, deliberate manipulation of public and professional opinion, and the power of the economic marketplace are assumed to be at work. But it is assumed also that free critical public and professional opinion remains both source and court of last appeal in the assessment of educational proposals—at least in the United States in the twentieth century. Upon this ground, then, proposals are treated as possessing a claim to truth and goodness. The pages that follow assess these intellectual and moral claims.

Today there is need for serious study of educational theory. What follows is important and relevant to the major problems of schooling in contemporary America. Educational policy is not the product of mindless political and economic forces shaped by institutions impervious to thoughtful human control. We still believe that men, by taking thought, can and do shape institutions. This book, then, lays out for inspection some things worth thinking about, for it treats of what has happened in American schools in this century as product of human intelligence at work on the question, "What shall we teach our young, and how shall this be done?"

Edwardsville, Illinois
January 1972

Contents

Introduction

FROM 1900 TO 1970 five different systems of educational theory strongly influenced schooling of children and adolescents in the United States. This book explains in some detail each of the five theories by describing and analyzing social events including published writings of persons advocating a particular theory's adoption. Thus each theory is treated as a social movement and a historical event. The chronological time of the movement and historical and social characteristics of its period are discussed. Major exponents and their writings are identified, and attention is given to formulation and explanation of the bibliography representative of each theory. Intellectual sources, both historical and current, are pointed out. Each theory is then reviewed with special reference to notions about human nature, values for living, crucial characteristics of reliable knowledge, and how we learn. Finally, and in summary, applications of the theory to schooling of children and adolescents is stated according to the educational aims, curricula, and method advocated.

The five theoretical movements to be thus discussed are:

I. The Liberal Arts Tradition
II. Progressive Education
III. The Structure of the Disciplines Movement

IV. Neo-Behaviorism
 V. Humanistic Psychology

A section is devoted to each of the above, the five headings constituting the five major divisions of this book. Discussion of each of the five is organized as follows:

A. Meaning of the title
   —other terms ascribed to the movement
   —explanation
B. Chronological period of the movement
   —difficulties in fixing chronology
   —narrow versus broad construction
C. Historical and social characteristics of the period
   —features of the movement seemingly inspired by contemporary social trends
   —features of the movement appearing to be a reaction against dominant social trends of the period
D. Theory supporting the movement
   —primary exponents
   —major writings
   —intellectual sources
   —descriptive statement of the theory—human nature, values for living, knowledge, learning
E. Educational applications
   —educational aims
   —curriculum
   —method

The justification for selecting these five topics as representative of twentieth-century educational theory is itself a theme developed and tested by the content of the entire book.

NINETEENTH-CENTURY BACKGROUNDS

The public school system of the United States at the outbreak of World War II (1939) was about one hundred years old. It had its inception in the fourth and fifth decades of the nineteenth century (1830–1850). During the first half of the nineteenth century the common man—the practical man of action—came into his own. Nineteenth-century farmers and trappers apparently believed that no man was absolutely wiser than another. The "three Rs" school expressed this notion; schooling meant training in basic skills, not necessarily in the arts of citizenship. Historic names of the public school movement are of the Jacksonian era: Horace Mann graduated from Brown University in 1819; Henry Barnard taught in Connecticut while Jackson was in the White House; Calvin Wiley graduated from the University of North Carolina in 1840; Caleb Mills began work at Wabash College in 1833. These men and others of like mind led in the definition of the scope, purpose, and philosophy of the American public, tax-supported school. They themselves were not men of the soil; they were intellectuals, in many cases motivated by missionary zeal. Nevertheless, these humanitarian leaders in the early-nineteenth-century public school movement succeeded in persuading legislators of the value of the common school.

The accomplishment of the educational evangelists in the train of Horace Mann before the Civil War was to establish the school as a public institution in the United States. They saw the public school as a powerful force contributing to the growing strength of a free society. However, various nineteenth-century cultural influences worked to restrict and limit the social functions of the schools.

Few of the leaders of the public school movement were themselves supporters of Jackson, but the movement achieved success during and after Jackson's presidency. Although the ardent supporters of Jackson gave little attention to public education, the one-room district school was, nevertheless, a part of the total social movement of the frontier which Jacksonian democracy represents. Jeffersonian democracy had involved the idea that political thinking and education for citizenship had no relation to religion. Jacksonian democracy apparently underwrote this, but added that political wisdom had no relationship to educational background and moral or philosophical outlook. There was no rule of religion in the Puritan sense; moreover, there was no rule of reason in the sense of the Enlightenment.

Howard K. Beale has suggested that while the evangelical frontier churches fostered an interest in education for literacy so that people could read the Bible, the emphasis upon emotional revelation carried with it a distrust of knowledge in social, moral, and religious areas. This influence persisted, according to Beale, so that a characteristic American trait is a tendency to take an emotional rather than an intellectual approach to important problems. A certain pervading anti-intellectualism has been fed by a tradition suggesting that too much learning proves a device of the Devil. Furthermore, claims Beale, the devotion to the Book fostered a certain authoritarianism, an acceptance of the Word rather than critical analysis and discussion.[1] The thrust of Beale's argument is that evangelicism, like Jacksonian political ideas, fostered artificial distinctions of the parts of knowledge. Political wisdom was thought to have relationship neither to

[1] Howard K. Beale, A *History of Freedom of Teaching in American Schools,* Report of the Commission on the Social Studies of the American Historical Association (New York: Charles Scribner's Sons, 1941), pp. 70–71.

book learning nor to religious nurture. Evangelical mysticism encouraged this compartmentalization by its emphasis on the possibility of knowledge of ultimate things by cataclysmic, emotional revelation. The revivals and camp meetings spread throughout the frontier country. In these emotional experiences, people believed that they found truth through their mystical experiences with the divine source of all wisdom. Thus, for people who saw the big moral and philosophical questions as settled not so much by thinking and study as by direct communion with God in prayer, the school did not need to give much attention to moral and philosophical problems.

Another cultural influence that tended to restrict the social role of the nineteenth-century school was the fierce antagonisms among revivalist sects. As communities grew larger and less homogeneous, it often became difficult for parents to find common religious ground. One reason why the schools eventually lost their religious orientation was that each sect became convinced that only a policy of religious neutrality would keep out the heresies of its rivals.[2] Each one thought it had the truth; if Methodists, Presbyterians, Baptists, and Congregationalists were to send their children to the same school, they were going to see to it that the beliefs of their children in matters of faith and morals were not undermined. Thus, a neutral public school, concentrating on reading, writing, and arithmetic, was necessary. The nonreligious, nonpolitical common school was resorted to partly because of the supicions of interest groups toward one another. The compromise was to exclude both politics and religion.[3]

Again, the general acceptance of the "graded school" after

[2] Ibid., pp. 208 ff.
[3] Ibid.

the Civil War encouraged formalized, factual presentation of subject matter. Graded schools made it necessary to measure the accomplishments of pupils to determine promotion. Memorization of facts could be measured, but development of ethical character could not be. Consequently, the "school machine" came to rest on facts and memorization of facts. Book assignments and recitation which was reproduction on call was the mode. The teacher, in turn, was under the control of a printed course of study, prescribed textbooks, and standardized examinations.[4] This educational practice, while frequently involving rote memorization of materials having some sort of moral significance, was not a practice that involved either students or teachers in value problems. The facts of history and government, but not citizenship, were the concern. Words printed in books, not understanding of the world around them, received the attention of children in the schools.[5] According to Reisner, every movement for school reform from the time of the Civil War to the years of the Great Depression was aimed at the mechanical system fostered by the graded school.[6]

Finally, an effort to locate the ideological and cultural foundations of educational theory in the nineteenth century cannot ignore the growing influence of the philosophy of reason of the Enlightenment and the impact of German idealism upon American intellectuals. Apparently Horace Mann looked upon impartiality as a positive educational value. He argued that the school must be above partisan rivalries; his view was that it is not the job of the school to inculcate opinions and beliefs. The school is dedicated to the pursuit of truth, and this means the ability to see a problem whole,

---

[4] E. H. Reisner, *The Evolution of the Common School* (New York: The Macmillan Co., 1930), p. 427.

[5] Ibid., pp. 537–538.

[6] Ibid., p. 428.

and impartially.[7] Henry Barnard, like Mann, consistently maintained during the Civil War period, as in the debates preceding the war, that the educator must remain nonpartisan and aloof, and that political differences lie outside the field of educational effort and discussion.[8] Neutrality, aloofness, and disinterestedness were educational values to which Barnard maintained high loyalty.[9] Again, William Torrey Harris, the most powerful leader in American public education after the Civil War, stressed the objectivity of truth and the importance of discipline and authority in schoolwork. While he and those who understood his philosophy were concerned about the moral effects of discipline and authority, classroom teachers were likely to interpret it in the narrow sense. For Harris emphasized authority, discipline, and traditional subject matter; such discipline and authority, he reasoned, encouraged self-realization in the lofty sense.

SCIENCE VERSUS THE HUMANITIES BEFORE WORLD WAR II

Theory affecting the high school before 1900 drew especially on notions such as those expressed by William Torrey Harris. The generally educated man was the liberally educated man; he knew the classical languages and had become familiar with the Great Books. High school should carry a young person as far as possible into this domain. Consequently, small country high schools early in the twentieth century taught much Latin, a little Greek, English and a few American literary masterpieces, and Greek, Roman, and

[7] Merle E. Curti, *The Social Ideas of American Educators*, Report of the Commission on the Social Studies of the American Historical Association, Part X (New York: Charles Scribner's Sons, 1935), p. 126.

[8] Ibid., p. 164.

[9] Ibid., pp. 166 ff.

European history. At best, the young people who completed
the course could write clearly and express themselves simply
and effectively. Moreover, they were committed to the moral
code of the Judeo-Christian ethic; they worked hard and
paid their debts. The relatively simple curriculum of the high
school at the turn of the century was concentrated on the
transmission to the young of the essentials of the moral tradition of Western civilization.

When education is looked upon as an endeavor carried
on in the light of tradition and involving transmission to the
young of the essentials of that tradition, it has unmistakable
direction and purpose. Teachers know what their objectives
are. They are in a position to devote their time and energies
to refining techniques for preserving and extending established tradition. The job of the schools, then, is to conserve
and extend the good, true, and beautiful things of life. The
curriculum of the American secondary school of the latter
nineteenth and early twentieth century supported an idealistic view of human nature. The notion was that mind is the
unique and precious part of man which deserves most of all
to be cultivated, and that man's purpose on earth is to use
his mind in the service of God and mankind. Not always—
for empty and rote verbiage was a curse of the late-nine-
teenth- and early-twentieth-century schools as of those of
today—but at best the upper division of the American school
system in the latter nineteenth century pushed young people
back to consider some of the fundamental problems of existence—questions having to do with the meaning of life, the
nature and destiny of man, the nature of the universe in
which men spend their days, and the natural abode which
forms their habitat.

By the end of the first decade of the twentieth century,
however, this conception of the role and purpose of schools
was being severely challenged in the name of the new sci-

ences of man. A scientific, experimental approach to education which de-emphasizes, leaves out, or sometimes clashes outright with the poetic dramatic approach to education based on tradition and religion was being forwarded by a significant group of scholars and educationists in America.

Historically, science made its first impact in material and technological fields. In astronomy and geology, men came to view the physical world as the product not of creative fiat but of long ages of gradual growth and development, in which chance had played a great part. The discovery of the "human equation" in physical measurements, evidence that matter and energy cannot be clearly separated, and—in biology—evidence that plant and animal forms cannot be clearly differentiated shook the former confidence of men in an ordered universe operating according to some fixed design. Even while physics, chemistry, botany, and zoology developed autonomy as separate "subjects" in school and college curricula, research and theory in these fields increasingly demonstrated the difficulty in discovering in the nature of things the essential differences between physical, chemical, botanical, and zoological change.

The latter nineteenth century saw tremendous strides in hybridization and plant and animal husbandry. Medicine became an experimental, laboratory science in the early years of the twentieth century. An experimental approach to the human and social fields began after 1900 as psychology, sociology, political science, economics, and education became independent fields of scholarly specialization.

At the turn of the century, through the epoch-making influence of thinkers such as William James and G. Stanley Hall, naturalistic, experimental psychology had its beginnings. In social studies and history, the work of such scholars as Carl Becker, James Harvey Robinson, and Charles Beard reflected the influence of science, naturalism, and evolutionary theory. In fact, the naturalistic, experimental, scientific outlook gained more and more headway in all areas of American intellectual life. It would thus be surprising indeed if theory and practice of public education had not shown the influence of such trends. Those who gave their major professional attention to the direct study of education as a human enterprise were, understandably, impressed by the apparent success of experimental scientific methods in the study of man himself. Scientists applying their intellectual methods to the study of man apparently provided evidence that disposition, temperament, intelligence were directly influenced by body chemistry. Experimentalists in anatomy and physiology found many direct similarities among the mechanisms of plant, animal, and human bodies.

Thus, psychology, literally the "science of the soul," came to be based upon chemical, anatomical, and physiological investigations of human behavior.

Edward H. Reisner, to whom reference has already been made, considers that the groundwork for the naturalistic movement in educational theory was laid as early as 1890. He cites William James' *Principles of Psychology*, published in 1890, as the first statement of a new viewpoint in psychology taking its fundamental concepts from Darwinian evolution. This work, according to Reisner, had great influence on educators and psychologists in the United States. He suggests that by the turn of the century it had come to be generally accepted by leaders in American educational work.[10] In 1916 John Dewey published *Democracy and Education* which was based on the notion of man as a natural biological organism.

Thus, on the one hand, we find the turn-of-the-century schools, and in particular the high schools, influenced by idealism and the liberal arts tradition as worked out by think-

---

[10] Reisner, *Evolution of the Common School*, p. 487.

ers such as Harris. At the same time, however, in the scholarship of James and Dewey, an attack on this educational tradition was embodied in the new sciences of man arising out of evolution. During the first half of the twentieth century—that is, through World War II—these two theoretical movements competed for the allegiance of American schoolteachers. Topics I and II of this book ("The Liberal Arts Tradition" and "Progressive Education") treat of these two movements. The discussion of these two topics comprises what might be called an analysis and interpretation of *American educational theory before World War II* or *American educational theory during the first half of the twentieth century.*

The course of American educational theory during the early decades of the twentieth century is to be understood as centering in the controversy over whether education is to be guided by science and a philosophy based thereon. Robert Maynard Hutchins, to whom extensive reference is made in subsequent pages, saw Dewey and progressive education as the enemy of the liberal arts.

In the light of the conflicting philosophical voices claiming to speak for public education in his day, Dewey identified two major positions:

I see but two alternatives between which education must choose if it is not to drift aimlessly. One of them is expressed by the attempt to induce educators to return to the intellectual methods and ideals that arose centuries before the scientific method was developed. The appeal may be temporarily successful in a period when general insecurity, emotional and intellectual as well as economic, is rife. For under these conditions the desire to lean on fixed authority is active. Nevertheless, it is so out of touch with all the conditions of modern life that I believe it is folly to seek salvation in this direction. The other alternative is systematic utilization of scientific method as the pattern and ideal of intelligent exploration and exploitation of the potentialities inherent in experience.[11]

EDUCATIONAL THEORY SINCE MID-CENTURY

Since the middle of the twentieth century, power, rather than individual cultivation, service to humanity, or aesthetic exercise, has become a habit of mind, and has come to function increasingly as an assumed criterion of excellence. World War II demonstrated that Germans and Japanese could build, maintain, and operate highly sophisticated military technology. With the end of the war it was increasingly evident that the United States could not assume continuing superiority over the Soviet Union, this realization dramatized in the shock of demonstration in the 1950s that Russia was ahead in nuclear technology if not in basic research. Moreover, continuing unrest at home among ethnic and minority groups as well as labor and political organizations representing ostensibly disadvantaged sectors of the society dampened optimistic assumptions. Unemployment, poverty, crime remained as the streams and the air became increasingly polluted.

The possibility arose that world leadership of the United States might be challenged, and that American social institutions might not survive the strains. That America might, after all, be vulnerable occurred to some for the first time. The power which advanced technology of production and communication generated possessed frightening and confusing manifestations, but even more impressive were the demonstrations that people supporting moral and political values quite different from our own might be as powerful as we.

World War II marked the end of the great European

[11] John Dewey, *Experience and Education* (New York: The Macmillan Co., 1938), p. 108.

colonial empires. As new nations clamored for admission to the United Nations the dismantling of Queen Victoria's British Empire proceeded apace. Although the United States did not officially annex any new territory, she became the unofficial custodian of the entire non-Communist world. The war in Vietnam was to secure American interests in Southeast Asia.

The United States took on the task of one of the great historic world powers after World War II. After mid-century American leadership functioned in the heritage of Alexander, the Caesars, and Charlemagne. The nation came to be led by an oligarchy; no one member had the heroic superiority of Alexander or Augustus, but the nation was doing what they had done. The United States took on the task of shaping the world for its national interests, in its behalf, in massive rivalry with the Soviet Union, and with China as a third contender for a role as a world power.

Schools as Instruments of National Purpose

In this view the tendency for educational standards to be shaped in the perspective of national destiny increased. Thus, more and more, a bright youngster coming along in school was thought of not as a future poet, painter, musician, literary critic, religious leader, philosopher, novelist, or even statesman. He was first thought of as a physicist, technician, engineer—a prophet and priest of technological power. Production and creativity were thought of as production of great machines and creation of new technologies.

To the schools fell the task of inducting the young into a civilization at once transformed yet threatened by the knowledge explosion and the race for power. As Francis Chase put it:

One of the functions of formal education has always been to

bring men (especially the rising generations) into possession of the culture; that is to say, of the world created out of the ideas of men. This function is more difficult today than at any time in mankind's past. Not only is the culture itself incredibly more complex and specialized than was true of a few decades past, but disjunctions in society have intensified and multiplied the demands for education. The present demands incorporate the old need to help man gain mastery of himself and free himself from the tyranny of external circumstances, but now for the first time, "man" means *all* men, and the external circumstances are global rather than local.[12]

The level of intellectual competence of the entire society rose enormously after mid-century. Moreover, a sizable and fairly powerful intellectual elite developed in a nation historically equalitarian and given to prejudiced attitudes toward intellectuals. A new white-collar middle class emerged made up of individuals who earned their livings in what came to be called the knowledge industry, persons for whom an analytical approach to problems was a way of life, persons who were at home with abstractions and generalizations.

Burton Clark referred to the new culture as "the expert society." [13] Elijah Jordan, and more recently James McClellan, referred to it as "the corporate society." [14] America became a highly regulated economy and an organizational society of an era of automated production. It became increasingly urban

[12] Francis S. Chase, "School Change in Perspective," in *The Changing American School*, ed. John I. Goodlad. The Sixty-Fifth Yearbook of the National Society for the Study of Education, Part II (Chicago: University of Chicago Press, 1966), pp. 275–276.

[13] Cf. Burton R. Clark, *Educating the Expert Society* (San Francisco: Chandler Publishing Co., 1962).

[14] Cf. Elijah Jordan, *The Good Life* (Chicago: University of Chicago Press, 1949); George Barnett and Jack Otis, *Corporate Society and Education: the Philosophy of Elijah Jordan* (Ann Arbor: University of Michigan Press, 1962); Solon T. Kimball and James E. McClellan, *Education and the New America* (New York: Random House, 1963).

and industrial. Organizations became larger and more complexly interlocked.

From 1940 to 1965 the population grew from 132 million to about 190 million—nearly one-third. Urban areas received most of this increase but the growth occurred around the old cities in the suburban fringes, not within the city limits. The central cities came to be populated mainly by ethnic minority groups with particularly large Negro concentrations in the great cities of the Northeast, Midwest, and South.

Although the population increased by less than one-third from 1940 to 1965, the number of government employees more than doubled in the period. The amount of federal taxes doubled from the end of World War II to the mid-1960s, and state and local taxes increased sixfold.[15] To meet the demands for conceptual competence and sophisticated organizational finesse, operating expenses of institutions of higher learning increased ninefold between 1938 and 1958. Large universities were looked upon as centers of a knowledge industry related at myriad points to government and business in sponsorship and sources of subsidization, with "spin-off" into the economy. That is, the university came to function as an important institution of capital investment; the knowledge industry was viewed as capital, coordinate with national resources and machines.

Many more areas of life came to be planned than in the past. The impact of such planning on individuals was usually through a government agency, but government was so dependent on big business, labor, and education that a vast network of interlocking organizations exercised influence.

Despite inflation and the large stratum of disadvantaged

[15] J. Steele Gow, Jr., Burkart Holzner, and William C. Pendleton, "Economic, Social, and Political Forces," in *The Changing American School,* ed. John I. Goodlad. The Sixty-Fifth Yearbook of the National Society for the Study of Education (Chicago: University of Chicago Press, 1966), p. 171.

poor, real income rose. The 1960 median in real income was double that of 1941. Combined with the rise in educational level and the impact of large organizations on daily living, it might be suggested that America was becoming a vast middle class of bureaucratic functionaries. There is question, however, whether this resulted in a more democratic society, for there was considerable evidence of strained, even frenetic, status seeking.

Formal higher education became an increasingly important factor in economic mobility, the young college graduate with some expert credential not infrequently being hired at a salary considerably above that of workers of less education with many years of experience. Moreover, as Gow, Holzner, and Pendleton put it:

In addition to specific occupational skills, social techniques of relating to others, of adjusting to the imperatives of life in formal organizations and between formal organizations have become increasingly important. Modern man must be able to present himself well, he must understand the subtleties of manipulating organizational relationships.[16]

Evidence showed that chances for occupational and social advancement were determined early in life by the amount and quality of formal education achieved. Many parents became convinced of this. Thus, strong pressure was exerted on youngsters to achieve in the competition for marks of educational success. Formal education yielded hard cash and social status. No longer was its purpose to develop the person, to extend the horizons of knowledge, to pursue truth as a good of beauty and nobility. Education entered the marketplace; teachers became the vendors; much haggling and bargaining ensued. Here is an important clue to the transforma-

---

[16] Ibid., p. 177.

tion of the school after mid-century. Measures of educational success became marketable commodities of considerable price. Teachers were pressed to become persons expert in the techniques of the marketplace to fulfill their role effectively.

Interestingly enough, the techniques of the market in postwar America were highly indirect and full of the hypocrisy of traditional polite societies. Decision-makers were members of a functional elite, their tenure in positions of power dependent upon their capacity to work smoothly within the organizational structure. Social finesse was crucial; the American style of leadership was transformed into a new version of the traditional indirection of polite societies.

Industries such as agriculture and mining which have been taken to represent hard, honest toil declined in relative importance while activities such as finance, communications, and public service increased. Note that these latter activities, again, were those which placed a premium on manipulation of symbols, analysis of systems and social finesse. Highly skilled, high-income white-collar occupations—managers, officials, proprietors, professional, technical—showed the greatest percentage increase. Higher than average unemployment rates prevailed in construction, mining, forestry and fisheries, and trade. Lower than average rates characterized service trades, government, finance, and public utilities. The highest unemployment rates were among fourteen- to nineteen-year-olds and nonwhites. Unemployment varied inversely with the number of school years completed and income directly with years of education completed.

There was some indication that flexibility was more important than mastery of specific skills, this because of the rapid obsolescence of many specific specialties. Thus, what was sought was not the specialization involved in highly specific trade and technical training but specialization as mastery of intellectual skills.

This way, formal education became an important factor in regional economic growth, producing and selecting persons to fill the roles.

The schools find themselves in a strategic place in the American social structure by being not only the agencies that provide general education to the masses but also that select persons and, at the higher levels, even award social status through academic degrees, which have a very real meaning in modern society.[17]

Except for the very lowest socioeconomic strata (i.e., inhabitants of Negro ghettos in the great cities, residents of Appalachia, and the Latin American and Indian minorities in the Southwest), class distinction based on race, religion, national origin, and family socioeconomic background were reduced. Success in formal education and social competence were rewarded. Thus, in an extreme way, high social mobility in a highly organized bureaucratic society accentuated competition and placed an inordinately high value on education and other status symbols.

Changes in the Teaching Profession

By any measurable criterion, the caliber of teachers rose after World War II. Most were college graduates whereas before the war between three and four years of post-high school formal education was the norm. The median age rose after the war; more men entered the field, and real income was markedly higher. A larger number of men entered elementary teaching, and with a median age of 45.5 years for women and 33.6 years for men in 1961, it was clear that teaching had become a life commitment for a majority of the members of the profession. Before the war, teaching had been a career for unmarried women, and the median

[17] Ibid., p. 191.

ages of both elementary and secondary school teachers had been below 30. Unquestionably, teaching, after the war, had become an occupation chosen as a life work by thousands of college graduates. Gordon Lee, dean of the College of Education at the University of Washington, said in 1966:

> . . . in terms of the role he plays, it is unmistakable that the American teacher in the 1960's is fast becoming something markedly different from his counterpart of thirty years before. Three central characteristics appear to be gaining in prominence, and it is abundantly evident that, to the extent that these become predominant, the position and the function of the American teacher are transformed. The three characteristic elements are: *specialization*—the concentration of focus and energy upon a narrower range of subjects and responsibilities; *intellectualization*— the assignment of clear priority, within the process of formal education, to the cultivation and refinement of the ability to use the basic disciplines; and *continuity*—the recognition of true education as continuous, self-generating, and independent.[18]

The teacher-training course was a tougher one than before 1950. More courses in science and the liberal arts were required. Faculty and administration outside the School of Education took more interest in it. Moreover, the conception of teaching as continuous inquiry gained considerable currency. That is, the notion of teaching as the fusion of research, scholarship, and teaching, with students seen as apprentices in learning the disciplines of inquiry—the idealized model of the career of the university professor—was to some degree extended downward to the lower schools. There was a somewhat greater tendency to think of teachers as scholars and

[18] Gordon C. Lee, "The Changing Role of the Teacher," in *The Changing American School*, ed. John I. Goodlad. The Sixty-Fifth Yearbook of the National Society for the Study of Education, Part II (Chicago: University of Chicago Press, 1966), pp. 24–25.

to expect that they demonstrate the vitality of scholarship in their vocational demeanor. The school curriculum was considered to be constituted of the major disciplines of scholarly inquiry and teachers were expected to inculcate the methods of scholarship in children and youth. The tools and methods of teaching, while resting heavily on such ancient means as books, talk, and written communication, came to include electronic data processors, film, television, and radio, and an array of teaching machines. Mere mechanical familiarity with the technical devices contemporary teachers were supposed to use constituted in and of itself an extensive body of knowledge. Finally, the diagnostic, clinical, and therapeutic instruments used by school guidance and counseling officers became so technical that these people more and more constituted a special group of professional staff psychologists. The trend in training policy was to produce counseling and guidance specialists with training quite different from that of classroom teachers.

Three Movements—Curriculum, Method, Guidance

In the postwar milieu described above, the old argument over the relative merits of the liberal arts vs. progressive education receded in significance. The new preoccupations were with power, national survival and destiny, business and industrial growth. During the 1950s and 1960s, against the background of a society preoccupied with power, a large number of academic scholars and a few leading educationists participated in a sustained effort to locate and define the basic structural elements of each of the major academic disciplines. These were to be organized according to their inner relationships to one another in making up a given intellectual discipline. The notion was that teaching in the schools should not impart to the young large bodies of information, or even skill as such, but mastery of the fundamental concepts of each subject field—mathematics, physics, chemistry, biology, history, and so on. This movement is called the *Structure of the Disciplines Movement*. It is also variously referred to as *Concept Teaching* or *Concept Learning*, and some have been fond of using the term *Inquiry* or *Inquiry Teaching* to refer to it. The names of Jerome Bruner and Joseph Schwab may be associated with this movement.

The structure of the disciplines movement is the third theory discussed in this book. It became important as such only after World War II, and has strongly influenced revisions of school curricula in a number of basic academic fields.

Inspired by the quest for knowledge as power, but embodying a special preoccupation with behavioral competence, another significant theoretical movement affecting teaching method in particular emerged after World War II. The emphasis in this instance was on learning as behavior modification. The question always asked was, "If a student has really learned something, what can he *do* now that he could not *do* before?" "What are the behavioral objectives of this course? of this lecture? How will you determine whether students have learned? What are the criteria? Exactly what will be the tests of learning?" Quite obviously, this suggests the psychology of behaviorism, which had been popular in the early part of the century, and some of the notions about teaching method hark back to Thorndike. The names of B. F. Skinner, Robert Glaser, and Jerome Mechner are associated with its more recent resurgence. The term *Neo-Behaviorism* has been applied to it, and since there has been considerable interest in the use of machines, it has been referred to as *teaching machine* theory. Professor Skinner used the technical term *operant conditioning* in developing his methodology. *Programmed Instruction*—as teaching machines require careful programming—is another term that refers to this general point of view and emphasis. *Neo-behaviorism,* then, is the designation used for the fourth theory discussed in this book. It became important as such after World War II at about the same time as the structure the disciplines movement was gaining popularity. The two are not clearly connected theoretically, however. Rather, they are different ways of responding to a concern about teaching more, teaching faster, and teaching more thoroughly. The underlying theories of the *structure of the disciplines movement* and *neo-behaviorism* are quite different. Both, however, emphasize competence and subject-matter mastery, the former influencing curriculum reconstruction in particular, the latter involving somewhat more explicit reference to method.

The fifth and final topic treated in chapters to follow has been most influential in school guidance and counseling circles. It appears in many ways to be a protest against the concentration on power, mastery, efficiency, and technical prowess emphasized so strongly by the *structure of the disciplines* advocates and the *neo-behaviorists.* It stresses the person—his feelings, hopes, fears, aspirations. Many of its advocates come out of a background of clinical psychology and consider psychology their major field of academic competence. As psychologists, however, they pride themselves on being primarily concerned about human beings, human experience, and the human condition. Hence the movement is called *Humanistic Psychology.* Because there is a strong interest in existential philosophy among some proponents of this theory, it is sometimes referred to as *Existential Psychology* or an *existential* point of view. The name of Carl Rogers, who advocated *nondirective counseling,* is an important one connected with *humanistic psychology.* Other leading advocates of this position are Abraham Maslow and Gordon Allport.

SUMMARY

This book is a treatment of "contemporary" or "twentieth-century" educational theory. Educational ideas discussed are ones that have affected the work of schools since 1900. Five theories, treated as social-historical movements, are discussed in this book. The first two, *the liberal arts tradition* and *progressive education,* were important mainly before World War II. The last three, *the structure of the disciplines movement, neo-behaviorism,* and *humanistic psychology,* have been important mainly since World War II.

In the years before World War II *the liberal arts tradition* and *progressive education* were very much opposed to one another. They were strongly competing or conflicting theories. After World War II we find *the structure of the disciplines movement* and *neo-behaviorism* not so much in opposition to one another but, rather, representing somewhat different approaches to similar educational ends: increased competence, efficiency, and intellectual power. There would appear to be opposition between *humanistic psychology* (the third postwar theory) and the other two, however. For the counselors advocating the viewpoint of humanistic psychology insist that the individual person—his feelings, his self-image—is far more important than either behavioral competence or intellectual mastery per se.

Probably important distinctions are likely to be blurred and confused if great effort is made to find similarities among the five theories. This much may be said, however. *Progressive education* before mid-century, and the *structure of the disciplines movement* and *neo-behaviorism* after 1950, make much more of science, the scientific method, experimentation and the experimental method than do the other two views. The *liberal arts tradition* and *humanistic psychology* seem to build more on art, literature, religion, poetry, and the realms of feeling and imagination than do the other three theories. Consequently, it might be suggested that the book examines three different types of scientific educational theory (*progressive education,* the *structure of the disciplines movement,* and *neo-behaviorism*) and two different types of humanistic educational theory (the *liberal arts tradition* and *humanistic psychology*).

I

The Liberal Arts Tradition

To POSSESS the ability to do something—build a house, play the violin, swim the breaststroke—is to command an art. The shoemaker has mastered the art of making shoes; the pianist, the art of playing the piano. Ancient Greek society, in which the idea of the liberal arts originated, distinguished between free men and slaves. Nonetheless, a slave who exhibited qualities deemed characteristic of a free man was sometimes given his freedom and the rights of citizenship. A free man was obligated to practice the arts of freedom. That is, he was to think clearly and logically, speak effectively, and read analytically. He was also supposed to have some knowledge of the world in which he lived, of human nature, and the ways in which the universe operated. He could not be a free man—that is, he could not exercise the necessary arts of freedom—unless he could read, think, and speak reasonably and with knowledge. Hence, the education of a free man, in contrast to the training of an artisan or slave, centered in grammar, rhetoric, and logic, with some attention also to mathematics, music, literature, and the sciences. The purpose of such an education was not to prepare a man for some economic vocation, but to prepare him for the moral life in which he used his disciplined intelligence in making choices affecting his nation, his family, and himself.

The fundamental purpose of liberal education was to produce the good man—the man who made right choices.

The word *liberal* comes from the stem *liber,* meaning "free." The liberal arts are the arts of freedom or the arts of the free man. This notion of freedom is incorporated in the conception of purpose surrounding study of literature, languages, and the arts; hence, the liberal arts tradition is also sometimes referred to as the *Humanistic Tradition* or the *Literary Humanistic Tradition.* The values and outlook of the liberal arts tradition have been very much bound up with various versions of idealistic philosophy—the philosophy which argues that Mind and Ideas are the fundamental realities. Therefore, *Idealism* or the *Idealistic Tradition* designates this general point of view.

Various philosophers—among them leading Roman Catholic scholars—have maintained that the emphasis on Ideas, Moral Choice, and the obligation of free men to the Truth is a kind of perennial philosophy or *Great Tradition* influencing education through the ages. Thus, *Perennialism* and *Traditionalism* are also terms referring to the liberal arts tradition in education.

CHRONOLOGY

The liberal arts tradition is the oldest educational theory of Western civilization. It began with the ancient Greeks, was extended and developed by the Romans of classical antiquity, and thrived in the schools of the church in the Middle Ages. In the late nineteenth and early twentieth century it represented the main line of secondary education in Europe and the United States. Shortly after the beginning of the twentieth century, however, the liberal arts tradition was challenged by progressive education, which derived its basic theory from

evolution and science rather than from the literary humanities. Public schools especially were influenced by progressive
education.

Around 1930 literary scholars in the colleges and universities became alarmed by the de-emphasis of literary humanistic studies involved in the scientific movement in education.
They began to write articles and give speeches calling attention to contradictions between the educational theory and
practice of the schools and the values they thought were
embodied in the humanistic tradition.

Although educational proposals of various participants in
the effort to revive the liberal arts tradition after 1930 differed
in details, they were in agreement on the following points:

1. The naturalistic, pragmatic, scientific philosophy and
practice of education which dominated the schools was inadequate.

2. Guiding values and standards coming from sources
other than naturalistic philosophy and pragmatic theories
were needed in the schools.

3. The needed values and standards were to be found in
the Greek, Hebrew, and Christian traditions of the Western
world.

Just what are these traditions? What is the tradition of
humanistic scholarship to which they said we should return?
What are the major tenets of the Graeco-Roman, Hebrew-
Christian heritage to which they would have had us turn for
guidance in education?

First of all, there is the persisting search for meaning in
all of existence. There is the reluctance to accept a world in
which human ideals and purposes are not given preeminent
and central status. The view is that mind is the unique and
precious part of man and deserves most of all to be cultivated. Despite the apparent success of the scientific method

as applied to the world of things, the philosophic presuppositions of philosophic naturalism are unacceptable. That our world and all things in it are the product of evolution, that man is a biological organism in a complicated society in which he learns to be "human," that change and flux characterize not only the realm of physical things but also the realm of ideals, purposes, and principles is denied. Yet it appears that such a world view is implied by, or at least most readily squared with, the thoroughgoing application of scientific method to all areas of human concern, and the progressives in the schools were insisting on just such a thoroughgoing application of experimentalism.

Progressive education built upon pragmatic theory remained vulnerable to critics who spoke for myth, tradition, and religion as against naturalism. For pragmatism questioned absolutes. Words such as *spirit, soul, mind, religion, God* appeared infrequently in the professional vocabularies of the progressives. Their school program was a this-worldly program, emphasizing problems of the here and now. Again, it was strongly equalitarian. The child-centered school romanticized equality and experimentalists attacked social distinctions as based on privilege rather than empirically grounded distinctions.

Between 1930 and 1950 there was a very special effort by humanistic scholars—philosophers, religionists, specialists in classical languages, literary men, and historians—to modify this scientific technological emphasis in the schools. The liberal arts tradition is discussed in this chapter most of all in terms of the interesting and exciting effort to revive it in the years before World War II and during the war years. Additionally, however, this was an effort to revive something older. From time to time the late nineteenth and early twentieth century will be treated as representing the "liberal arts point of view." When this is done the reference will be to the time immediately before the scientific movement took hold in the schools—or to the situation in the schools at the time when John Dewey began to write on education. Again, there may be some allusion to the liberal arts tradition as it prevailed in the Middle Ages; in explaining some of its basic doctrines it may be helpful to go all the way back to Plato and Aristotle.

CONTEXT

All of the progressive education leaders—to whom the twentieth-century traditionalists objected—took Darwin very seriously, extending the implications of evolution to realms of human, moral, social, and educational domains. They began together with an evolutionary, naturalistic set of assumptions.

This outlook views the universe in all its phases as a product of evolutionary change, and says that such change continues. Thus, social and moral principles as well as principles of the physical world are constantly changing. Man is a highly complicated organism whose contemporary nature is a product of biological and social evolution. His destiny is to achieve vitality, poise, and a sense of achievement in this changing world of which he is a part. The methods appropriate to, and demonstrably most effective in, achieving such a life for individuals and for societies are the methods of science and democracy.

The most influential philosophy influencing public schools during the first half of the twentieth century was pragmatism. This is not to say that all schoolteachers and administrators during the first half of the twentieth century accepted and applied all the pragmatic ideas. In every field there is a lag between theory and practice, and there are all sorts of arguments and disagreements down the line. Nevertheless, pragmatism and progressive education were a kind of vanguard movement that expressed a central theme or emphasis in educational work and in theorizing about education.

Evidence of strong counter-movements in educational thought in the United States began to appear after the Great Depression which began in 1929. Although an experimental, scientific approach to the enterprise of schooling had come to dominate the thinking of professional leaders in public school policy, traditional ways of thinking about life, learning, behavior, the good life, and the good society had continued to exert force in areas of informal education—in homes, in social gatherings, and in the stories and myths of common people. Increasingly, a degree of conflict between informal and formal education characterized our society. Informal education tended to be regulated more by tradition and religion, while the deliberate educational enterprises conducted by the schools, in the light of professional policy, were increasingly influenced by science and a philosophy of education based on science. Informal education comes out of the social habits or mores and folkways of a culture. It is frequently guided by unexamined, habitual assumptions about the world in which we live, the nature and destiny of man, and the purposes of life. The guiding values of informal education—the education of home, street, club, and neighborhood—are expressed in the novel, in music, in art, in drama, and not so much in the critical, scientific formulations.

The literary humanists were concerned not only about public education but also about the state of the arts, the theater, literature, recreation, and religion. The leaders in religion who criticized the public schools were also critical of certain tendencies in American religious life, home and family living, and social and economic outlook. The conservatives were vigorously critical of certain political institutions, economic movements, and social customs of the day. Although informal education in the culture remained relatively more traditional than education in the schools, tendencies criticized in the schools were bound up with certain broader cultural characteristics reflected not only in the schools but also throughout American life. The public school controversy was one particular dimension of the impact of science, technology, and naturalism upon American society.

With all their differences, the humanists, conservatives, and religious leaders joined in struggling to revive what they considered to be the Great Tradition of Western thought. The institution through which they hoped to accomplish this was the school. As we have seen, they claimed that the *philosophia perennis* or perennial philosophy has persisted in Western civilization since the fifth and fourth centuries B.C. when Socrates, Plato, and Aristotle stated its fundamental tenets. In twentieth-century debate, literary humanistic scholars, religious leaders, and conservative political theorists, basing their arguments on the philosophy of the Great Tradition, criticized the public schools and advocated fundamental changes in curriculum and method.

The so-called Great Tradition in Western culture holds that we live in an intelligible world based on stable principles that can be understood by man. It holds that man is capable of achieving a reasonable grasp of his nature and the world in which he lives because he is endowed with mind. The mind of man transcends man's biological and social nature and is his most precious endowment. The primary purpose of education, then, is to train and develop the mind of man. In this connection traditional literature, philosophy, art, religion, and history are of central importance, because the unchanging principles of reason are demonstrated therein. A philosophy of education based on the Great Tradition is one of integrity and responsibility. If the world view of the Great Tradition is accepted as authentic, traditional education at its best is effective education, judged by the criteria provided. Were these, however, the criteria appropriate in twentieth-century American society? Was the traditional world view that by which American citizens should measure their schools?

SOURCES

Two writings of Plato dramatically express fundamental notions which, through the centuries, have been associated with the liberal arts tradition. One of these is the dialogue *Phaedrus*, in which Plato explains the nature of the soul, the reason for the soul's search for truth, the reason for differences among men, and the purposes of education. The noblest educational aim is to bring men to recollection of the vision of the good which lies within all men, but buried, so that teaching is required to bring forth the memory.

The other writing of Plato which deserves careful study for its educational implications is the *Republic*, in particular Book VII. The first part of Book VII tells the story of the cave, in which it is explained that man lives in a world of shadows, but that the function of true education is to bring him from the shadows into the light. In response to the question, "How is this to be accomplished?" Plato, in the concluding pages of Book VII, outlines the curriculum of the liberal arts embodying the seven medieval studies plus gymnastics, which Christians of the Middle Ages tended to ignore.

The educational doctrines of Aristotle are more widely scattered throughout his writings, no one title really constituting a specialized work on educational theory. Nevertheless, references to child rearing, the family, and individual differences in the early books of the *Politics* are relevant. The distinction between the intellectual and the practical virtues in the *Nichomachean Ethics* is of some importance. In particular, it is to be noted that Aristotle, while giving highest place to the intellectual virtues, nevertheless teaches that the life of mind can only be pursued effectively by those who have been nurtured in practical virtues.

In the *De Anima* Aristotle distinguishes among levels of soul—the plant soul, the animal soul, the human soul. His view is that all living things are possessed of soul. Soul is the life principle. Souls are of different orders, however. The human soul is unique in that it alone possesses reason. Inasmuch as the very meaning or purpose of any soul is to realize its highest potentiality, it follows that the education of man should endeavor most of all to realize—that is bring out or "make real"—mind or reason in man. Futher elaboration of the doctrine of act and potency may be found in the *Physics*, especially Book VIII, and the *Metaphysics*, Book XII. It is in the latter that the distinction between man and God is clarified—God being prime cause, the unmoved mover yet the source of all movement. Only God is pure mind, pure intellect, pure act. But man has the potentiality to aspire toward perfection; education should work to bring him as close as to God as his potentiality will allow.

The listing of the seven liberal arts accepted as authentic during the Middle Ages left out medicine, gymnastics, and architecture which had been important to the Greeks and Romans, because these studies would be of no importance to angels, who have no bodies. But angels, as disembodied spirits, will nevertheless practice the trivium (grammar, rhetoric, and logic) and the quadrivium (arithmetic, geometry, astronomy, and music). These were the seven liberal

arts pursued in the medieval church schools and the arts
faculty of the universities.

Of the twentieth-century writings advocating the liberal
arts tradition, Mark Van Doren's *Liberal Education* is the
finest statement. Dr. Van Doren was a professor at Columbia
when this book was published in the early 1940s. Philosophical works of importance are Jacques Maritain's *Education at the Crossroads* and Étienne Gilson's *The Unity of
Philosophical Experience.* Maritain and Gilson are highly
respected Catholic scholars, authorities on medieval philosophy, who taught and lectured at both secular and church
universities before and during World War II.

Leaders of what was called the "new humanism" in American universities during the 1930s and 1940s are A. J. Nock
(*Theory of Education in the United States*), Irving Babbitt
(*Humanism and America*), Paul Elmer More (*The Greek
Tradition*), Norman Foerster (*The American State University*), and Gilbert Highet (*The Art of Teaching*). All were
professors of classics in various American universities before
and during World War II.

T. S. Eliot, the poet and dramatist, added support to the
movement in his tiny volume, *Notes Towards a Definition of
Culture,* which was widely discussed and received a Nobel
Prize for literature.

But the two most influential protagonists for a return to
the liberal arts are Robert Maynard Hutchins and Mortimer
Adler, who were both associated with the University of Chicago in the 1930s. Both remain active as lecturers, writers,
and molders of public opinion in the 1970s. Hutchins and
Adler are rightly given credit for the strong movement of
criticism of, and opposition to, progressive education in the
mid-twentieth century. Among Hutchins' more important
writings are *The Higher Learning in America* (1936), *The
University of Utopia* (1953), and *The Learning Society*

(1968). Adler wrote *Art and Prudence* (1937) and *How to Read a Book* (1940), and edited the massive collection of *Great Books of the Western World.*

THEORY

Proponents of this educational theory identify a set of doctrines about the universe, man, and nature as "our tradition." They then propound that this tradition provides us with a body of established truth, and that currently unsettled questions of belief, action, and policy in human affairs, and specifically in education, should be settled by reference to this body of truth.[1] There is a sympathetic reversion to conceptions of human nature and the world derived from Greek philosophy and Hebrew-Christian religious thought. Emphases such as those on the liberal arts, the importance of the humanities, and a return to the classics are justified by a system of metaphysical conceptions.

Traditionalists held that there is meaning, pattern, and design in the universe. The eternal ground of this order may be personified and designated by the religious term *God.* The possibility that all movements in our universe have a direction, and that consequently human and natural events are to be understood in the light of cosmic purpose, is viewed sympathetically. Moreover, in this sort of world, nurture of the young comes to be seen as progressive actualization of potentialities unique to man. Certain generic characteristics of man as human mark the course educational practices should take. Fundamental themes developed by contemporary literary humanists, religious leaders, and conservatives are beautifully stated in classic myths, such as the fable of

[1] A. E. Murphy, "Tradition and the Traditionalists," in *The Authoritarian Attempt to Capture Education,* ed. Conference on the Scientific Spirit and the Democratic Faith (New York: King's Crown, 1945), p. 13.

the cave in the *Republic* of Plato or the fable of the chariots in *Phaedrus,* and recur in the teachings of thinkers like Aristotle, Augustine, Aquinas, Calvin, Leibniz, Kant, and Hegel.

The Universe

This universe, so the teaching goes, is governed by eternal laws and principles. The eternal principles that are the ground of intelligibility are those of truth, goodness, and beauty. These principles, by which the world is governed and by which it is to be understood, are independent of time and place, and independent of particular social conditions. Chance and contingency operate in natural processes, but since natural processes are grounded in an intelligible and orderly universe, even chance can be studied and plotted. The world finally "makes sense." Man is at home in this world.

Man

Man, in contrast to the plants and lower animals, is endowed with the capacity to understand the principles that govern the universe, for man is a reasonable being. The principles of reason are within him, although they may have become blurred as he has lived his life in the cave of the everyday world. He lives in a world he can understand, when he has been disciplined by an education appropriate to his nature. The universal principles by which the world is governed are the basis of human knowledge. The secret of the good life is to know them and to govern one's life by them. They are not only intellectual guides; they are also ethical ends.[2]

Awareness of Universal Principles

These principles originate in the common experience of

[2] Norman Foerster, *The American State University* (Chapel Hill: University of North Carolina Press, 1937), pp. 219 ff., 247.

all men. The basis of philosophy is man's common experience in living. Progress in philosophical thought is not a matter of adding to past knowledge but, rather, of increasingly adequate analysis of the meanings of our experiences. The basic truths—the guiding principles that are principles of the universe, eternal and unchanging—are finally self-evident. You see them the way you finally grasp the truth of a theorem in geometry.[3] In a sense, they are grasped intuitively, as if they were laws written in the heavens.

Humanism is not to be identified with this or that body of traditional precepts. The law of measure on which it depends becomes meaningless unless it can be shown to be one of the "laws unwritten in the heavens" of which Antigone had the immediate perception, laws that are "not of today or yesterday," that transcend in short the temporal process. The final appeal of the humanist is not to any historical convention but to intuition.[4]

Moral Standards

Questions of good and bad, right and wrong, are to be decided in the light of these principles. They transcend society. Moral questions are questions of principle, not questions of public opinion. Society can sometimes be wrong. Although the state is superior to the individual on many counts, questions of good or bad, right or wrong, and true or false are personal questions—to be decided by moral individuals in the light of absolute and universal standards.[5]

[3] Mortimer Adler, *Art and Prudence* (New York: Longmans, Green and Co., 1937), p. 248.

[4] Irving Babbitt, "Humanism, an Essay at Definition," in *Humanism and America*, ed. Norman Foerster (New York: Farrar and Rinehart, 1930), p. 27.

[5] Mark Van Doren, *Liberal Education* (New York: Henry Holt & Co., 1943), p. 40.

Man Essentially Intellect

Human nature does not change. It is the same at every place and at every time. Even when people say that human nature changes, they are referring to something permanent in their very use of the term *human nature*. There is something eternal behind the apparent differences. Now what features or characteristics of man can be considered distinctively human? To be sure, we share many characteristics with animals and even plants. The student of general zoology does not find many uniquely new features in a study of human anatomy and physiology. The skeleton, the internal organs, the musculature, and reproductive system are very much like those of the other mammals. A good many of our desires and enjoyments we share with the animals; dogs enjoy riding in automobiles and frequently take pleasure in food prepared for humans. The family cat gets as much enjoyment from the favorite chair as we do. The philosophy of the classical tradition sees us as partly animal—in a way, brothers of the cats and dogs, butterflies and apes. According to this tradition, however, of all the living creatures, man alone is endowed with mind or intellect. Of all man's characteristics, the most distinctive and most intrinsically valuable are the intellectual virtues.[6]

The Good Life

It is good for a human being to develop his mind because he is a human being. But again, it is good to develop the mind because it is good to understand. It is good to know reality because reality is there to be known. Knowledge and understanding, that is, are intrinsic goods. It is good to know

[6] R. M. Hutchins, *The Higher Learning in America* (New Haven: Yale University Press, 1936), p. 67 and *passim*.

just because it is good to know. The attitude is like that of the mountain climber who spends a lifetime working to scale a peak, just because the mountain is there. It is like the attitude of the astronomer who studies the stars just because they are there to be studied. Attainment of the ideal of completeness of life, of a human nature rounded and perfect on all its sides, is for greatest worth.[7] Attainment of this ideal of completeness of life depends on the exercise of intelligent self-restraint,[8] and such discipline or self-restraint consists of the ability to relate facts to principles and see things in perspective.[9] The process of self-realization may be looked upon as one in which the potentialities of the person are actualized. Inasmuch as man is a rational being, however, his achievement of form and his actualization of his potentialities are directed by himself.

Means to the Good Life

To the extent that a person has been educated, he possesses not only the power to grow but also the ability to shape, form, or direct that growth. Human form is something achieved out of potentiality. The potentiality for form is given, but struggle under discipline is necessary for the realization of form. Self-direction is accomplished as the individual discovers and incorporates into his personality certain attitudes and modes of behavior supposed to be universal. The individual becomes a *person* as the universal or generic in him is actualized. The self is realized as the individual becomes humane, a practitioner of the intellectual virtues, a pursuer of truth, goodness, and beauty, a cultured

[7] Norman Foerster, "Preface," in *Humanism and America* (New York: Farrar and Rinehart, 1930), pp. xiii–xiv.

[8] Ibid.

[9] Foerster, *American State University*, p. 247.

individual, and a disciplined, balanced person. The life of reason is the distinctively human life. The goodness of living humanly or living reasonably needs no defense. One who questions the goodness of a life of reason is questioning the goodness of life itself. One who rejects the life of reason for a life devoted to the pursuit of physical comforts is rejecting himself as a human being. He is living like an animal. He is merely vegetating.[10]

Happiness and the Good Life

There is no conflict between this emphasis and values such as happiness and a good society. Intellectual virtues are good in themselves, but they are also indispensable to goods such as happiness, peace, and social productivity, for individuals and for societies.[11] For true happiness and a truly good society are only possible as men pursue truth, goodness, and beauty. The self-realizing person is in possession of a balanced, poised personality. This is the product of intelligent, disciplined control. Such people are the happiest people and the best citizens.

EDUCATIONAL APPLICATIONS

In the light of the theory of the universe and of human nature outlined above, what educational practices are advocated? How is it proposed to develop reason in men who live their lives in this reasonable, intelligible universe?

Purpose of Education

The general conditions for achieving the good life are the general principles of education. Certain characteristics of

[10] Mortimer Adler, *How to Read a Book* (New York: Simon and Schuster, 1940), pp. vii–viii; also Adler, *Art and Prudence*, p. 213.
[11] Ibid.

man that mark him as human are to be drawn out and given expression. Education is to concentrate on bringing out and developing those features of man that make him different from the animals. Thus, there is a sense in which we can say that the best-educated person is the most human person. To be sure, the rest of us are also human, but we are inferior in our humanity to the person who has been more completely, more fully, educated. The purpose of education is self-realization, for if the self can be made real through expert cultivation by a master teacher, then we can most completely express our humanness.[12]

A truly educated person exhibits poise, self-control, and culture because he applies the eternal standards to specific situations. He is a master of situations because of his wisdom. His is a noble spirit because his life is guided by truth.[13] Education is development; education is drawing out; education is self-realization; education is becoming human by becoming progressively aware of the truth. Such education is good because it is real.

An education that develops reason is good education because reason is there to be developed. More than that, it is good education because it enables man to understand his world. But more, since man is a reasonable being living in a reasonable universe, an education that concentrates on the development of reason will also work out to be the best education for developing good citizens holding good jobs in a good society. These principles of which we have spoken are basic to everything—to science, life, liberty, and the pursuit of happiness.

The chief and fundamental function of education is to shape man as man, to draw out and develop the distinctively human in him. Education, to be sure, is something that goes

---

[12] Van Doren, *Liberal Education,* p. 23.
[13] Babbitt, "Humanism, an Essay at Definition," pp. 42–43, 49.

on in different times and in different places, but always its chief function is to shape man. It does not matter whether the individual is living in the twentieth century or in the second. He is a human being, and because of this, the central task of education is to bring out and develop his potentialities as a human being. The obligation of the school is to bring out his essential humanness. People thus educated can operate well in all fields. An education that develops reason is best, in and of itself; it is best as a means to happiness; it is best as a preparation for citizenship; it is even the best vocational education.[14]

Content of Education

The discipline of the Western intellectual tradition is that which literary humanists recommend as the one that will develop minds and contribute most to self-realization. The methods and content of Western thought demonstrate the eternal principles; thus, so the reasoning goes, men must be disciplined in the methods and content of classic thought before they realize the inescapability of the eternal principles and understand the applications to life which follow from them. In this sense it may be said that the source of regulating principles is the thought of the past.[15] Wisdom comes as we steep ourselves in study of our traditions. Thus seen, wisdom is fundamentally traditional and conservative. To be human, then, is to be in possession of knowledge, to have developed the capacity for judgment, and to be morally virtuous. It is to be a part of one's cultural heritage. These things come about as an individual is liberally educated; that is, as he

---

[14] Hutchins, *Higher Learning in America,* p. 63.
[15] Foerster, "Preface"; Adler, *Art and Prudence,* pp. viii–ix; Van Doren, *Liberal Education,* p. 148.

comes to know history and literature, and as he has been disciplined by the study of languages and mathematics.

The aim of education . . . is to guide man in the evolving dynamism through which he shapes himself as a human person —armed with knowledge, strength of judgment, and moral virtues —while at the same time conveying to him the spiritual heritage of the nation and the civilization in which he is involved, and preserving in this way the century-old achievements of generations. The utilitarian aspect of education—which enables the youth to get a job and make a living—must surely not be disregarded, for the children of man are not made for aristocratic leisure. But this practical aim is best provided by the general human capacities developed. And the ulterior specialized training which may be required must never imperil the essential aim of education.[16]

Function of the Elementary School

Dispositions to be fostered in the young child are those which finally make possible a mature life ruled by reason. Love of truth, love of good and justice, and a conscientious, responsible attitude toward work have an important place among these. Self-discipline and good moral habits are objectives, but the emphasis on habits and habit formation need not necessarily issue in an elementary education that is repressive and negative. The task of the teacher might be thought of as that of liberating the good energies so as to help children achieve control of the bad ones.[17] The moral disciplines that elementary education should cultivate and develop may be thought of as the reasonable control of desires. It is the habit of wanting the right thing at the right

[16] Jacques Maritain, *Education at the Crossroads* (New Haven: Yale University Press, 1943), p. 10.
[17] Ibid., pp. 36–39.

time.[18] Habit, thus conceived, plays an important part in moral virtue. In adulthood, morally mature and morally immature persons may be distinguished by the degree to which habits have become fixed. We speak of the stable personality. The stability of such a person—a trait which makes him dependable and admirable—has been achieved because he has made a habit of virtue. He has built certain ways of acting into his disposition, so that he is a person of integrity.[19] The basis for such integrity is laid in childhood. Children must be led to form good habits, for moral maturity is based upon habituation. We may say that elementary schoolteachers need to help children build good habits into their lives. When people become older, they need to maintain the good habits by exercising them—by continuing to live the good life.[20]

In addition to the foundation of moral habituation, which is a prime responsibility of the elementary school, this institution also introduces children to the first steps of mastery of the tools of learning. Elementary education may well be based upon experience, although there is some question as to whether it is the job of the school itself to provide the experiential basis of learning. The work of the school is primarily in moral habituation and in the beginnings of intellectual discipline.

In general education . . . we may wisely leave experience to life and set about our job of intellectual training.[21]

Function of the Secondary School

Once the foundations for learning are laid in the elemen-

---

[18] Mortimer Adler, *How to Think about War and Peace* (New York: Simon and Schuster, 1944), p. 232.

[19] Adler, *Art and Prudence,* p. 177.

[20] Ibid., p. 178.

[21] Hutchins, *Higher Learning in America,* p. 70.

tary school—in the time before the mind is ready to do its
work—liberal education begins. Literary humanists generally
frown upon permitting students wide choice in general education. Some would insist there be no electives whatsoever,
the argument being that the immature mind has no criteria
for making intelligent choices.

Mastery of the arts of language is fundamental in liberal
education.[22] Reading is a basic tool for living the good life,
for to read thoughtfully and analytically is to reason.[23] In
meaningful reading, one finds himself in a discussion with
the writer. One comes to reason with a book and think
through the issues raised.

The mind which is trained to read well has its analytical and
critical powers developed. The mind which is trained to discuss
well has them further sharpened. One acquires a tolerance for
arguments through dealing with them patiently and sympathetically. The animal impulse to impose our opinions on others is thus
checked. We learn that the only authority is reason itself—the only
arbiter in any dispute is the reasons and evidence. We do not try
to gain ascendancy by a show of force or by counting the noses
of those who agree with us. Genuine issues cannot be decided by
mere weight of opinion. We must appeal to reason, not depend on
pressure groups.[24]

The study of language comes to include not only reading,
but also analysis of the structure of language, of logic, and
persuasion. Mathematics, too, contributes to the development
of orderly reasoning and careful analysis of meanings. Upon
such a basis of careful intellectual discipline, further and
more advanced study of philosophy, history, natural science,
literature, poetry, and the fine arts may contribute to the

[22] Van Doren, *Liberal Education,* p. 131.
[23] Adler, *How to Read A Book,* pp. vii–viii.
[24] Ibid., pp. 362–363.

refinement of liberal discipline. The student grounded in the study of grammar, rhetoric, logic, and mathematics will recognize intellectual order in new forms in these studies.[25]

The great masterpieces of our literary heritage are the carriers of the cultural tradition. That a classic is old is not important. The important consideration is that the classics are the great minds of Western civilization in action. We can become liberally educated as our minds are disciplined by the great minds. The classics are classics because they demonstrate superior methods of thinking. The acquaintance with great literature and great thought which thus develops is not a mere passive awareness. The Tradition becomes a part of one as he controls his thinking by its perennial arts. The elements of our common human nature are discovered here. Our minds are thus made.

In addition to all this, however, the content of the great books is vital. That is, the great books not only demonstrate the way to think; they also treat of the things men ought to be thinking about. It is only by acquaintance with the past that the present can be understood. The educated person can maintain his poise in times of personal and cultural stress— and thus exert leadership—because his feet are solidly planted. That is, he has cultural and intellectual roots; he has developed a scale of values which gives him strength and guidance; he understands the agonies and passions of his forebears.[26] This is so because certain great human problems are perennial. Liberal education deals with that portion of the past which is always present, with the art and discipline of thinking significantly. Liberal education, rooted in the wisdom of the past, thus remains forever contemporary.[27]

[25] Maritain, *Education at the Crossroads,* pp. 55 ff.
[26] Van Doren, *Liberal Education,* p. 131.
[27] Ibid., pp. 144–145.

Here, then, we have the point of view that should guide general or liberal education. Liberal education, thus defined, is seen as development of the intellectual disciplines and prolonged study of the literature of the humanistic tradition. Many of the literary humanists do not make a clear distinction between the high school and the undergraduate college. Apparently some have doubt about the appropriateness of the American high school in its present organization. Thus, the colleges at the University of Chicago and at St. John's accepted qualified young people at the age of sixteen, upon completion of the customary tenth grade. Mark Van Doren asserts that the high school is an anomalous institution which must either disappear altogether or distribute its effort forward into college and backward into elementary school.[28] However the educational ladder be arranged and administered, the curriculum during the adolescent years should, so it is claimed, involve learning the arts of investigation, discovery, criticism, and communication, and developing first-hand an intimate acquaintanceship with the great books in which these arts are demonstrated.[29]

Importance of Cultural Heritage

Realization by men of their ideals of truth, goodness, and beauty depends upon effective transmission and preservation of the cultural heritage. Man is an animal of culture and he cannot become mature except as he is disciplined by the collective experience of his society.[30] It is not enough to master the Tradition as a body of subject matter. One must be able to use it. The past must be brought to bear upon the present.

[28] Ibid., p. 98.
[29] Ibid., pp. 144–145.
[30] Maritain, *Education at the Crossroads*, p. 8.

Thus it may be that locating a problem to be solved—the very awareness of a problem—depends upon mastery of traditional insights and approaches. The ultimate educational ends are the eternal principles which distinguish man from the animals. In general education we are devoted to drawing out the elements of our common human nature, not so much to the cultivation of individual differences among men.[31] Incorporated in the literary tradition are the eternal principles that have relevance and validity always. The principles to guide us in approaching contemporary problems—in art, in politics, in morals—were discovered long ago. The classics containing the traditions of European wisdom throw light on these problems.[32] Thus, we should not talk about education for democracy, or education for world order, or education for this, that, or the other. We simply need good education, and there are standards in the nature of things and in man for determining this.[33]

A liberal education is the study of the eternal and unchanging. The curriculum may well be thus organized. It should have a design that makes clear which studies are central and which are secondary, and students should be led through this curriculum systematically. The so-called "problems approach" must be used with great care as a pedagogic method, for it may be dangerous. Such a procedure may confuse proper educational sequence and order, and it is impossible to have social order without intellectual order. It is through such analysis that Hutchins has arrived at his conclusion, highly publicized, that metaphysics is the study that should unify all elements of liberal education, and that,

[31] Hutchins, *Higher Learning in America,* p. 73; also R. M. Hutchins, *No Friendly Voice* (Chicago: University of Chicago Press, 1936), p. 30.
[32] Adler, *Art and Prudence,* pp. viii–ix.
[33] Van Doren, *Liberal Education,* p. 38.

at the same time, the study of basic principles is the best guarantee of world peace, good citizenship, and prosperity.[34]

Role of Science

Traditionalists draw a distinction between facts and values. The values are the ultimate moral and metaphysical truths in the light of which facts must be judged. Experimental science may help us in determining the facts, but what to do with these facts may be decided only in the light of the eternal principles of Tradition.[35] Science confers power, but the power has to do only with the mastery of means. Philosophy must determine the ends. Thus, philosophy, religion, and the humanities are superior to science at all points. They tell us what to investigate and set the foundation for empirical research; then they come in again to tell us what to do with the facts discovered by scientific analysis.[36] Thus, more emphasis is placed on literature and philosophy than on experimental science. There is the fear that science and technology will make men slaves of a technocratic society—that modern science may become a kind of soulless Frankenstein which will finally sap the roots of liberty. Thus, Maritain warned in the years of World War II that if we held everything that is not subject to experimental demonstration a matter of myth, although we might conquer the Nazis on the battlefield we would lose to them in the realm of human values.[37] Hutchins, Adler, Maritain, and Foerster, insisting that science confers only mastery of means, make science of subsidiary importance in liberal education. Mari-

[34] Hutchins, *Higher Learning in America,* pp. 95 ff; *No Friendly Voice,* pp. 31–32, 66 ff., 105.
[35] Adler, *Art and Prudence,* pp. 148–149.
[36] Ibid., p. 250.
[37] Maritain, *Education at the Crossroads,* pp. 113–114.

tain and Hutchins take the explicit position that, although specialized scientific institutes may be affiliated with universities, training in such institutes is not to be a part of liberal or general education.[38] Such specialized training has its place only at the higher levels, and those who are allowed to pursue such specialized training must have a well-rounded liberal education first.[39]

The important truths for living are embodied in the literary tradition, not in modern experimental science. Not the specifics of the technician's laboratory, but general principles or theories are the proper subject matter for education.[40] The development, elaboration, and refinement of principles, which in turn are ordered by the Tradition, are the functions of the university. The laboratory sciences do not develop their own theoretical principles of organization. There are actually philosophical assumptions in the organization of every science. Science may confer mastery of means, but philosophical analysis based on self-evident principles common to the experience of all men is needed to determine the ends they should serve. The facts discovered by scientific inquiry are of value only as they are ordered by disciplined minds toward true ends.[41] Thus, we return again to the emphasis on language, literature, mathematics, and the great books of the Western Tradition. They, not the empirical sciences, are the center of the curriculum in this view.[42]

Education for Leadership

To advocate that education be geared to eternal values involves the conception that there are objective standards of

---

[38] Ibid., pp. 83 ff.; Hutchins, *Higher Learning in America,* passim.
[39] Van Doren, *Liberal Education,* p. 167.
[40] Hutchins, *Higer Learning in America,* p. 48.
[41] Hutchins, *No Friendly Voice,* pp. 56–57.
[42] Hutchins, *Higher Learning in America,* pp. 80 ff.

human excellence. Thus, one of the chief functions of the school will be to sift from the inferior those whose native aptitude makes them better than others. Educational procedures to accomplish this will involve adjustment of materials to the capabilities of students. Those of lesser ability will be given a shorter training period and training of a different kind. The able and industrious who survive the intellectual rigors will receive education to develop in them the intellectual power that comes from thorough discipline in Tradition.

Even so, it will be to the good of society if the level of excellence as measured in terms of truth, goodness, and beauty can be raised to a maximum. Good education will help each human being become as good as he is capable of becoming. A democracy will give each of its members as much liberal education as he can take; in fact, no individual will be allowed to escape it. Finally, it must be recognized that men are of different potentialities. Some men cannot be as human as other men; some men are not by nature as good and wise as others. Liberal education for all is to produce a pyramid with the best men on top.[43] It is assumed that most men do not have the ability to become aristocrats, princes, and philosophers, but that society is more healthy when each individual is helped to become as princely and as philosophical as his abilities allow.[44]

Thus, a course of study designed to produce an intellectual elite may also be a course of study in which all are carried as far as their abilities will allow; the ability of the individual may determine how far he should go in such a curriculum. The education that prepares for the good life also prepares for citizenship. Individuals are good citizens to the extent that

[43] Van Doren, *Liberal Education*, p. 33.
[44] Ibid., p. 31.

they are good people. The quality of a democracy—the very possibility of its continued existence—depends on the degree of goodness achieved by its citizens through liberal education. Because men's basic mental processes are the same and because practical wisdom is à product of the intellectual virtues operating in experience, a liberal education oriented toward truth, goodness, and beauty constitutes an effective preparation for practical affairs and vocational life.[45] Yet it may be that some people must be vocationally trained while others, destined to lead these workers, are educated for leadership. A democracy must have its leaders, and those leaders must be liberally educated. A protection against totalitarian mob rule inheres in educational provisions that identify and cultivate respect for those who can think.[46]

Mortimer Adler interprets the American tradition of equality in proportional terms. He interprets the maxim that all men are born equal to mean that they should be treated equally. Then he argues that since there are natural inequalities among men, "equal treatment" must mean treatment proportional to the natural inequalities. This principle of proportional equality—that is, of freedom and responsibility proportional to natural ability—is applied to education and suffrage. He denies that democracy means giving equal amounts of suffrage or education to all men.[47] Thus, when truth, goodness, and beauty are held as standards against which all men are ranked according to their excellence as men, many fall short and a few rank high on the scale. However, since these standards are the measure of a good society as well as of a good man, society should be led by the best

[45] Hutchins, *Higher Learning in America*, pp. 63 ff.
[46] Adler, *How to Read a Book*, pp. 98–99.
[47] Adler, *Art and Prudence*, p. 99.

men and educational practice will have as one of its major functions the selection of such.

CHANGES RECOMMENDED

Literary humanistic scholars believed the schools should modify their concern about the social and vocational adjustment of boys and girls and return to the emphasis on basic intellectual skills to which they gave relatively more attention before progressive education became influential. The crudities and absence of intellectual design in our public schools were attacked. It was said that progressives must be rooted out of the teacher-training institutions to bring about improvement of the work of the schools. Naturalism and pragmatism were blamed for deplorable conditions in educational institutions and a renewed emphasis upon traditional humanistic studies in the schools and colleges was recommended.

T. S. Eliot argued that society must be headed by a hereditary aristocracy made up of savants in all fields. These members of an elite would be supported by the people, and would guide and direct the community as well as preserve and contribute to the culture. Education of the highest order would be for these elite individuals. They would be liberally educated in all fields of scholarship, and each would be a specialist in one of the arts or sciences. Thus, the evils that have resulted from the lowering of educational standards to educate too many might be ameliorated. Equality, for Eliot, is an impossibility; therefore, attempts to attain it are self-defeating. Culture, then, is to be preserved and extended by the gifted few who are to be liberally educated and then, perhaps, even subsidized by the masses.

Albert Jay Nock was similarly critical of equalitarian democracy and an educational program to preserve and extend it. Nock claimed that our educational system was founded on three false ideas—equality, democracy, and the literate society as the good society. Here, he argued, are the roots of our educational difficulties. Equality is a false ideal because not everyone is equal—not everyone is educable.

The philosophical doctrine of equality gives no more ground for the assumption that all men are educable than it does for the assumption that all men are six feet tall.[48]

Democracy is an inadequate educational ideal, for it reduces ideals to the level of the average man. Literacy as an ideal is false, for by itself the ability to read does not relate to wisdom in human affairs. In the light of these false ideals, we have attempted to educate all the people, but this can only pervert education, for the masses of men are ineducable. Only a few are educable; they are those who can profit from the study of Greek, Latin, and mathematics. The classical curriculum remains that most appropriate for the nurture of an intellectual elite.

Nock insisted that the difference between education and instruction or training must be recognized. Training for literacy should be continued, for although wisdom does not issue from this, there are advantages in having a literate citizenry. A genuine educational program for those who can profit from it must be developed.

As for the educables, Nock would emulate European educational procedures. On the Continent there have been fewer pseudo-equalitarian and pseudo-democratic notions. Educables have been recognized as rare and valuable. The Continental system has also done reasonably well by the in-

[48] A. J. Nock, *Theory of Education in the United States* (New York: Harcourt, Brace & Co., 1932), p. 44.

educables. There is no romantic nonsense about their capacity. Training is given to those who will accept it.

In the United States, suggests Nock, independent schools and colleges supported by private philanthropy might dedicate themselves to the selection and nurture of an intellectual elite, thus preserving true education. He is apparently aware that support of such a notion on the part of the American public might be less than enthusiastic, however.

Robert Maynard Hutchins, who was probably the most vigorous and influential critic of progressive education, apparently shared much of the Eliot-Nock point of view regarding the importance of an intellectual elite to ensure the future of Western civilization. But Hutchins did not propose to curtail the freedom of the masses, nor did he advocate the sort of subsidy of the intellectuals recommended by Eliot. Neither did Hutchins draw a sharp line between the educables and the ineducables, as did Nock. Nevertheless, he proposed a fundamental reorganization of American education in the view that democracy's future depends upon a liberally educated leadership.

In Hutchins' book *University of Utopia,* published in 1953, a detailed plan for revising the educational system was presented. Since education is "a conversation aimed at truth," children should spend the first ten years of the school life learning the techniques of communication, that is, reading, writing, and arithmetic. Along with this should go study of great literature, history, and geography. A foreign language should be mastered; some study of science should be included, and there should be some emphasis on appreciation of art and music. Hutchins maintains that subjects that depend on experience should not be taught to the inexperienced; thus, children should not be involved in social studies programs that center in examination of current social problems.

Their efforts to discuss such material will be superficial and ineffective because they do not have sufficient experience to understand the issues in depth.

At the age of sixteen or earlier, according to Hutchins, the student should pass into college. Here he continues to study the same subjects, but the emphasis shifts from learning how to communicate to developing familiarity with the leading ideas that have been developed by mankind. The appropriate method for teaching in such a program centers on discussion, criticism, questioning, and debate. The curriculum from early elementary school through college is designed by educators and allows no student electives. There is no credit system; when the student is ready, probably at about the age of eighteen, he takes examinations to determine whether he has acquired a liberal education. If he passes, the Bachelor of Arts degree is conferred.

After leaving college, he chooses one of two paths open to him. He may start to earn a living. If so, his education does not cease; he continues it in adult study groups all his life. On the other hand, after college he may enter the university where, if he is qualified, he may begin specialized study. Only the occupations that have intellectual content are represented there, however, and all departments must be able to maintain conversation with one another.[49] The ideal university is responsible to no authority; it is a center of independent thought and must maintain complete academic freedom.

Hutchins makes a sharp distinction between the experimental sciences and the humanities; science has its own disciplines and methods of achieving results, but there are other methods of reaching truth. Historians, philosophers, and theologians have come to conclusions using disciplines

[49] R. M. Hutchins, *The University of Utopia* (Chicago: University of Chicago Press, 1953), pp. 59–61.

other than those of science.[50] The supreme educational aim which all scholars hold in common, however, is the improvement of men as moral, spiritual, and political beings; this is to be achieved as the primary emphasis of all education remains intellectual.

A somewhat more moderate position is developed by Gilbert Highet, according to whom a liberal curriculum is made up of the classics in their original form, religion, politics, art, history, sociology, and the sciences, in addition to reading, writing, manual arts, and shop. Such a liberal education is the answer to the challenge of preparing the population for the life and responsibilities it must assume. Men must have minds disciplined by the lessons of history to deal with life in our kind of society. This means a deep and complete study of the classics. A liberal curriculum, according to Highet, should include the study of all things that make up the history of man's life and thought. Everyone should have equal opportunity for such study, he insists. No differentiation should be made between rich and poor, but only as much vocational training may be included in the liberal curriculum as can be afforded after the more important work is thoroughly and carefully done. This more important work is that of achieving a general education based upon the classics.

Highet believes that the mind is man's director and most precious possession. Without a highly trained mind, man is not in any way the custodian of his own destiny. The ability to think, precisely and correctly, separates man from the rest of the animals. He holds that competition is a natural instinct of the young, and that it can, if properly directed and used, be a powerful educational asset. Tradition, he holds, can be a motivating power in educational work. It can offer

[50] Ibid., p. 16.

encouragement in learning, provide a range of possibilities, instill a sense of order, impress the sense of responsibility, and constitute a challenge to the student. He believes that punishment is a stimulus to learning, and recommends repetition of work badly done as the punishment for poor work, and the loss of privileges as the punishment for misbehavior.

All people in all walks of life are teachers, according to Highet. The methods of these teachers are as varied as their jobs and characters, and they are all artists. In their work and in their speech—in their instructions to employees, and in the counsel they give their friends—they are conveying what they believe.[51] Highet maintains that in Western civilization all modern teaching stems from two lines: the Greek teachers who claimed to follow reason, and the Hebrew prophets who knew that they were voicing the will of God for men.

We admire both, but we are apt to think that while a group of men who are in touch with God can change the world by a rare and miraculous intervention, it needs the steady work of reason to keep the place going and to train the young.[52]

In summary, humanistic scholars favoring the liberal arts tradition objected to the extreme concern in modern schools with the vocational and social adjustment of young people, the absence of intellectual design in the work of schools, and the lack of respect for intellectuals and the work of the mind, which they thought was prevalent. They were critical of the efforts to popularize education and considered that children and young people have mistakenly been led to believe that

[51] Gilbert Highet, *The Art of Teaching* (New York: Alfred A. Knopf, Inc., 1950), p. 277.
[52] Ibid., pp. 174–175.

learning can always be pleasant and need never be painful. Despite the emphasis on individual differences in modern schools, humanistic scholars considered that educators had failed to deal realistically with the fact that not all young people have the same capacity for education. This is partly because they did not see that the primary function of education is to provide intellectual discipline. Confusion about the real purpose of education resulted in a tendency for schools to take over guidance functions which properly belong to other social institutions, such as the family and the church. Finally, they were critical of the tendency of modern schools to treat science and the scientific method as if they were appropriate to all fields and to all sorts of problems. They considered that the scientific method cannot be applied to the humanistic fields, and they doubted the possibility of scientific social and economic planning.

As literary humanistic scholars forwarded proposals for education, they consistently advocated recognition in educational programs of intellectual methods and criteria in humanistic studies which are somehow different from those of experimental science and unique to the humanities. Every school program must exhibit intellectual design; thus, the liberty of students to elect various courses must be curtailed. The school program that is appropriately designed will recognize distinctions among liberal, technical, and scientific studies. Central emphasis should be given to the basic intellectual skills, and relatively more attention must be given to the literary humanistic fields, in view of the strong tendency of American education to overemphasize the technical and the scientific. The classics and history should receive more emphasis, particularly social and intellectual history with special emphasis upon Western civilization. The school regimen should be more demanding. Special educational opportunities for gifted and able students should be provided, and poor work should be recognized as such, with appropriate penalties and punishments attached. Schools and the society at large must recognize, respect, and reward intellectual achievement.

II

Progressive Education

Progressive Education is a term applied to changes in schools which occurred between 1910 and 1950. These changes were to make schooling more practical, that is, more capable of dealing with the day-to-day concerns of common people. More activities, more vocational and technical courses were introduced, and much more attention was given to social, personal, and vocational adjustment of young people. Emphasis was placed on science and scientific studies; moreover, courses of study, methods of teaching, and ways of thinking about human nature and the purposes of life and education were adopted from science. School became secular, scientific, practical, and technical, as theoreticians came to accept the notion of the world as product of long ages of evolutionary change, man as a natural biological organism, and scholarly inquiry as an extension of problem solving.

These changes were so far-reaching that the movement is sometimes called the *New Education* or the *New Education Movement*. The philosophy behind these changes was basically naturalistic and Darwinian; thus, the term *Evolutionary Naturalism* or simply *Naturalism* may be applied to it. Science received much emphasis; terms such as *Scientific Humanism* or *Experimentalism* refer to the philosophy of progressive education. Among the naturalistic philosophers who led in theorizing about education in the early twentieth century were pragmatists (i.e., William James and John Dewey), hence the term *Pragmatism* also appears in references to progressive education. Dewey also used the title *Instrumentalism* for his philosophy.

CHRONOLOGY

One hundred fifty years ago the schools were paid for and controlled by the fathers and mothers of children attending the schools. The child was considered the ward of his parents. The parents in the neighborhood decided what their children should be taught in school. Minority privileges involved the right of parents to place their children in parochial schools if they so desired. But minority penalties such as compulsory school attendance and principles of common law regulating parent-child relationships might be invoked. This was a workable arrangement. Inasmuch as the school curriculum was meagerly utilitarian, most property owners were parents, and the schools themselves were small and simply administered, they were democratic institutions controlled directly by the people of the community.

However, with the establishment of public secondary schools and with the expansion of offerings in the historical and social fields at the turn of the century came certain industrial and social changes which influenced location of authority in public education. American society changed from a primarily agricultural to an industrial one. Large cities grew up, and along with the growth in cities came a corresponding growth of city school systems. State departments of education became tremendously powerful, often to the point of recommending textbooks, and in nearly all states to the point of specifying teacher-training requirements.

Within local communities, public-spirited and progressive school boards increasingly adopted the attitude of sanctioning the judgment of the superintendent on professional matters, restricting their activity in the main to one of trusteeship of school funds. A high percentage of the parents in big cities were now renters rather than property owners. Consequently, they paid their school taxes painlessly as indirect taxes, and became indifferent to school policy except as some personal dissatisfaction developed. Thus, policy making and curriculum construction increasingly was done by members of the teaching profession rather than by the parents. The complexity of the modern school systems made many school problems more difficult for the layman to understand. Moreover, many intelligent citizens deliberately adopted the attitude that teachers were specialists who should be allowed to ply their trade without lay interference. The philosophy of education held consciously or accepted more or less unconsciously by teacher-education institutions, state departments of education, and in-service teachers and administrators was expressed in school practices. A body of professional literature on education came into being. Courses in education were offered by reputable colleges and universities, and education was recognized by university graduate schools as a field in which candidates for advanced degrees might study. That is, education became a specialized field of professional study and practice.

These more recent developments connected with the rise of professional education in the United States did not, however, result in the elimination of local school boards and committees. There was continued support, among both professional educators and laymen, for the local school board as a policy-making body, and school issues continued to generate interest in many American communities.

The enterprise of deliberate, formal, institutionalized education became a special science and subject matter after 1900. Education as a field of study emerged in the same chronological epoch as psychology, the scientific study of human behavior; sociology, the scientific study of social organization; and pragmatic philosophy, the expression of the influence of science upon philosophy itself. The point of view that has most influenced the public schools in the past half century has emerged from a background of scientific thought in the wake of nineteenth-century Darwinian evolutionary theories.

These early scientific philosophies took various forms. For a time, the works of Herbert Spencer were widely read in the United States. A politically conservative Social Darwinism arose, which emphasized the relationship between survival of the fittest and laissez-faire economic competition. Mechanistic, thoroughly materialistic philosophies such as that expressed by Bertrand Russell in his famous "A Free Man's Worship" were propounded. Likewise, the earlier work in the scientific study of education was socially conservative and, as to methodology, strongly influenced by mathematical-physical models. The testing movement in education was probably an expression of this tendency. E. L. Thorndike's psychology, with its emphasis on "connections," suggests the structure of a machine. Other leaders in the study of education were more influenced by scientific biology than by physics. Thus, for them, the scientific study of education was the study of types, life histories, growth, and individual differences.

Since 1900 many competent men have devoted their lives to the application of scientific theory and practice, in some form, to formal educational work. Their efforts took hold, especially in the public elementary and secondary schools, so that the theoretical foundations, curricula, teaching methods, and measurement and evaluation have ostensibly been grounded scientifically. The naturalistic, empirical, pragmatic philosophy of education which was most influential in American public school work from 1900 to mid-century was based on science and evolution as conceived by nineteenth- and early-twentieth-century American scholars who were profoundly influenced by Charles Darwin and Darwinian ideas.

As early twentieth-century educators worked to build an educational program in the light of a scientific ideal, three quite different types of educational emphasis took form. For some, the effort was to make of education a science like physics or chemistry. For others, the effort was to secure an educational scheme that would give each child as much freedom to explore, invent, investigate, and create as possible, as if each child were a creative researcher in the laboratory of life. For still others, a major emphasis was on educational conditions for establishing a cooperative, planning society in which men had sufficient social and economic security to free them for creative living.

Each of these movements made an impact on American schools and contributed to the new education. At the same time, each must be looked on as a historical phenomenon to be recognized as a part of the development of modern education, not necessarily as a contemporary live option. The American public school never became a child-centered school or a social reconstructionist school. Furthermore, despite the wide use of various devices invented by the technologists, the school never became a technological institution.

The course of educational theory and practice in the twentieth century before World War II paralleled the course of social thought in the period. A persisting influence was the impact of experimental science on the spirit of the times. It was not that science made it impossible for men to hold to a traditional world view, but that experimental science, reflected upon and held to as a primary intellectual resource,

encouraged, supported, and tended to bring about fundamental shifts in philosophical orientation.

Criticisms of the progressive education movement were
myriad, violent, and frequently virulent. Early progressive
education was criticized for its individualism, for its lack of
system, and for a pervading sentimentalism. The concern in
later years for programs of social action to establish a cultural
context in which the ideals of child-centered education might
be more broadly achieved was attacked as socialistic. The
pressure of these dissensions was most certainly a major factor
in the weakening of the Progressive Education Association
which was finally officially dissolved in the summer of 1955.
Nevertheless, the notion that the movement was somehow subversive, manipulated by evil men motivated by greed for
power, is absurd. The ideals, values, and political and educational practices advocated have been a part of broad social
and intellectual movements of the twentieth century. Since
these movements have been of the warp and woof of our
contemporary culture, all twentieth-century men have been
part of them.

Public schools across the land were never generally characterized by the extremes represented in the so-called child-
centered school, nor did public schoolteachers and administrators in large numbers flock to the banners of the social
reconstructionists. On the other hand, the pedagogic and
administrative devices invented by the educational technologists were widely adopted. How much of the theory
preached by the professional educationists did get into the
schools? What, after all, did the American public, tax-
supported school of the mid-twentieth century stand for?

CONTEXT

During the first half of the twentieth century educational

theory was gradually emancipated from its age-old domination by theology and transcendental or idealistic philosophies. Yet the "great debate" over educational policy which literally raged during the war decade and the early 1950s was ostensibly an effort to revive the Great Tradition. Perhaps it could be understood as an ideological effort to counter the vicious atavism of Hitler which was, quite properly, looked on in the 1940s as a challenge to civilization. Robert Hutchins, Mortimer Adler, and Mark Van Doren all used this argument. They insisted that, as a weapon against the horrors of Nazism, the humane tradition of the Greeks, Hebrews, and Christians had to be revived and indoctrinated.

John Dewey held that the function of the school was socialization—the induction of the young into a civilization—and that this was to be accomplished by simplifying, purifying, and balancing the environment. But this formula involves overwhelming difficulties. The highly specialized nature of knowledge tends to make each segment the private preserve of a group of specialists. How can these specialized disciplines be simplified for the young? The total body of knowledge in all fields has been somewhat reshaped by scientific discovery. How can knowledge be purified to insure its valid contemporaneity? Again the notion of the human community has been extended to include the vast non-European and non-Christian cultures. How can the understanding of man and the human condition be balanced to include all dimensions of the experience of universal mankind?

American teachers in the interregnum between the two great wars were strongly humanitarian and imbued with an almost evangelistic fervor for the uplifting of boys and girls in character and service to their fellow man. The purpose of education was to shape the person who would take his place as a worthy citizen in a community of free men.

Although the impact of the educational theorists and scientists who worked in shaping the professional preparation of teachers before 1950 was thoroughly naturalistic, it was overwhelmingly moral in tone. Before 1950 teachers were generally committed to the nurturing of social and moral attitudes. The importance of emotional and personal elements in the character of a person was seen to be as important as specific command of subject matter. The school was viewed as a specialized extension of the total process of nurturing, and schools and teachers were seen as engaged in the process of character formation. Social and recreational activities, guidance and counseling, the clubs, dances, and athletic events were looked on as of equal or even greater importance than the strictly academic curriculum. At extreme, the view considered seriously the possibility that the school might be a vestigial institution. For the theory was that the community served as educator, and, especially in the American small-town context, the notion of merging school with community to make education an actual novitiate in community living was seen as a distinct possibility.

For most youngsters the twelve-year school was a terminal school. Not more than one in four went on to college. School, then, was looked upon as an induction into adult life, with citizen participation in community activities rather than specific vocational skills as the center of emphasis.

SOURCES

Of the ideas which shaped the progressive education movement, the influence of Darwin is by far the most important, for the psychology and social philosophy of the pragmatists was inspired by Darwinian notions. In *Origin of Species,* Darwin presented empirical evidence that the various forms of life were products of long ages of constant change, this involving continuing alteration of all distinguishable forms of life. In the *Descent of Man,* this thesis was applied to man himself, to show that man, too, is a product of evolution.

The influence of Marx upon educators is direct only in the case of a specific subgroup of progressives who, in the 1930s, became interested in using the schools in a very specific way to bring about social change. There is no evidence that any of the major leaders in progressive education were Marxists. However, the Marxian notions that man is a material being, that society is the product of economic struggle, and that man is motivated more by material than ideal forces supports the naturalistic implications of Darwinism. In *Das Kapital* and the *Communist Manifesto* Marx expresses some of these basic ideas.

Sigmund Freud, whose major influence came somewhat later than that of Marx and Darwin, actually lived and published at about the same time as Dewey. His emphasis on the physical basis of much human motivation, the importance of sexuality in the stages of maturation, and the underlying biological significance of many social institutions reinforces the naturalistic outlook. Enthusiasts for the child-centered school and some specialists in early childhood education were especially influenced by Freud.

In American philosophy, the four great pragmatist philosophers, Charles S. Peirce, William James, George H. Mead, and John Dewey formulated ideas applied to education by the progressives. References to each of these philosophers are made in the pages that follow. Two essays of Peirce, "How to Make Our Ideas Clear" and "The Fixation of Belief," deserve attention. We have already mentioned William James' writings on psychology. His books *Pragmatism* and *A Pluralistic Universe* are also referred to later in this chapter. George H. Mead supplies an explanation of mind arising out of language in *Mind, Self, and Society* and *Movements of Thought in the Nineteenth Century*. Dewey, of course, is the most important, and the following works by him deserve attention: *The Influence of Darwinism on Philosophy, Reconstruction in Philosophy, Experience and Nature, Democracy and Education, Essays in Experimental Logic, Experience and Education*.

Finally, several philosophers and school leaders interpreted the theory and applied it directly to school practice. Carleton Washburne, William H. Kilpatrick, and Harold Rugg represented the child-centered emphasis in progressive education in the late 1920s and early 1930s. George S. Counts and Theodore Brameld were social reconstructionists.

Interpreters of pragmatism who worked to develop carefully and rigorously a conception of educational content and method emphasizing the scientific method and experimental criticism—avoiding the extremes represented by the child-centered group and the reconstructionists—were Sidney Hook, Boyd H. Bode, John L. Childs, and R. Bruce Raup.

THEORY

Advocates of progressive education are preoccupied with change. For them, change is the basic characteristic of our world. The physical universe, the geography of the earth, and biological forms exhibit a long history of change and development. Hypotheses supporting this view have been established by scientific inquiry, only to pave the way for further discoveries in the light of which specific theories are refined and modified. There is no clear evidence at any point that an overall design or pattern governs changes in our world. In any case, analysis and control of the changes, rather than formulation of overall theories of origin and design, is the central task. Naturalists, characteristically, are not particularly interested in speculation about first causes. They are too busy working to understand specific instances of change in specific areas.

Man himself has evolved from lower biological organisms. His fundamental drives he shares with other living creatures. His guiding moral values are constructed, not established in the nature of things. Truth, goodness, and beauty are culturally defined. The rules man observes in living with his fellow men are rules that have evolved through social processes; there is nothing absolute about them. Man's social life is much more complicated than that of most other living things, because of man's proficiency in using language. Nevertheless, it too is looked on as a product of evolution. Mind comes to be spoken of as a "bio-social emergent." What has been called mind is not really a substantive part of a person but is, rather, man's symbolic behavior (i.e., acting with or by means of symbols). Men have learned to stand and walk upright; thus the arms have been freed. The thumb-forefinger opposition makes it possible for them to use tools, and the mouth has been freed from the carrying and grasping tasks it serves in other similarly constructed animals. There is a loose lip and tongue structure with a highly developed musculature. This mouth and tongue musculature, coupled with a highly adaptable vocal structure, provide conditions necessary for the development of language. There is a large brain and a centralized nervous system. The life span is long enough to make a long period of learning possible.

The physiological uniqueness of man is not a sufficient explanation of civilization and learning, however. Here a sociological theory developed primarily by George H. Mead is drawn upon.[1] Language emerged at the human level; it was

---

[1] George H. Mead, *Mind, Self, and Society* (Chicago: University of Chicago Press, 1934). See also A. S. Clayton, *Emergent Mind and Education* (New York: Teachers College, Columbia University, 1943).

an emergent, not an inborn capacity or a preordained gift of some great prime mover. A mystery—yes. Perhaps even a miracle. But no more so than the emergence in time of mountains and valleys, and of the endless varieties of living things on earth. With the emergence of language, what traditional philosophers had called "mind" appears. For intellectual activity is still activity—behavior. To do something by means of language is still to *do* something. "Mind" is symbolic behavior. "Mind" is not a substance; it is a way of behaving; it is acting through symbols. "Mind" is "minding"—this way, it is a verb, not a noun.

Man is considered a product of evolution connected by a long line of descent with prehuman ancestors. Now he holds a place of prominence among the primates, having exhibited an unprecedented power of mastering his environment. He is more abundant and more widely distributed over the earth than any other primate species.

The universe in which he lives out his days includes compact masses such as the earth formed by condensation from a primordial cloud of cosmic dust and gas. Life itself is considered to have been a chemico-physical emergent, the process of its emergence subject to scientific analysis.[2] Although we have knowledge only of life on earth, enough is known about the physical makeup of other planets to suggest that life may also have arisen elsewhere in the universe.

If life could arise spontaneously from nonliving matter on the primordial earth, might it also have arisen elsewhere in the universe? This is a question that intrigues modern biologists and astronomers. So far no one knows the answer. Life may be

[2] See, for example, William T. Keeton, *Biological Science* (New York: W. W. Norton & Co., Inc., 1967), pp. 765 ff.

unique to the planet Earth. But few scientists working in this branch of biology think so; most are convinced that life has probably arisen many times in many places. They point out that there is no reason to think that any unduplicated event was necessary to the origin of life on earth, that, on the contrary, all the events now hypothesized and all the known characteristics of life seem to fall well within the general laws of the universe, i.e., that they are natural phenomena susceptible of duplication. Given the immense size of the universe, they argue, it would actually be unreasonable to think that life is restricted to one small planet in one minor solar system.[3]

Those biologically unique features of man which contributed to his rise to dominance on earth are his large brain, the development of a motor-speech center in the brain, the thumb-forefinger opposition of his hands making possible manipulation of tools, his high reproductive efficiency, and the slow rate of development from birth to adulthood which provides time and opportunity for influences of deliberate education.

These biological conditions have provided necessary but not fully sufficient conditions for the emergence of civilized man. With the development of language—itself a natural phenomenon—human culture begins and a sociological or cultural force is introduced which shapes continuing evolutionary process. The phenomenon of language, which makes possible, by the intervention of symbols, reflection upon experience, provides a means by which experience can be identified, criticized, and evaluated or judged. To put it another way, language makes it possible for men to think about and assess what has happened to them. And when we do this, our decisions about future events are affected; we

[3] Ibid., p. 772. See also pp. 772 ff.

direct our endeavors accordingly, and these endeavors, fac-
tored in purely as force of energy, affect the future.[4]

Nature is the all-inclusive category. Man and his universe
are natural. There is nothing over and above the realm of the
natural. Man is an organism struggling to satisfy his needs
and perpetuate himself in a natural world. The methods that
appear to have been most successful in conserving life and
contributing to the satisfaction of man's basic drives are
those we call scientific or empirical. Thus, while there is no
eternal truth, the *scientific method,* sometimes called the
critical method or the *method of intelligence,* is the best way
to get the best possible answers to all sorts of questions.

A New Logic

In the most fundamental and technical sense, the idea of
evolution was of greatest importance as it gave rise to a new
conception of the very nature of thought and inquiry. Older
formulations of the method of intellectual work had, in one
way or another, finally assumed the underlying presence of
an eternal, unchanging structure in the world. The Aristotelian conception of change which had persisted for centuries in the minds of Western men, although it involved
ideas such as *development* and *potentiality,* had not allowed
for genuine novelty. The Aristotelian view was that the process in which anything is involved is, after all, only a specific
instance of the eternal forms.[5] When terms like "development" or "evolution" were used by pre-Darwinian thinkers,
they did not mean the origin of new forms or a mutation
from an old species. Rather, change, growth, development,
and evolution were thought of as the traversing of a pre-

[4] See T. A. Goudge, *The Ascent of Life* (London: Ruskin House, George
Allen and Unwin Ltd., 1961), especially Chap. IV, "The Evolutionary Account of Man," pp. 133–151.

[5] John Dewey, *Reconstruction in Philosophy* (New York: Henry Holt &
Co., 1920), p. 58.

viously plotted cycle—as having been somehow planned before.[6]

When the modern conception of evolution was introduced, on the other hand, the idea of the underlying presence of a structural design and of a prior intelligence and prime mover working in and through it was called into question and discarded. Organic adaptations were attributed to constant variations, with elimination of the less fit variations in the struggle for survival. There seemed to be no need for postulating a prime mover as an eternal planner or designer.[7]

This was thought to be the case, not only in nonhuman nature but also in situations involving human beings. The center of human behavior was no longer considered to be in the relation between God and man. As in nature new forms emerge and new mutants spring from old species, so in the life of man new and unforeseen modes of behavior emerge. Man and his enterprises are placed in a natural environment, and they, like any other natural phenomena, are considered to have a natural origin and a natural setting. Thus, the fundamental importance of evolutionary thought lay in its implications for intellectual method.

It has now grown clear that the fundamental importance of evolutionary thought, like that of . . . earlier naturalisms, lay primarily in its methodological significance: there was to be no sharp difference in intellectual methods in treating man and the other aspects of the Nature of which he was taken to be a part.[8]

This point of view accepts novelty as a constant feature of the world—novelty in the very forms or species of occur-

[6] Ibid.

[7] John Dewey, *The Influence of Darwin on Philosophy* (New York: Henry Holt & Co., 1910), pp. 11–12.

[8] John Herman Randall, Jr., "The Nature of Naturalism," in *Naturalism and the Human Spirit*, ed. Y. H. Krikorian (New York: Columbia University Press, 1944), p. 357.

rences as well as in details of specific processes. Man and his experiences are seen as parts of nature. The gulf between the "nature" studied by chemists, physicists, and biologists, and the "nature" studied by sociologists, psychologists, and educationists is closed.[9]

In his essay "The Influence of Darwinism on Philosophy," John Dewey points out three positive characteristics of the new logic arising out of evolutionary naturalism:

1. Inquiry comes to be directed to how special changes serve and defeat our purposes rather than to the discovery and statement of some ultimate meaning or eternal essence back of the special changes.

2. The concern of inquiry comes to be with the present use and meaning of experience, its qualities and values being taken as they come. The attempt to justify wholesale certain qualities and values of existence and to disparage others is given up.

3. Such a conception of inquiry injects responsibility into life. We are seen as having a real part in determining the future, in that our actions are viewed as having power in indeterminate situations. We can actually have a part in creating the future—in making our own good world. We can to some degree affect the future development of situations in which we are involved.

In fact, this effort to control or create a future emerges as the central purpose of all thought. The function of inquiry is to control special changes so that our purposes are served rather than defeated, and it is to this end that the exercise of intelligence is supremely valuable. Seen this way, morality is the exercise of intelligence in life situations. The good life is the life devoted to inquiry for the purpose of enhancing

[9] Ibid., p. 356.

the values of future experience. It is to make future experiences more accessible to us, to make them enjoyable, and to make them valuable.

William James viewed the self as a stream of consciousness. A mysterious transcendental ego or Aristotelian soul was considered not necessary to explain human behavior. The part of oneself which knows, and the part which "knows that it knows" are simply different aspects of one unity, argued James.[10] He maintained that the hypothesis of the soul was superfluous for psychology, and that human behavior could be explained by states of consciousness.[11] The eternal principles of logic or ethics about which philosophers of the past had spoken are simply the content, whatever it may have been, of the understanding. It is the thoughts that do the thinking. There is no substance or entity which may rightly be called *mind* or *soul*.

The states of consciousness are all that psychology needs to do her work with. Metaphysics or theology may prove the Soul to exist; but for psychology the hypothesis of such a substantial principle of unity is superfluous.[12]

For James, all knowledge arises out of direct experiences of or acquaintanceship with things. The world of things outside the individual really exists. Things are interrelated and can be experienced, thus known by an individual. James called himself a pluralist. He referred to our world as an "open universe." What he consistently denied was that there was any overall universal plan or scheme by application of

[10] William James, *Psychology* (New York: Henry Holt & Co., 1892, 1920, 1935), p. 176.
[11] Ibid., p. 203.
[12] Ibid.

which the whole could be understood. The world is a world of many things, many relationships, and many principles.[13]

These were important ideas, for they were in conflict with traditional philosophies. Traditional philosophies had taught that there was somehow a final end or overall principle which included everything else and in terms of which everything else could be understood. Pluralism took the stand that there is no such principle. The world is many things; and we must simply learn to live with it that way.

As an organism moves in this world, obstacles to ongoing activity arise. Problems constituted by such blockings of activity stimulate inquiry, and the acts of inquiry, which are in the nature of problem-solving activities, are initiated. A problem is viewed as a blocking or inhibition of ongoing activity; the criterion of whether or not a problem is solved is whether or not the sort of activity that was going on before the rise of the problem can be continued. The so-called "true" is to be found in the working of the hypotheses devised to release the inhibited or blocked activity. A hypothesis works when a process that has struck a snag can start working again and go on.[14]

The way a scientist tests a hypothesis resembles the way an animal works to get out of danger by finding an escape and running away. He burrows around in the problem. He tries one thing, then another. A scientist seeks a way out of a problem, just as the animal looks for a hole in the fence through which he can escape from the enclosure in which he is trapped.[15] The scientist works for months on a complicated research problem. Then one day he hits upon a theory, acts upon it, and gets away—or escapes from the difficulty that has

[13] William James, *A Pluralistic Universe* (New York: Longmans, Green and Co., 1909), pp. 321–323.

[14] George H. Mead, *Movements of Thought in the Nineteenth Century* (Chicago: University of Chicago Press, 1936), p. 349.

[15] Ibid.

held up his work. The test of his theory or hypothesis is, of course, crucial. If he "escapes from his difficulty" or "gets out of the hole," he pushes ahead into another phase of the work. If not, he starts burrowing again to find another clue.

Critical and competent interpreters of pragmatism have never made it a justification for anarchy or shallow expediency. Yet the biological context in which pragmatic thought and exposition moved at the beginning of the century was not fully adequate to explain and justify social controls. A vulgarized educational and moral interpretation of pragmatism came to be that truth is whatever works; whatever produces desired results in a given context, regardless of further-reaching consequences. In the popular mind, pragmatism came to mean an individualistic relativism such as that attributed to the Greek sophists by Socrates.

James was understood to advocate a psychological, behavioristic pragmatism that sanctioned any solution of any problem which allowed activity to proceed. Whatever the individual found to resolve his difficulty appeared approvable. It was sometimes pointed out that James found it possible to encourage people to "will" their beliefs, whether or not the beliefs were critically formulated.[16] It appeared that he was willing to sanction superstition and humbug in religion as long as the religious experiences afforded were in some way satisfying to believers.[17] The implication seemed to be that one person's solution is as good as another's, and that individuals should be free to explore and invent—to discover or create beliefs that satisfy them as individuals, with little or no concern for the long-term social consequences.

The fight against absolutes in the early years of our cen-

[16] William James, *The Will to Believe* (New York: Longmans, Green and Co., 1917).

[17] William James, *Varieties of Religious Experience* (New York: Longmans, Green and Co., 1902).

tury was frequently waged in the name of James. The influence of the more humanistic, emotionally toned pragmatism associated with James remains with us to some extent and continues to exert a degree of force in morals and education.

Influence on Social Science

The impact of pragmatism can be seen in the social sciences as they developed after 1900. One of the most impressive examples was the so-called New History of scholars such as James Harvey Robinson and Carl Becker. This was a move to relate historical scholarship to contemporary concerns and tensions. The view was that historical scholarship is an intellectual instrument for dealing with social problems. In all probability, the shift from conventional systematic history to the social-problems approach, sometimes referred to as the *social studies movement* in the public schools, was inspired by the New History.

Carl Becker compares the twentieth-century outlook with the thirteenth-century world view of Saint Thomas Aquinas. The arguments of Saint Thomas can neither be affirmed nor refuted by moderns, he asserts. They are simply irrelevant, for men can no longer think of existence as a divine drama having a meaning and purpose as the creation of some great mastermind. To the contrary, modern men must regard the world as a continuous flux, as in constant change in all its phases.[18] History, as a record of past experience which may furnish principles for guiding present effort, does not render impartial directives. Men find what they wish to find in the past; they prove what they wish to prove. Although an actual series of events once occurred, we cannot get to the original, and consequently, we are forced to identify history with knowledge of history or what may be designated simply as "memory of

[18] Carl Becker, *The Heavenly City of the Eighteenth Century Philosophers* (New Haven: Yale University Press, 1932), pp. 11–12.

things said and done." [19] The present includes a past and a future. History is a dynamic, moving function of a human being. It is a different record, depending on who is doing the writing, his culture, and his values.[20] Each age writes its own history. The history of one generation differs from that of another, because to different ages the past means different things. Every generation must understand the past in terms of its own needs, tensions, and issues. Every generation ". . . must inevitably play on the dead whatever tricks it finds necessary for its own peace of mind." [21]

Like Becker, James Harvey Robinson disparaged the quest for objective history. All students of the past, he maintained, have to pick and choose, and their selections are governed by many unrecognized assumptions.[22] To justify one set of aims over another is scarcely possible, according to Robinson. There are many possible points of departure and as many endpoints.[23] Thus, past experience can scarcely be a nonpartisan guide to men in times of perplexity. For the history written is a function of the aims and purposes of the historians doing the writing, and one aim or purpose is about as defensible as the next. Continuing evolution of society and continuous reconstruction of the past by a moving present is assured. Each person who discusses human affairs has his peculiar frame of reference. Study of the points of view from which opinions proceed thus becomes a major task of scholars in the social fields.[24]

Thus, since human interests are always prior to facts, it

[19] Carl Becker, *Everyman His Own Historian* (New York: Crofts Publishing Co., 1935), p. 235.

[20] Ibid., pp. 242–243.

[21] Ibid., p. 253.

[22] J. H. Robinson, *The Human Comedy* (New York: Harper & Brothers, 1937), p. 380.

[23] Ibid., p. 378.

[24] Charles A. Beard, *The Discussion of Human Affairs* (New York: The Macmillan Co., 1936), pp. 123–124.

appears that records of past experience are relative to time, place, and the causes, interests, beliefs, and prejudices of those doing the recording. All social investigation may be seen as proceeding from immediate concerns of the present. A corollary to the "cash value" interpretation of pragmatism is provided. The new historians appear to say not only, "Whatever works is right," but also, "One person's idea of what has worked is as good as the next." The new historians seem to be contending that the interests of the observer condition what he sees, so that interpretations of past experience are relative to time, place, and the causes, interests, and beliefs of those doing the recording. If human minds are biosocial products, the individual must think with the categories that his environment has given him. Thus he can scarcely transcend his place in time, space, and class to view the whole. He is a part of the process and he can see the process only from his vantage point.

EDUCATIONAL APPLICATIONS

When intelligent direction of present experiences to make specific changes serve our purposes becomes the center of concern, a theory of education markedly different from classic theories emerges. Now the educational task is to foster in the young this ability to control and direct experience. Education is seen as an effort to control the future. In educative experiences we learn how to direct our present experiences so as to achieve control of future experiences. To be an educated person is to be in command of skills and knowledges to meet and master the new problems that come our way as we live our lives. The purpose of education, then, is to help us grow,[25] but inasmuch as we must grow in a world char-

[25] See Sidney Hook, *John Dewey, an Intellectual Portrait* (New York: The John Day Co., Inc., 1939), p. 179.

acterized by constant change, education devoted to the end of growth in this changing world must foster flexibility and adaptability.

Here, then, we have the philosophical foundation for a new education. In a changing world involving no absolutes, wherein man is looked upon as a natural emergent in a long evolutionary process, education is released from its bondage to tradition and social class. As has been suggested, there were some who found in science and democracy, taken as educational ideals, support for a relativistic, almost anti-intellectual kind of educational individualism. They frequently used the terms *science* and *democracy* together. They saw the method of science as tentative and hypothetical rather than didactic and authoritarian. To them, the scientific ideal meant a way of life—a way that liberates men from convention, arbitrary authority, and dogma. They held in mind the long history of conflict between empirical method and deductive or authoritarian method; it appeared to them that science had always been iconoclastic; it had always challenged vested power. To them, to be scientific meant to enter into free, open questioning of all established routines. They found in science justification for a kind of romantic laissez-faire in school practice. Thus arose the claim of critics of the schools that in the name of vulgarized, pseudo-scientific point of view, a certain softness and intellectual and moral flabbiness sometimes developed.

Still others, men of different temperament and attitude, were inspired by the possibility that education could itself become a science. As they saw it, to be scientific meant to apply techniques of quantification and mathematical measurement in order to discover more efficient ways of teaching, building school buildings, working out school financial problems, and managing equipment and personnel. The scientific ideal meant, quite literally, making an experimental science of the educational enterprise. The methodological model was drawn from the physical sciences in which techniques of quantification and precise measurement had been most evidently successful.

For a third group, the ideals of science and democracy in education came to mean the systematic effort to build a reasonable social order. It seemed to them that it should be possible to predict and control social events for the health and welfare of men. This was to be accomplished by applying to social problems those techniques that had proved so successful in medicine, public health, and engineering.

The Child-Centered School

The revolt against the Dewey who seemed to say that the school should be adjusted to the child began almost as early among the progressives as it did outside their ranks. Yet, with all the modifications and explanations, Dewey's pedagogy remained an application to the school of the ideals of democratic liberalism which were popular in America during the first three or four decades of the present century. Dewey's social theory is of the milieu of Woodrow Wilson or Robert LaFollette. What was different about Dewey the educationist was that he put the social philosophy to work in the very halls, rooms, and grounds of schools. His justification was that schools were in and of the society; he could see no ground for one social morality outside school and another inside. Why? Because children and adolescents are people. After all, it was not until 1920 that women were finally recognized as people in American political life. Seen this way, progressive education was to children and adolescents what the women's rights movement was to women, and what the fair employment practices and civil rights movements have been to Negroes. The notion can be supported intellectually, and its educational applications can thus be seen as grounded in an understandable theory. The notion is also one of sentiment and romance, however, like the other liberal democratic notions with which we have compared it. Eccentric people given to extremes, governed more by feeling than intellect, and lacking good common sense, have been swept up by abolition, women's rights, the temperance movement, and various civil rights crusades. Progressive education, likewise a humanitarian movement, gained its coterie of people of warm sentiment and rattling brains.

Insofar as fundamental educational theory is concerned, the overweening emphasis on emancipation of the child passed in the early 1930s. Since then, fundamental educational theory in the train of John Dewey has moved to a much more sober consideration of the educational significance of the logic of science and a concern about the social conditions of educational liberalism. Nevertheless, the child-centered sentimentalism of early progressive education did not pass from the scene so quickly. Freud provided a new kind of supporting rationale, and the study of child development gained enormous momentum.

The educational liberalism of the 1920s must be distinguished from the liberalism of the classical tradition and of the Judaic-Christian tradition. It has more in common with the earthy liberalism of Walt Whitman. It is an emphasis on the individual human being as he comes, naked and unschooled into his culture. There are elements of Rousseau in the ideals of the child-centered school. There is the suggestion that man liberated from the conventions of his society is far more blessed than man nurtured by these conventions. It is not absurd to hold in mind that the decade of the child-centered school was also the decade of Prohibition, of the Charleston, of the flapper, of F. Scott Fitzgerald, and of wild speculation on the stock market. While special economic, political, and social forces were at work, the iconoclasm of the 1920s found intellectual grounding in the new relativism of the philosophy called pragmatism. For the pragmatic philosophers seemed to advise people to test everything against experience (*their* experience), and it was interpreted to mean that whatever appeared not to "pay off" in immediate gratification might well be discarded.

This way, education has its locus in the experience of children. Who is to judge whether these experiences are worthwhile? The people who are having them, of course. Then what if some things done in school appear not to be received favorably by children? What if the experiences provided by the school do not meet criteria of satisfaction in the lives of the children in the school? Then the school should be fitted to the child.[26] The task of the school is to meet the needs of children, and the sense of need held by the children is to be studied, respected, and honored.

But what happens to subject matter in such a school? Are there not certain things that must be learned, willy-nilly? Perhaps, but any subject matter that remains dull, boring, and apparently meaningless to children at the time when they are assigned to work upon it must be viewed with extreme caution. Children, not subject matters, are of prime importance. When a matter becomes important to young people, in their terms and in their own lives, they will want to learn it. It is better to wait. Subject matter laid out in advance has no special sanctity; in fact, it is likely to be inappropriate, for who can predict ahead of time where the interests and concerns of children will lead them?

Does this mean that a group is to sit Quaker-like waiting

[26] See Carleton Washburne, *Adjusting the School to the Child* (Yonkers: World Book Co., 1932), Caroline Pratt, *I Learn from Children* (New York: Simon and Schuster, 1948), W. H. Kilpatrick, *Foundations of Method* (New York: The Macmillan Co., 1925).

for the spirit to move? No. This assumes, again, a false conception of learning. Learning is doing. We learn what we live. Therefore, the school should be a living place—a place where young people do things together, things that seem important to them. As they do things together, there will be things to be learned, and here the teacher can help. School becomes more like a settlement house or like the older rural community in which young people learned most of the important things in life not by precept, or even by example, but by active apprenticeship in the activities of the community.[27]

Actually, fundamental educational theory moved to provide important qualifications to the slogans of the 1920s during the second quarter of the century. It is interesting to note, however, that as the educational theorists moved away from the slogans, the child study movement, which was ostensibly experimental rather than theoretical, picked up and gave form to the slogans. The influence of psychoanalytic thought on child psychologists reinforced the emphasis on permissiveness and adjustment of the school regimen to the "self-demand schedule" of the child. Forcing children to do things that they did not want to do was considered to have harmful psychological effects. Psychologists presented evidence to show that tiny babies thrive when they determine their own schedules for feeding, evacuating, and sleeping. It was demonstrated that when children were allowed to choose freely from foods available on an open cafeteria line, they chose well-balanced meals. The evils of parental overprotection were pointed out; children must be free to develop in their own way. The authoritarian school was said to present

[27] See Joseph K. Hart, *Education in the Humane Community,* a John Dewey Society publication, ed. with an intro. by H. Gordon Hullfish (New York: Harper & Brothers, 1951), L. Thomas Hopkins, *Integration, Its Meaning and Application* (New York: D. Appleton-Century Co., 1937), Elsie Clapp, *Community Schools in Action* (New York: The Viking Press, Inc., 1939).

all the psychological hazards pointed out in the authoritarian, overprotective family. A school must be democratic in order to nurture strong, self-reliant young people.

It was recognized that the democratic school is not the same as the anarchic or laissez-faire school. Some sort of order must emerge. Nevertheless, the order was to emerge not by being imposed from above by authority figures, but according to the needs of children in the school as these are expressed. Again, the analogy of Arnold Gesell's self-demand schedule is appropriate. There is to be order, but the order must arise out of the felt needs of the people involved. In school, this is to be achieved by pupil-planning of activities, in which the teacher is to act as adviser and counselor.

With this tremendous emphasis on meeting the needs of children and youth—on their own terms—the role of the teacher increasingly becomes that of counselor or adviser. Thus, much interest in, and concern about, guidance develops. Young people must be helped to make their decisions, but *they* must do the deciding; they must not be told what to do. They must be helped to do what they want to do. This way, guidance is seen to be close to the center of the work of the school. Not teaching subjects to students but guiding students in their decision-making is the task. Choice of school studies, choice of a life work, choice of a college, choices in the more intimate matters of personal and social life—the trained guidance counselor works in this realm.

Not only psychology but also aesthetics of a sort was drawn upon to support the practices of the child-centered school. A group of educators, literary critics, and artists stress the importance of art and the art experience as neglected dimensions in educational work. These thinkers may be seen as developing a sophisticated educational theory which is in the heritage of the child-centered school.

In a world of ever-increasing change, so their reasoning

goes, teachers cannot foretell what children will need to think. Faced with new problems in a new age, it is extremely important, they argue, that sources of unique, creative insight be tapped. If men are to meet change and mold it to their advantage, sources of creative thought and action, warped and suppressed by traditional disciplinary educational practice, must bloom. Our modern interdependent world society cannot trust its affairs to blind forces. If freedom is to be preserved, intelligent, cooperative struggle for freedom is necessary. The struggle demands creative social thinking of a high order, and it is of crucial importance that the schools produce individuals capable of such creative thought. As change is so deep-cutting that order and design cannot be discovered, but must actually be created and imposed, likewise change is so inclusive that an attempt to deal with it by isolating specific problems for experimental treatment is inadequate. Ends and ideals must be projected. The situation must be sized up and structured as by a creative artist.

American life is characterized by a shallow materialism and opportunism. The artists in America, maintained Lewis Mumford, have not been recognized as they should have been because of this expedient, opportunistic materialism.[28] The artist's vision—his design or ideal in the light of which great plans are made—comes as a deeply personal experience. It is a "one-man job" finally. It is not a problem-solving experience in the narrow sense. It involves the feelings, emotions, and total sensitivities of a person. Thus, to treat the method of scientific problem-solving as if it were the only possible educational method is incorrect. There is another method to which attention must be given, designated by Rugg as the

[28] Lewis Mumford, "Pragmatic Acquiescence: a Reply," *New Republic*, 19 January 1927.

method of "organic awareness." [29] This is the method which characterizes the work of artists—in music, the drama, literature, sculpture, and painting.[30] It is this method which should be applied to social problems; man can be a craftsman in the social scene. He can design and operate his own good world.

There is an element of the artist in all men. Each person is to some degree a creator. All products of human endeavor partake of a degree of quality, form, style, and breeding. This is the artistic quality, and it is the product of human creative activity. The artist is an organizer. He is always trying to give form or pattern to life. Yet each person who does creative thinking gives a different expression to life; each expresses what he sees, and each sees it differently. A criticism of the tendency in American schools to emphasize values bound up with production, business, and industry appears. It is said that we have worked for efficiency, adjustment, and equality in such things as employment and housing, but that we have neglected the drama of human living. There has been too much of a tendency, it is asserted, to think of people as machines. People have not been treated as people—as living, feeling human beings with lives full of sorrows and a few joys.[31]

Educational practice must, then, break with the dead hand of the past in order to free human beings to create the new forms of order which are a condition of survival. Educational freedom, the kind of educational freedom that the slogans of the 1920s and the pronouncements of the child psychologists suggest, is a condition of the good life in a

[29] See Harold Rugg, *Now Is the Moment* (New York: Duell, Sloan, and Pearce, 1943), p. 37.

[30] Ibid., pp. 104–105.

[31] Lewis Mumford, *The Story of Utopias* (New York: Boni and Liveright), 1922.

beautiful society. The reason for a child-centered education is to build the future-centered society.

The Science of Education Movement

In every enterprise some division exists between the theorists and the technologists. The latter are the people who "get things done." They are expediters; they concentrate on acquiring and putting to practice "know-how." They are frequently impatient with the theorists, who keep asking, "Why do we do it this way?" The theoretical mentality has more to do, however, with policy formation, or at least with the framing of statements of policy. Some might argue that framing of policy is often a rationalization after the fact, merely a kind of "public relations" device. This latter view would make of the educational theorist an "educational journalist." On the other hand, many would counter that the proposals of the theorists have great significance in pointing the technologists one way or another, that they play a leadership role in creating policy, and that they do more than merely report policy.

Professors of education earlier in the present century were frequently technologists rather than philosophers. That is, they gave their attention not so much to fundamental questions of educational aims and purposes but to techniques of pedagogy. Their concern was to make pedagogy scientific; it was with the technology of teaching rather than with the goals of education, and educational technology has not passed from the scene. A formidable array of test batteries, manuals of instruction, and pedagogic machines has been built into American education. The popularity of devices such as the College Entrance Board examinations and the services of the Educational Testing Service would suggest that technology is here to stay—even in higher education. Intelligence testing, vocabulary grading, various methods of homogeneous grouping for instructional procedures, curriculum organization based on surveys of tasks performed by adults in various occupations, specialization in school organization and instruction, and application of techniques of business management to school administration were proposed by the educational technologists.

It must be emphasized that the "gadgetry" of modern education, epitomized in the minds of some in the so-called true-false test, is not inescapably involved in progressive education. In fact, the literature of progressive education is replete with criticisms of such devices, and leading educational technologists such as E. L. Thorndike were sometimes vigorously critical of so-called progressive education. The more vigorous advocates of educational television as a substitute for face-to-face contact between teachers and pupils have been associated with the Fund for the Advancement of Education, which, again, cannot be seen as under the special aegis of progressive education. Actually, Dewey and his followers in progressive education had little if any interest in educational technology of this sort. All modern schools make use of educational technology, but pragmatic or progressivist theory is not responsible for it. Rather, it was educational psychologists under the leadership of Thorndike who gave it stronger support. George D. Strayer, who was perhaps the pioneer figure in the development of a so-called science of school administration, was a student and disciple of Thorndike. Probably the educational psychologists rather than Dewey and the "progressives" should be given whatever praise or blame is to be attached to the development of educational technology in twentieth-century America.

To some who view modern public education with alarm, there is too much machinery in schools. Children are constantly being tested—not in the subjects they are studying, but as to personality, mechanical aptitudes, interests, and social adjustment. Printed workbooks are used in many courses; a synthetic, "graded" vocabulary constitutes the books read. There is a plethora of charts, graphs, models, and audio-visual aids. The machinery of the modern school impresses some as having been complicated beyond all reason.

Certainly much of the educational gadgetry is here to stay. Insofar as this involves measurements and computations having to do with construction and maintenance of school buildings, a sober critic can scarcely raise objection. Attractive, hygienically correct school buildings are all to the good. To romanticize old, smelly buildings more or less efficiently managed is farfetched. Furthermore, to the extent that techniques of the efficiency expert have been applied to the business management of schools, probably the public has gained. Modern public schools are big business. Expert management of funds and records can do no harm.

Much more dubious, however, may be the values accruing from the application of mass-production, assembly-line techniques to the process of instruction. How can learning be a creative adventure when it moves in a maze of standardized, carefully graded, mass-produced workbooks, charts, and film strips? Again, if the acid test of learning is the ability to use knowledge in fresh situations, does the standardized multiple-choice test do it? The essence of standardized tests is the controlled response. Alternatives are strictly limited; one of four or five buttons must be pressed; there is no opportunity to explain why. Nevertheless, to reject these devices out-of-hand may well be like refusing to ride in an automobile or make use of the telephone. Use of devices such as the American Council on Education Psychological Examination and the Miller Analogies for college entrance determinations is not likely to pass away in the near future. Even the College Entrance Examination Board tests are now cast in such form that they can be machine-scored. Moreover, it cannot be claimed that the Educational Testing Service at Princeton, New Jersey, has been boycotted by educational traditionalists.

Although unquestionably the science of education movement was, like the child-centered school, inspired by the ideals of science and democracy, its products cannot be evaluated solely in terms of these origins. Nor can educational technology be looked on as a direct application of pragmatic or progressivist educational theory. How the educational machines invented by the technologists are to be used, and to what extent, are questions that cut across the major lines of educational controversy in our day.

Social Reconstructionism

A strong case can be made for the view that the very rise of *Education* as college and university subject matter was brought about by the ferment of evolutionary, naturalistic ideas among American intellectuals, and the consequent effort to apply scientific ideals in education. Nevertheless, an evolutionary, naturalistic ideology may also suggest basic changes in the conceptions of the purposes of education that men hold; and the literature of educational controversy demonstrates relatively more concern about these changes in educational goals than about the impact of educational technology.

Thus, regardless of the special techniques used in classrooms of schools, what are schools really for? Whose values are to be served in the schools? One answer, inspired and supported to some considerable degree by the theories of evolutionary naturalism, is that the schools are really for the children and that the values of the children are those to be served in the schools. Yet, some who began with this individualistic emphasis were struck by the miseducative forces affecting the lives of children and young people outside the school. Thus they tended to emphasize in their educational theorizing the importance of the social context, and the ideals of science and democracy came to mean working deliberately through the schools to achieve a rational social order. The notion that a just society may be established and sustained by an educational program devoted to that end has appeared many times in the history of thought. It is present in Plato's *Republic* and in Comenius's *Great Didactic*. The works of Herbert Spencer and other late-nineteenth- and early-twentieth-century writers such as Edward Bellamy involve the idea of a deliberately planned society. Single-tax theorists and supporters of technocracy have, in different ways, suggested the possibility of a planned and planning society through education. Some of the twentieth-century educationists considered that if the mission of the schools is to develop intelligence, this meant being critically intelligent about social problems. It also meant, so they reasoned, that the schools would thus teach young people to be critically intelligent about their society, and to try to apply to their roles as citizens the knowledge and methods appropriate to social problems. It was argued that the essence of intelligence is planning—foresight. An unplanned society would therefore appear to be a society dedicated to chance rather than controlled by intelligence.

In organization and support, the public schools are tax-supported cooperatives. More than that, however, the public schools are inescapably committed to transmitting the official morality. The society does not wish the school to teach how to cheat on the income tax return, how to keep a member of a minority group from buying a home in one's neighborhood, or how to win at a gaming table. Even though some might consider these things important, they nevertheless do not belong to the official morality; therefore, if they are to be acquired, they must be learned outside and not taught formally and deliberately in school.

What is the official if, at points, perhaps unrealistic morality we affirm as that to be taught admittedly and publicly? It is comprised of honesty, candor, concern for others, sharing, and cooperation. The official morality, in other words, is the morality of brotherhood, but an obvious dualism exists in the society with regard to it. We seem to wish it taught, but not too well, for the official morality may become embarrassing if taken too seriously. Nevertheless, there have been some master teachers in the schools, and as they teach the official morality, youngsters are likely to begin to work with it meaningfully and critically. When they do this, some of the customary ways of businessmen and politicians appear morally questionable.

Over and above the ideological and sociological factors mentioned in preceding paragraphs, it should be pointed out that in the 1920s and 1930s educationists, like sociologists, historians, economists, and philosophers, frequently discussed current social and economic theories. Of course there were some socialists in education, as there were in other fields of research and inquiry. In the deepest years of the Great Depression some of these considered the possibility that the public school might be used as a deliberate instrument of social reconstruction to bring about a social organization grounded in critically intelligent planning rather than laissez-faire. The movement gained a few able disciples. After the beginning of World War II, however, it received less attention. Nevertheless, a handful of leading educationists worked to keep such considerations alive. They continued to provide a target for those who could criticize the public school for a so-called socialistic bias.

It is now a commonplace that the depression of 1929

extending into and through the 1930s carried with it a deep-moving shift in cultural outlook in the United States. The exuberant immaturities of the 1920s were supplanted by a more somber concern about the economic future of our nation. Were the characteristics of the 1920s completely lost, however? Recall the political and economic iconoclasm of Franklin D. Roosevelt and the "Happy Days Are Here Again" campaign song. Moreover, the repeal of the Eighteenth Amendment in a sense brought to reality a persisting fantasy of the 1920s. The question raised is whether the values of the 1920s has changed. Perhaps not. Perhaps what American people still wanted was liberty to have a good time in their own way, making their own rules. It may well be, then, that the so-called mentality of the 1930s had to do with changes in strategies for realizing the values of the 1920s.

Here we mean by "the mentality of the 1930s" a set of ideas about economy and politics in the United States. As the depression dragged on, with many Americans experiencing misery in a land of plenty and with the more fortunate looking backward with sadness at the passing of the great fun of the previous decade, some concluded that social control of the means of production was the answer. Apparently capitalism had failed. Apparently the liberal ideals of the 1920s were only to be realized as the people took over the means of production. Was it possible that a new social order was demanded in the United States? To be sure, this did not mean a society in which the basic civil liberties had been surrendered as in totalitarian states; nevertheless, a society in which wealth was more equitably distributed to those whose sweat and pain had been instrumental in producing it. But why? What was the appeal? What values was it thought might be thus achieved? Notice that the values were finally those of food, clothing, shelter, and security—

they were economic values. They were the values of the realm of the natural, rather than those of the realm of the supramundane. The values of the depression years were similar to those of the 1920s. The change of mentality had to do with proposals for achieving them.

Thus it becomes possible to understand how educators who, in an earlier day, had given adherence to the child-centered school movement, began after 1929 to give more and more attention to ways and means by which the school might contribute to the building of a new social order in which such depressions did not occur. Writings by John Dewey, W. H. Kilpatrick, and their followers and colleagues throughout the country reveal this shift in emphasis. Whereas before 1929 these thinkers devoted their major statements on educational matters to proposals for providing more creative freedom for youngsters in schools, after 1929 they gave much more attention to the social conditions for such freedom. Once again this is understandable, and it does not mean that the positions of the pre-depression years were being completely negated. A modicum of security in the possession of food, clothing, and shelter is presupposed in any efforts to bring about greater liberty for children in schools.

The argument over means and ends during the depression years produced the internal dissension among progressive educationists which contributed to the collapse of organized progressive education. The social reconstructionists held that experience-centered, pupil-planned, activity schools, although in many ways ideal schools, could not cope with the problems of social reconstruction demanded during the depression. Our society was seen as engaged in a fierce class struggle, and control of the schools was one of the issues at stake. The free, open, pupil-planning advocated earlier by most followers of Dewey and Kilpatrick was viewed as lending itself to subtle propaganda by the power groups in Amer-

ica motivated by their own selfish interests. Some concluded
that the experience-centered, pupil-planned activity school
could only exist in a society in which economic justice had
been achieved. This being the case, certain educational tasks
having to do with reconstruction of the social order must take
priority over the demands of the ideal school talked about
in the 1920s.

A credo for the social reconstructionists was furnished
when George Counts published his sensational *Dare the
Schools Build a New Social Order?* in 1932.[32] A book edited
by Kilpatrick, to which a number of pragmatist educators
contributed, developed the theme of social action through
the schools.[33] Two educational journals, *The Social Frontier*[34]
and *Frontiers of Democracy*,[35] became organs of discussion
and controversy, the persisting theme being the role of the
schools in bringing about social change.

The social reconstructionists argued that some sort of
indoctrination is inescapable in educational work. Their
argument was that of the "frame of reference" as developed
by the new historians. A point of view always operates, so
they argued. Teachers cannot be neutral. This being so, it is
important to decide deliberately and critically which point
of view is to dominate educational work. At a time when a

[32] George S. Counts, *Dare the Schools Build a New Social Order?* (New York: The John Day Co., Inc., 1932).

[33] W. H. Kilpatrick (ed.) and others, *The Educational Frontier* (New York: The Century Co., 1933).

[34] *Social Frontier: a Journal of Educational Criticism and Reconstruction* 1–10, no. 81 (October 1934–December 1943). Published in New York by The Social Frontier, Inc., 1934–1943. Subtitled in October 1937–June 1939, "A Medium of Expression of the John Dewey Society for the Study of Education and Culture."

[35] With the October 1939, issue, the title *Frontiers of Democracy* was substituted for the former title. From October 1939–December 1943, the reference to the John Dewey Society was dropped. *Frontiers of Democracy* was published by the Progressive Education Association; publication ceased with vol. 10, no. 81 (December 1943).

great nation is in deep economic difficulty an educational sine qua non is an intellectual orientation that places the school on the side of social justice. There is a moral obligation here—the moral obligation for organized, institutionalized education to dedicate itself to bringing about the social conditions that make freedom possible.

When this is done systematically and deliberately, however, what happens to the freedom, the activity, the deeply sensitive concern for the individual about which the earlier child-centered-school people had talked? To some considerable degree they go by the board, at least until the crisis has passed. Thus, so far as pedagogy is concerned, the social reconstructionists might be said to have been conservative or traditional. More didactic, more formally structured methods of teaching were suggested. Certainly, using the school to build a new social order demands a structured curriculum.

The progressivists who continued to hold to the values of the child-centered school were at first confused, then indignant. They claimed that the social reconstructionists were violating the avowed ends in the means. They insisted that liberty, democracy, experience, and activity in schools with aims and ends determined as much by the children as by the teachers were unqualified goods, and that no economic crisis could justify giving up these educational means.

During the years of World War II the social reconstructionist discussion gradually faded. So many far-reaching social reforms had been achieved during the Roosevelt Administration that some educators considered the battle for social justice won. In any case, unemployment and overproduction were problems no more, and the moral issues posed by Nazism and Fascism overshadowed domestic concerns. Then too, extremists among the child-centered group had, on their own and in response to the social changes of the years, become less extreme. Once more the values of liberty, experience, and activity, along with cooperative planning in classrooms had not been forsworn. More and more attention was being given to the importance of order in educational work, however, and more and more educators were ready to grant that children grow up not in a vacuum but in social conditions of a special sort in special times and places. Yet the social reconstructionist point of view did not die out completely. Harold Rugg, B. Othanel Smith, William O. Stanley, and Theodore Brameld [36] are among educators who continued to use the term and devote thought to the ways in which the school can function as an instrument of social reconstruction while preserving essential democratic civil liberties.

The reconstructionists argued that creative social thought must be inspired by a vision, by a kind of imagined Utopia. The vision is grounded in critical intellectual formulations, yet it is held as a far-off goal or target, the complete fulfillment of which is not expected in the near future.[37] What America needs, they said, is an organic order that takes form as creative geniuses work on the social scene. This will arise, so we are told, from the creators of new ideas.[38]

[36] Theodore Brameld, *Towards a Reconstructed Philosophy of Education* (New York: Dryden Press, 1956); Harold Rugg and William Withers, *Social Foundations of Education* (Englewood Cliffs, N.J.: Prentice-Hall, Inc., 1955), pp. 623 ff.; B. Othanel Smith, William O. Stanley, and J. Harlan Shores, *Fundamentals of Curriculum Development* (Yonkers: World Book Co., 1950), pp. 187, 724–743.

[37] See Mumford, *Story of Utopias*, p. 252. Karl Mannheim, *Ideology and Utopia* (London: K. Paul, Trench, Trubner, 1936), and Mannheim, *Man and Society in an Age of Reconstruction* (London: K. Paul, Trench, Trubner, 1940), are works occasionally cited by those who would advocate social reconstruction through education.

[38] See Theodore Brameld, *Patterns of Educational Philosophy* (Yonkers: World Book Co., 1950), pp. 511 ff. and *passim*. See also Brameld, *Towards a Reconstructed Philosophy of Education.* Mannheim's discussion of the role of intellectuals in bringing about social change as well as the work of Gunnar Myrdal are considered to be relevant. See also Waldo Frank, *Re-discovery of America* (New York: Charles Scribner's Sons, 1939), p. 154.

CARL A. RUDISILL LIBRARY
LENOIR RHYNE COLLEGE

Since the method of creation is seen as a method over and above the method of problem solving, there is some considerable criticism of the experimentalist preoccupation with the methodology of problem solving as the complete delineation of intellectual method. The method of experimental science is not fully adequate for this creative task.[39]

The experimental method applied wholesale has destroyed old objects of loyalty, but it has failed to point out and define new objects to take their place.[40] It presents a valid description of psychology of democratic action, but it needs supplementation in the location of goals, aims, and values.[41] In certain situations one does not respond as one would to a problem.[42] One of these is that of meeting complicated social situations. The effective approach to social problems is the method of creating and designing; this is the method by which order and unity are achieved in complicated situations characterized by disorder and lack of unity.

Although an effort may be made to develop creative ability in all, actual social control at a given time and place may come to reside more directly with a few outstanding artist-planners. These leaders must have a comprehensive grasp of the genius of America, from which they state the elements of design toward which we must strive. Artists, engineers, and intellectuals must proceed to put the plan into effect and operate it. Organized leadership in such a

[39] Harold Rugg, *Culture and Education in America* (New York: Harcourt, Brace, & Co., 1931), pp. 141, 215; *American Life and the School Curriculum* (Boston: Ginn and Co., 1931), p. 440; *That Men May Understand* (New York: Doubleday, Doran & Co., 1941), pp. 361 ff.; *Now Is the Moment* (New York: Duell, Sloan, and Pearce, 1943), *passim*. Also Harold O. Rugg (ed.) and others, *Democracy and the Curriculum*, Yearbook No. 3 of the John Dewey Society (New York: D. Appleton-Century Co., 1939), p. 251.

[40] Rugg, *Culture and Education in America*, p. 141; *Democracy and the Curriculum*, p. 251; *That Men May Understand*, p. 112.

[41] *That Men May Understand*, pp. 320 ff.

[42] Ibid., pp. 326, 328.

great social enterprise is essential. The leaders are the artist geniuses. They must lead because they have unique ability to impose order on what seems to lesser men chaos. Rugg believes that these leaders are masters of a certain method, different from that of science, unique, distinctive. It is the method of organic awareness or intuition. It is the method of poetry—the method of creative imagination. The artist's vision is better, truer, more beautiful than the partial insights of his fellows.

Through education, a deliberate effort is to be made to persuade people that this is the best way. Nevertheless, discussion, challenge, disagreement are not to be disallowed; they are to be encouraged. The educational technique advocated is not that of propaganda but of persuasion. A deliberate effort should be made to organize the school studies and activities around the aims and goals involved in the utopian vision. Thus the educational program advocated is a "future-centered" one.

Through mass education, therefore, an effort is to be made to develop the artist in all men, and to bring all men to an appreciative understanding and commitment to the utopian ideal. Force is not advocated as a means for bringing about commitment, but persuasion is. The techniques of persuasion include myth, religion, art, and group dynamics. The aim is to achieve democratic consensus through an educational program arranged to persuade but not to coerce.[43]

The position of the reconstructionists was an unusually controversial one because of its emphasis on social planning. If social planning be art, a crucial question would seem to be whether the method of the artist can be shared by all. It may be questioned whether a method of communication has yet been devised which makes possible democratic shar-

[43] Ibid.

ing of the insights of artists and intellectuals. This being the case, to advocate that artists and intellectuals do the planning may be to insist that the democratic method be sacrificed for the sake of efficiency and beauty. If the masses cannot communicate with the artists, establishment of a bureaucracy of artists would appear to be an undemocratic move. Rugg and Brameld maintain that the values for which they stand are individual values. At the root of their educational concern is the concern about full, rich, creative living for men and women, boys and girls. It is in the name of the intrinsic values of individual expression that they advocate social planning; hence, there is clear continuity between the values of the child-centered school of the 1920s and the social reconstructionism of the later years. The planned society is a means, not an end in itself. Nevertheless, there is ground for concern that the means advocated may endanger the ends-in-view.

EXPERIMENTALIST REVISIONS OF PROGRESSIVE THEORY AND PRACTICE

Before 1930, leaders in the Progressive Education Movement—Childs, Bode, Kilpatrick, and Dewey himself—sensed intellectual weaknesses in the movement, and insisted that a pragmatic philosophy of education must include conceptions of educational controls. But laymen and numbers of classroom teachers, for that matter, continued to interpret progressive education to mean random, uncontrolled school situations and a kind of romantic idealization of creativity.

In 1928, Dr. Dewey addressed the Eighth Annual Conference of the Progressive Education Association on the subject, "Progressive Education and the Science of Education." He suggested that progressive schools shared in common an emphasis upon respect for individuality, increased freedom, informality, and a disposition to build on the experiences of boys and girls instead of imposing external subject matter and standards.[44] However, at this early date—before the Great Depression and long before the disillusioning experiences of World War II and its aftermath—Dewey strongly insisted that the extreme emphasis on individuality and freedom characterizing the progressive schools was a negative or protest emphasis, and that workers in the Progressive Education Movement should assume responsibility for intellectual organization of their work.[45] Stressing that he was not advocating a return to a rigid, formal type of organization characterizing traditional schools, Dewey insisted that improvisation is no substitute for planning, and that planning of a high order must go on in progressive schools. To be sure, the very word *organization* suggests something external and set, as in traditional education. When we give up the type of organization which the traditionalists advocate, however, it is desperately important that we provide some other sort of organization to take its place. Pragmatists hold no brief for chaos. The experimental schools, said Dewey, are under constant temptation to improvise, but if there is improvisation day after day, meaningful command of subject matter does not build up. Although Dewey denied that any one subject matter must be taught, he argued that some subject matter must always be undergoing formulation. That is, there must be consistent, meaningful learning and growth.[46]

A few years later Boyd Bode, professor of education at the Ohio State University, urged that emancipation from a vicious traditional formalism in the schools only sets the task of finding valid principles of order and control. He maintained

[44] John Dewey, "Progressive Education and the Science of Education," *Progressive Education* 5 (July–August–September 1928): 197–204.
[45] Ibid., pp. 200–201.
[46] Ibid., p. 201.

that progressives had not accomplished this important task and suggested, perhaps with tongue in cheek, that some teachers who belonged to the progressive movement had no clear conception of what they were doing and why.[47] Bode, himself a pragmatist, said that progressive education appeared to be motivated by a vague mixture of sentimentalism,[48] reflection of a growing demand for recognition of the common man,[49] Rousseauism and instinct psychology,[50] and nineteenth-century romanticism.[51] He said that its central connotation had been that of "child-centeredness," in that values such as interest, freedom, and self-activity had been stressed. In methods of teaching, learning by doing had been the motto, and a social outlook emphasizing cooperation rather than competition and the worth of the individual had received emphasis.[52] Nevertheless, he pointed out that the progressives had generally assumed that respect for personality and maximum development could be achieved simply by becoming emancipated from traditional formalism and improving conditions of learning.[53] This assumption, argued Bode, was fallacious.

A number of leaders in progressive education agreed with Dewey and Bode in criticizing the child-centered school. They maintained that the pragmatic reliance on experience must be interpreted to mean the critical, controlled kind of experiencing and learning exemplified in science. According to these thinkers, who sometimes used the term *experimental-*

[47] Boyd H. Bode, *Progressive Education at the Crossroads* (New York: Newson & Co., 1938), p. 84.
[48] Ibid., pp. 11–12.
[49] Ibid., p. 49.
[50] Ibid., pp. 37 ff.
[51] Ibid., p. 99.
[52] Ibid., p. 4.
[53] Ibid., pp. 4–5.

ism to designate their philosophy of education, neither the intellectuals, the artists, nor the saints have special authority in the modern democratic community. For them, the methods of criticism, full public inspection, and testing become moral principles to guide educational work. Dependable, publicly verified knowledge is to be respected, mastered, and applied to use. Although life is more than a series of scientific operations, all life experiences are to be subjected to critical examination and validation. In the last analysis, the authority of our myths, our poetry, and our ideals must rest upon open, public criticism.

Centrality of Critical Intelligence

With this reinterpretation of pragmatism to mean reliance on critical use of intelligence, the romantic individualism of the child-centered-school group in the new education movement was modified. Here we have an emphasis upon intellectual rigor. The exponents considered themselves pragmatists. Moreover, they remained active in the Progressive Education Association. However, within pragmatism and within progressive education important divisions developed between experimentalists and apostles of the child-centered school. Let us now turn to an examination of the theory and the educational practice advocated by those who considered critical intelligence a primary educational ideal.

In this view, each individual has the right and the obligation to present his insights and his beliefs for public inspection and testing. But individual insights become truth-claims only to the extent that they are validated through public inspection and test. Thus, social institutions that make possible free, open communication and cooperative criticism are indispensable instruments of intelligence. Transmission of dependable truth-claims to the young and cultivation of scientific attitudes and habits are prime educational values. These traits differentiate human behavior from animal trial and error. They are, thus, of primary educational importance.

The principle at the heart of the child-centered-school movement, that of learning through personal experience, is granted. But when the importance of personal experience is emphasized in educational method, a need is created for guidance and direction of learning which makes the teacher even more important than he was in the traditional school. The teacher must now guide and direct learning without violating the principle of learning through personal experience. Not every experience is of equal educational value; some experiences restrict rather than extend the possibilities of future growth in learning.[54] Once more, disconnected experiences are miseducative when they are not organized in such a way that their interconnections become clear. Field trips and casual use of moving pictures for instructional purposes frequently exhibit this weakness. Experiences are educative only when they make possible desirable future experiences. That is, when they are meaningful, so that they make possible greater intelligent control of events in the future.

Learning by experience is never learning in a vacuum. There must always be interaction between an individual learner and certain objective conditions—things and events in his environment. These may be people, toys, materials of an experiment, or imagined persons and things called up by reading, by talk, or by pictures. The point is that an experience is an interaction between objective conditions and the needs, desires, and purposes of a living being.[55] Now the role of the teacher is to work with the objective conditions that

[54] John Dewey, *Experience and Education* (New York: The Macmillan Co., 1938), pp. 8–9.
[55] Ibid., pp. 41–42.

make up learning situations.[56] He works, then, by exercising discriminating choice in setting up learning situations. His responsibility is to set up conditions in the environment of students that will bring about learning—not any learning, but learning that will have a favorable effect on the future.[57] To permit free play and individuality, and to foster creative critical inquiry, flexibility is advisable.[58] There must always be limits to this flexibility, however, for the function of the school in a free society is to educate for freedom. Men cannot be free except as they are made capable of intelligent, that is, discriminating, choice.

People are not actually born free. They achieve freedom as they master intellectual tools that make it possible for them to control their own destinies. These tools are the knowledge and intellectual methods that come out of past experience. Thus, education for freedom demands knowledge of past experience. The tools of freedom come out of past experience as that experience has passed through repeated testings.[59]

The great and awe-inspiring power of a teacher is to manipulate objective conditions to bring about learning. This is the way he works, and society sanctions his exercise of this power. Educational guidelines are laid down. An educative experience, then, is one that makes for growth, that leads on, and that increases power of control over the future. Such power is freedom. An essential condition of genuine freedom is that it be intelligently exercised. The decisions of the free man are made in the light of past experience and the knowledge coming out of past experience. Hence, a primary concern of a teacher in setting up learning situations will be to

[56] Ibid., pp. 43–44.
[57] Ibid., p. 52.
[58] Ibid., p. 65.
[59] John Dewey, "Individuality and Experience," in A. C. Barnes *et al.*, *Art and Education* (Merion, Pa.: Barnes Foundation Press, 1947), p. 40.

see to it that knowledge—that is, useful generalizations built on past experience—is used in solving problems.

Thus, the responsible theorists in progressive education were clearly not advocates of random, uncontrolled, unorganized activity in the name of education. Constant critical selection as a responsibility of teachers was emphasized. In fact, Dewey argued at one point that this uncompromising emphasis on critical selection is the strongest asset of progressive schools.[60] Thus, the new experiences must always be connected with what has gone before. Learning must involve organization. Experiences must connect meaningfully with one another. New objects and events must be seen as related to, connected with, and developing out of earlier experiences.

It is a mistake to suppose that the principle of the leading on of experience to something different is adequately satisfied simply by giving pupils some new experiences any more than it is by seeing to it that they have greater skill and ease in dealing with things with which they are already familiar. It is also essential that the new objects and events be related intellectually to those of earlier experiences, and this means that there be some advance made in conscious articulation of facts and ideas. . . . Connectedness in growth must be his [the educator's] constant watchword.[61]

If the position of the systematic philosophers of the New Education had been adequately treated in the preceding exposition, the question may be raised whether they had not, in effect, broken with progressive education. Whence this emphasis upon subject matter? Whence this emphasis on the importance of organizing concepts, of mastery of knowledge? It remains to demonstrate that this view, despite its differences with the child-centered school, retained an edu-

[60] Dewey, *Experience and Education*, p. 26.
[61] Ibid., pp. 89–90.

cational theory in opposition to conventional education under the continued influence of the literary humanistic tradition.

Objectivity of "Needs"

The view was that school studies should be based on needs, but the concept of need was interpreted in a significantly different sense from that in which it had been used in conventional educational parlance. First of all, the limitations and controls inherent in man's external world are to be taken very seriously. Thinking goes on in a context which is not itself constituted out of thought. This is not a subjectivism, making of experience something unrelated to an external world of hard limitations. There are certain "brute existences," as Dewey called them, within which or out of which we live and grow.[62] There is a real external world. From time to time living human beings are involved in incomplete, disturbed, unbalanced situations. A situation may be incomplete if there is an absence of food or drink; it may be disturbed, as in a traffic jam at rush hour; it may be out of balance.

Problem situations such as these, so the argument goes, constitute needs, and needs call forth inquiry. Note, however, that *needs* thus conceived are not narrowly personal. Situations become needy; although the human agent is a part of the situation, the needs are not somehow deep down inside the skin of the agent; they are in a situation, not inside the viscera of an organism.

Thus, *problems* are constituted in situations, of which human individuals are a part—but only a part. Now every such situation has a history. Moreover, in a changing, dynamic, evolving world, every such situation is also seen as having a future; it is bound to become something other than it is "right

[62] John Dewey, *Essays in Experimental Logic* (Chicago: University of Chicago Press, 1916), p. 35.

now." This way, *needs, needy situations,* and *problem situations* are conceived dynamically or genetically; that is, as extending through past and present into the future.[63]

The position is that needs are properly the basis of education; inquiry has its origin in *need* situations. Any process of inquiry begins, then, within a context whose important elements have been set by past events. Thus, there are things to be known about a situation, and to the degree that other human beings have been involved in the situation, cooperative work may be possible—that is, shared inquiry.[64] The products of inquiry we call *knowledge.* Let us recapitulate: the purpose of education is to meet the needs of people; needs exist in situations, not somehow merely inside people; meeting needs, then, means reconstructing situations; this is accomplished through inquiry; inquiry yields knowledge that is instrumental in further inquiry. How do we inquire? What is the procedure by which we may work fruitfully to meet human needs, to inquire, to gain knowledge?

Achieving Reliable Knowledge

Data are useless if they are not appropriate to the realities of a disturbed situation. But they are not exactly the same as the external reality out of which they arise. Data are means to knowledge, not ends. They are the raw material out of which inference is made. Technical as this argument may appear, it has important relevance to educational work. Laying bare the data is basic to inquiry, we are saying. Needs of children can only be met as we get to the data, and until we gather them, we can never get started on a sound educational base. This calls for order, precision, and genuine research. The needs of children and youth can only be met as we use

[63] John Dewey, *Logic, the Theory of Inquiry* (New York: Henry Holt & Co., 1938), p. 228.
[64] Ibid., p. 8.

subject matter grounded in competently formulated data to meet them. In other words, there can be no opposition between a concern about careful, competent primary scholarship and "meeting the needs of youth."

It is in the process of laying bare data, which occurs in problematic or indeterminate situations, that meanings are constructed. Meanings arise as the organism, caught in a needy situation, begins overtly or imaginatively to move around in a situation in an effort to reconstruct it. Such "moving around" is guided by the location of the data, already accomplished in part. Whatever "moving around" occurred prior to location and collection of data was random, unintelligent, not free; it was meaningless. On the other hand, when the "moving around" begins to be guided by data, then meanings and interpretations can arise.

Data and meanings applied to reconstruction of a situation—getting out of the traffic jam, securing food or drink—result in knowledge. Thus, a total situation generates or gives rise to needs. Needs are not narrowly personal or private. A disturbed or incomplete situation indicates and brings about the need for an agent to investigate, to plan, and then to test the plan as a way or reorganizing the situation.[65] What we finally call *knowledge* comes out of this sort of need-data-meanings background. What we call knowledge is a body of tested conclusions that have been sifted through past experience. It is based on data and meanings, and it has been tested by inquirers making use of it in problem situations.[66] That is, it has been subjected to experimental verification. Responsible inquiry yields conclusions that are to be respected in further inquiries.[67] Now, since all situations have trails into the past, and since living is essentially a social experience, a

[65] Dewey, *Essays in Experimental Logic*, p. 70.
[66] Ibid., pp. 46 ff.
[67] Dewey, *Logic, the Theory of Inquiry*, p. 12.

problem situation with regard to which absolutely no inquiry has been made is almost inconceivable. Thus, responsible inquiry must grow on a foundation of scholarship. Postulates or principles derived from past inquiry are resources for future inquiries. Professor Dewey maintained that principles —tested ways of doing things coming out of previous inquiry— are *operationally a priori* with respect to further inquiry.[68]

If this be the case, then teachers must indeed be reluctant to set up instructional units that lead students into areas of inquiry for which their lack of knowledge makes them incompetent. If principles are "operationally a priori," serious questions might be raised with regard to so-called experiential units which ignore the importance of a background in history and theory.

Nevertheless, we do not have here a mere restatement of the classical tradition in education. Human experience, in this view, is considered part of a natural and evolving process. Thought is looked on as instrumental to human and social well-being, not as a *summum bonum* in itself. The function of the intellectual life is to look into the future and project hypotheses for future action; to speculate about past and present experience is of significance only as hypotheses for future action are to be made. Dynamic reconstruction of a moving present, not perfect description and contemplation of absolute reality, is the ideal. The function of intelligence is to attack problems actually faced by people in living their lives in specific times and places.[69]

This means that the school curriculum should be constructed to treat areas of experience in which there is stress, strain, or imbalance. The criterion in curriculum construction is need. If life adjustment means reconstruction of disturbed

[68] Ibid., pp. 13–14.
[69] John Dewey, *Reconstruction in Philosophy* (New York: Henry Holt & Co., 1920), p. 51.

situations in life for the maximization of human satisfactions in life, then education for life adjustment is not an improper or a mean educational goal. We ought to think about the things that need thinking about. The past is gone; the present cannot be other than it is, but we may hope to reconstruct the future to some degree. Problems of the present and hopes for the future fix the content of the school curriculum. The mightiest resource at hand for building a future is in the data, meanings, and knowledge at hand. We select from this fund, which is our heritage from the past, according to present need and our hopes for the future. There is no corpus of subject matter from the past which is somehow sacred. Knowledge is instrumental to our present problems and future hopes.

Of course, this never means that knowledge remains fixed and unaltered. In the process of using knowledge instrumentally, theories are altered and refined. Knowledge coming out of the past is constantly reconstructed in the present. This constant refining through criticism is finally what distinguishes critically grounded meanings from those coming out of daydreaming or free fantasy.[70] This is to say, experience is meaningful in terms of its background. An argument, an idea, or a scientific generalization cannot be understood except for its matrix extending back into the past and involving purposes, interests, and intents of the past which gave rise to it. Moreover, the past renders certain dependable generalizations or tested ideas. These are tools that the inquirer uses in coping with his problem. He is obligated to master these tools—to know these truths, and to respect them. Such truths provide assurance to those in their command. They are not absolute and they are not eternal, how-

[70] John Dewey, *Experience and Nature* (Chicago: Open Court Publishing Co., 1925), p. 339.

ever. They are finite, and they are always subject to criticism.[71]

This should make clear that experimentalists, although accepting evolution, denying metaphysical absolutes, and applying the pragmatic test, do not deny that certain tested ideas deserve a relatively permanent status. The experimentalist does not advocate that the inquirer adopt a skeptical attitude toward all universals. His is certainly not the view that all results of past inquiry should be open to constant doubt. The point is, rather, that scientific generalizations must be recognized for what they are—products of human inquiry, not eternal revelations. At the same time, the notion is that the relatively permanent conclusions of past inquiry must undergo constant modification and change. New discoveries will constantly impinge upon the body of scientific generalizations. The past runs into the future. Past, present, and future are connected. History does not stop with the present; it moves on into a future in which there are always elements of emerging novelty.[72] The emerging situations are never completely new, but novel elements may exist within them. New situations have trails into the past, but they are new in that there is an unexplored part of them. Principles coming out of past inquiry should be venerated and respected, but even the most respected of truths, respected because they have been dependable, must bear scrutiny in the light of the needs of the present. It is only relatively that they are unchanging. The oldest and most dependable of truths are to some extent remade as they are used instrumentally in coping with current problems.[73]

[71] John Dewey, *The Influence of Darwin on Philosophy* (New York: Henry Holt & Co., 1910), pp. 151–152.

[72] Dewey, *Logic, the Theory of Inquiry*, p. 501.

[73] Dewey, *Influence of Darwin on Philosophy*, p. 152.

Source of Moral Order

Now if science deals with facts but not with values, although the scientific comprises the realm within which education should do its work, what supports the moral teachings? Sentimentality? Custom? As teachers work to impart scientific habits of mind in the young, the young cannot be expected to refrain from raising critical questions about values. However, when we teach them to criticize everything, to subject all assertions to critical test, inspection, and experiment, and to hold all propositions tentatively, subject to alteration with the appearance of new evidence, the moral codes will also be questioned. Thus, why should we respect human life, tell the truth, cooperate, or support the Constitution? These questions will be asked in a school that dedicates itself to teaching young people to be critically intelligent.

It may appear that moral sanctions finally have their ground only in some form of self-interest. To be sure, self-interest can be extended to include interests of "my family," "my race," "my clan," and "my country," but whether a scientific humanist can extend self-interest to include all of mankind may be a moot question. Is there any reason why one should live a life of pain and suffering for all mankind? Perhaps one can critically establish the advisability of ten or twenty years of pain and suffering for others, with the promise that the joys will eventually be greater as the investment in pain contributes to a group enterprise from which one will profit. In this view, however, there would appear to be no ground for an ultimate personal sacrifice in the name of a cause greater than oneself.

Paradoxically, it would appear that progressive education involves a moral fervor rarely matched in the long history of education. How can this be, when the philosophy supporting it appears to elevate self-interest to such a high plane? One explanation has been that teachers who joined the movement were ladies who loved children but who had none of their own; thus, the romantic conception of childhood expressed in the maxims of the child-centered school captured them. Another suggestion has been that the moral fervor of the movement is derived from Christianity; that is, that a fundamentally Christian morality of love carried over, as a phenomenon in cultural lag, when the metaphysical dimension of Christianity had been discarded. That Bode and Dewey came out of Calvinistic Christianity and that some of their more eminent interpreters were men reared in evangelical Protestantism are cited as examples.

What these suggestions fail to take into consideration is the understandable devotion that men have demonstrated in various ages to the cause of human freedom. Progressive education at its best has a place in the liberal tradition. It stands for intellectual and moral freedom, a freedom which takes form as men forge their own criteria for judgment out of their experience in living. The moral fervor involved in such a movement is generated out of compassion for man's fellows, indignation at the forces that oppress them, and a clear vision of the means of their deliverance.

The most impressive rejoinder to criticisms of pragmatism and progressive education as involving a moral vacuum comes from educational theorists who see connections among science, freedom, and democracy. They find a ground for morality in those methods and institutions which make possible realization of human values by human beings. They grant that it is the earthly joys and satisfactions which count, but they find it possible to dedicate themselves critically to the means of their preservation. That is, the critically established cause—a cause somehow greater than self-interest

—comes to be the cause of preserving and extending those social methods and institutional forms that enable man to be "for himself." This cause is the method of disciplined intelligence. Ground for devotion to it is the empirical evidence of its fruitfulness in producing joys for people like ourselves. The method of critical intelligence is viewed as a way human beings have of working together. If this be the case—if the critical method is a way of accepting one another, working with one another, listening to one another, watching one another—then it must have moral significance. If this be the case, then it may well be that educators can find a fruitful, dynamic scheme of educational values built on the content and method of intellectual criticism.

The method of criticism is seen as the method of democracy. That is, it is the method of free, open examination, with decisions always subject to revision on the basis of overt test. It is the method of science, broadly construed.[74] It is to be skeptical, critical, and open-minded; it is to accept as true or reliable only that which is demonstrated openly, publicly, honestly, and obviously.[75] Faith in human intelligence thus broadly construed has been the faith of progressive modern educators. That is, they have been passionately devoted to inquiry, criticism, and experiment—to systematic, careful, alert, unprejudiced observation and testing. In other words, for them human intelligence has been the supreme authority and prime educational value. The basis for giving intelligence to this preeminent position is that it has been more fruitful in producing richer lives for more people than any other method.

A great moral commitment is involved in the faith that

[74] Sidney Hook, *Education for Modern Man* (New York: The Dial Press, Inc., 1946), pp. 128–129.

[75] John Dewey, "Antinaturalism in Extremis," in *Naturalism and the Human Spirit,* ed. Y. H. Krikorian (New York: Columbia University Press, 1944), p. 12.

intelligence is the prime educational value. It is a commitment to the view that systematic, controlled, unprejudiced
observation and experimentation, subject to critical testing by
all comers, is better than unsystematic, careless, uncontrolled,
biased procedures claiming special authority. Truths thus
established always have a provisional status. They rest on
public acceptance by individuals whose criterion of acceptance is the evidence of experimental testing. Verification by
others is not something grudgingly tolerated. It is a positive,
constructive, necessary element in the making of truth. It is a
protection against hallucination and vagary. It is the process
by which truth is created; but this process is never completed, for verification by individuals comprising an unlimited
community would be the condition for complete establishment of a proposition's truth-claim.

Political and social institutions rest on the same foundation as truths. They rest on public acceptance by individuals
whose criteria of acceptance have been criticized. Just as no
particular truth-claim has a privileged status, so no political
or social institution is good in itself. Just as a truth-claim
may continue to serve in the absence of negative or unproductive instances of its application, so a political or social
institution may be used as an instrument as long as it actually
continues to serve. This is true of democratic institutions.
Although democracy as a method is correlated with the
method of intelligence, specific institutions and specific
social forms are open to continuous criticism, inspection, and
revision. The democratic faith, in this view, is simply faith in
intelligence; it does not attach itself to any particular form
or organization.

At the same time, as dependable, usable truth-claims are
treasured for their instrumental value while recognized as
constantly subject to change, so dependable, usable political
and social institutions are appreciated. But we are the masters;

we pass judgment on institutions. Human institutions are to be judged and controlled by human intelligence; there is no form of social organization whatsoever which is above or beyond criticism.

The ground for holding that all men should participate in criticism and decision-making in a democracy is the recognition that all men have something to contribute to the process of criticism. Since the view is that no absolutely fixed or permanent truths exist, human beings are both subjects and objects in the working out of social-scientific generalizations. That is, every proposal for social action proposes modes of association among individual human beings. Thus, each individual is a part of the material of the experiment. Nevertheless, since the consequences of the experiment—where people are involved—can be measured only by human satisfactions and dissatisfactions, each individual must also be one of the experimenters, recorders, and reporters. Since social experimentation extends through time, it becomes extremely important that all men remain free to speak honestly and freely, and to record and publicize their reactions.

Here we have a powerful justification for freedom of speech and press, and a strong argument against censorship. Seen this way, when we refuse to hear men speak or when we forbid circulation of what they have written, we hurt ourselves. Since truth is wrought out of human experience, a continuing refining edge in the building of truth is the voice of the dissenter. Actually, he is extremely important to us; he helps us discover where our ideas and institutions are weak. The spoken or recorded word coming from the dissenter is like pain in the body. He is unpleasant; he disturbs us; but he lets us know where there may be weakness or incipient social disease.

Of course, the process of governing ourselves is inexact.

The effort to manage human affairs intelligently is always hampered by the inescapable personal equations of observers (the prejudices and vested interests of legislators and voters). There is the muddling of records (editorial policies of newspapers and piques of reporters). There is the elusiveness of subject matter (How many Communists were there in the State Department?). But these are difficulties every scientist faces; we always work with imperfect and incomplete tools. The advantages in the method of intelligence inhere in the frank recognition that this is so, and the consequent continued effort to improve tools recognized as imperfect.

If it is good to be intelligent and thus free, then a method of intelligence exists to which we must cleave in order to preserve freedom. Beginning with the commitment to intelligence as a supreme moral value, we derive certain "oughts" for personal conduct and for education as we examine what it really means to be intelligent.

First of all, a man cannot be intelligent alone. The method of intelligence is social in nature. A generalization simply is not a generalization if it holds "for me alone." Reliable generalizations, then, are those that hold for a large number of people occupying places in time, space, and class. The extension of the community is the mission of intelligence, and it is also of the very substance of intelligence. The point is that the safety, security, and happiness of each person depend on persisting critical sensitivity to the appearance of negative, unproductive instances in the use of generalizations. Every human being may make some contribution to the testing of all generalizations. Since the biological makeup, environment, personality, and position in time and space of each individual in history, in the present, and in the future are unique, each individual represents a unique dimension of intelligence. He can criticize from his point of view—from his position. Thus he can make his contribution to human intelligence.

There is a sense in which this way of thinking of human intelligence—as a great community enterprise—makes human life valuable. If life is precious for this reason, it immediately follows that a moral commitment to education and the provision of health and welfare services is involved. If people are valuable because of the contribution they make to the community of intelligence, this contribution is to be maximized in worldwide efforts to support and nurture their contributions. However, this effort is seen as extending through time, through an unlimited community. Here is the suggestion of a kind of brotherhood among men of all ages—the suggestion that all are engaged in the cooperative task of seeking truth. Having forsaken metaphysical presuppositions holding for absolute, completed truths, we must look on the human community as our one best source of wisdom. We need each other desperately in a world in which cooperative inquiry is seen as the primary source of dependable principles to guide action.

It may also be pointed out that in this conception of social democracy, status is a function of earned esteem. An insight that stands the test of action is of value regardless of its source. Race and lineage are of no account in the method of intelligence. Conversely, even the wisest and the most far-seeing of men must recognize how limited and fallible his concepts are, and how minute his own personal contributions have been. His wisdom is the wisdom of the community that nurtures him, and his wisdom is constantly confounded by new insights coming from his peers. The point is that in this way of thinking of human intelligence, we have the ground for an ethic of equality and of personal humility. There is here the suggestion of awe or even reverence for the community which extends through time and to which one is both an heir and a contributor.

Finally, we may point out the tremendous emphasis upon

honesty and integrity, which is a part of the democratic-scientific ethic. Accuracy is a virtue; deliberate falsification makes one a traitor to his fellows and to himself. One must tell the truth, for only thus can others learn from him and can he be true to the ideals that have made him and that sustain his freedom.

How, then, are moral values to be taught in a secular school? What does all this mean for the establishment of guiding value commitments? What faith remains to sustain boys and girls, and men and women in times of crisis?

In the first place, there is loyalty to, and respect for human beings in their exercise of intelligent living. This loyalty is to men in community, men at work at the arts of civilization, men at the task of perfecting the disciplines of freedom—the method of intelligence. This becomes a supreme educational value, because it is the means by which goods are created and recreated. It is the ongoing method for making and remaking the good life among men. The method of intelligence is that method which thrives on creation of human goods. It is the method most fruitful and dependable in the long run. Thus, it becomes of supreme educational value, and educational practices that make for growth in intelligence are deemed indispensable.

Another loyalty, which we would wish to keep alive, is to the total range of human experience expressed in folklore, the arts, and play. Enjoyments are many and various, and every enjoyment is, as such, a good. Although teaching the supreme value of cultivated, disciplined intelligence is central, it would be unfortunate to teach that intellectual experience is itself the only enjoyment. Everyone has occasionally enjoyed foolishness. The fortune teller's predictions did, indeed, come to pass; the star was wished upon on that memorable night, and good luck did come. Deliberately non-intellectual play may certainly be indulged in from time to time, clearly identified as such. *Beowulf's* dragons, the fairies of *Midsummer Night's Dream,* the Lord speaking to Moses have a part in our literary tradition, and ought not to be obliterated.

In addition to the intrinsic delight which the arts and humanities may provide, taken on their own ground as imaginative creation, a case can be made for the possibility that novel creative insights providing avenues into new, valid knowledge may arise initially from nonscientific sources. Free imagination, whimsy, lore from the ancients or contemporary primitives may contribute novel styles of perception. Thus, in work with the young, respect and generosity toward various sources of traditional wisdom are to be taught. Nevertheless, in a spirit of gentleness and humility—inasmuch as elements of the folklore are not infrequently held to with great intensity—criticism of these nonscientific insights must not only be encouraged but demanded.

The fixing of belief must be upon evidence. When the question is one of truth or falsity, with the fixing of belief at issue, the critical stance must prevail. For a notion may be beautiful, intriguing, satisfying, even plausible, but subject to rejection on evidence as a candidate for belief. The field of candidates for belief entertained at the initiation of inquiry should be as broad as we can make it. The field is narrowed, however, not by whim nor by traditional doctrine, but by intelligent criticism. Ideas come in from all sources, but every notion is to be assessed critically. This is what it means to be reasonable. The task of teaching is one of structuring minds—the concern, to determine what method provides the most adequate foundation for strong minds. The scientific, experimental, secular humanism here under discussion as an educational theory holds that minds constituted by loyalty and adherence to critical methods are, in the long run, most blessed. This is because the critical method is most productive of human goods of all sorts. Children and youth thus educated survey with sympathy and appreciation assertions and records of assertions coming from traditional and noncritical sources. The critical mind, however, in contrast to the authoritarian or noncritical mind, will arrive at choices experimentally, making use of technological information and philosophical analysis.

A school dedicated to development of intelligence as a prime educational value will use every technique of pedagogy not in contradiction with the faith in intelligence to inculcate the moral traits involved in the method of intelligence. Moral virtues will indeed be viewed as a central part of the concern of free nonsectarian education. Specific moral habits and attitudes will be encouraged in the young, but the morality will be a secular, public morality.

Since the morality of intelligence and democracy, as outlined above, does have a clear cutting edge, undoubtedly any school dedicated to this morality will frequently be subjected to community criticism. Existence of individuals and blocs within communities purposefully advocating private and uncritical commitments in preference to public, critical problem solving is likely to be the rule rather than the exception. Although the position of the school must be uncompromising in its dedication to the free mind, it must always be remembered that a means which, when challenged, moves contrary to the end for which it is advanced is dubious. Certainly if freedom is endangered by the operation of authoritarian groups within society, it is lost indeed when members of the community of intelligence become authoritarian in the name of freedom.

Children and youth in the schools should be taught that the method of intelligence must remain true to itself. Use of force is the ultimate indication of failure of intelligence. If there is a justifiable use of force, it may be to see to it that authoritarian groups submit their propositions for public inspection rather than be allowed to maintain secrecy. So long as an authoritarian group allows its books to remain open, democratic persuasion rather than force is always to be preferred. Thus, young people in the schools, while being taught the morality of criticism, must always be reminded of the dignity of dissent, even when the dissent comes close to the roots of the faith to which the school is dedicated.

Children and young people in the schools will, therefore, be constantly reminded that resort to coercion, force, subterfuge, or deliberate "shading" of evidence falsifies the faith of the community of intelligence. The young should be taught that the greatest evil is concerted, organized effort to discredit the method of intelligence in favor of some authoritarian method. Political maneuvering by any group which involves deliberate weighting of evidence in favor of some preconceived and invulnerable point of view is wrong.

SUMMARY—THE EXPERIMENTALIST POSITION

In summary, the educational platform of those for whom free intelligence is the educational ideal defines human inquiry as problem-solving activity. Problems arising out of situations continuous with the past are to be confronted by the use of certain intellectual tools or instruments. These instruments include data, meanings, results of past inquiry, and human institutions which make possible communication and testing of hypotheses. Complex problems may be recognized and attacked only as data, meanings, and funded knowledge are mastered. Educational efforts will involve laborious and careful surveys of fields of knowledge to acquaint persons with data, meanings, and results of past inquiry essential for their activities as creative members of a democratic community dedicated to freedom. Conceivably, years of study devoted to mastery of intellectual instruments may be necessary before creative problem-solving activity can be completely undertaken in a given area. Sound analysis of the method of intelligence by no means issues in support of an educational practice lacking order and rigor. Individuals must be thoroughly acquainted with pertinent data and meanings before they can sense problems, locate them by intelligent analysis, and proceed to construct hypotheses for their solution.

The faith represented by the school in an open society is that maximal enjoyment of life in all its myriad forms is to be established and secured by intelligent rather than nonintelligent means and methods. Intelligent living makes full use of meanings and knowledge coming out of past inquiry and gives loyalty to the moral canons of the method of intelligence. The primary job of the school, in this view, is to foster and develop intelligence in the young. Not the least important reason for loyalty to the critical method as supreme authority is that adherence to it does not circumscribe or limit the field of human enjoyment. It represents a morality that points toward the future rather than toward the past. It expresses a philosophy that minimizes authority and insists that authority when exercised must be public rather than private, and functional and dynamic rather than static and absolute.

There is a stubborn insistence that problems are tackled intelligently only as significant data, meanings, and knowledge are used. Great attention must be given in schools to mastery of important data, meanings, and knowledge. Responsible progressives would emphasize as strongly as traditionalists that students must master knowledge. The distinctions come at the point of selecting the items of knowledge to be mastered, and in relating the total educational enterprise to the field of reliable knowledge. Thus, the frequently voiced criticism that pragmatism in educational theory advocates carelessness and irresponsible expediency in scholarship must be discounted.

The experimentalist progressives considered that the best way to teach young people to be critically intelligent is to organize the work of the school around significant problems. This was sometimes interpreted to mean that a school course should be organized around problems that students said they wanted to investigate. There was ample evidence that when people worked on something they wanted to work on, and that they considered to be important, they worked harder. However, most school people were careful not to elevate this principle of pedagogy or teaching method into an adequate principle of curriculum organization. To say that students learn more rapidly and thoroughly when allowed to follow out their interests did not imply that school programs should be organized solely around the immediately felt and directly expressed interests of students. They realized that there may be serious problems of which the individual is unaware. Serious needs may exist in the situation, yet people may be unaware of those needs. The distinction between felt needs and interests and objective needs, as made by Professor Sidney Hook, was accepted by most school people:

As a term it [the word *need*] is ambiguous and slippery but in educational context it can be given sufficient precision to rescue it from those who use it interchangeably with interests, preferences, likes, and desires. A need in education is any want, absence or lack whose fulfillment is a necessary condition for the achievement of a desirable end. It follows therefore that needs are *objective*, not errant offsprings of fancy, and that they are not only individual but also *social*, related essentially to value-norms rooted in the community. If health is a desirable educational goal, then the needs of a child for proper food, or for special treatment to counteract a deficiency, are objective even if he is unaware of them. . . . When these needs become *felt* needs, the specific processes of interaction between the individual and his environment by which these needs are fulfilled will be reinforced by the powers of organic impulse. When these needs become *intelligently* felt needs, the individual displays a greater initiative and responsibility in determining the quality and direction of his educational experience. He learns more, integrates better, sees more deeply. The drive to fill his needs becomes voluntarily sustained against obstacles. Out of this voluntarily sustained—because intelligently felt—drive, there is born a discipline more pervasive and more reliable than any imposed by external rewards or fear of punishment.

What determines the existence of needs in the individual are natural structures and social institutions and the operation of intelligence. Their recognition, in the first instance, is the task of parent and teacher, family, and school. The child, and later the student, actively cooperate in setting needs; but until full maturity is reached they cannot assume total responsibility for the decision as to what constitutes their educational needs.[76]

In setting up a curriculum, then, it was considered desirable, but not essential that students want to study certain subjects. A better learning situation was considered to exist when the need is felt. When the need is not felt, the teacher certainly faced a more difficult teaching situation. Nevertheless, immediate felt needs of school students were not to be the significant determiners of the curriculum. The curriculum, it was thought, must be organized around problems, but these are to be real issues of currently objective significance, not passing whims of young people. Organization of subject matter and systematic, orderly teaching of subject matter was respected, but the traditional customary list of required and

[76] Sidney Hook, *Education for Modern Man* (New York: The Dial Press, Inc., 1946), pp. 145–146.

elective courses was subjected to thoroughgoing, ruthless criticism. The criteria of tradition and ornamentation were not accepted as adequate. The demand made by the experimentalist progressives was that any subject matter must have demonstrable worth in the kind of world in which the shared lives of boys and girls are to be lived. It must be what they need, and need was to be determined on the basis of an objective, critical, empirical examination of the stresses and strains, the demands and opportunities of the foreseeable future in the time and place in which they were living their lives.

Granted that there was a strong iconoclastic bent among the progressives, including certainly the experimentalist group. Nevertheless, an important and recurring aspect of the system of thought which inspired these men has been conservation in the name of continuity. Dewey makes this most clear in the work *Experience and Education*, to which frequent references have been made in preceding pages. The book is a severe indictment of the individualistic excesses of the child-centered school.

As viewed by the experimentalist progressives the popular slogans of the activity-school movement failed to provide criteria for distinguishing between more and less worthy learning experiences. There is strong criticism of teachers who follow momentary and passing interests of students in the name of "progressivism." This is a gross distortion of the meaning of criticism and scientific method in education.

The view is that problems arise out of the past, and that data, meanings, and knowledge coming from past inquiry must be brought to bear on problems of the present. Every situation extends through past, present, and future. Because a situation is thus continuous through time, the situation cannot be understood except as its history, including data and meanings, is known:

1. The situation as it now exists is a product of the past.

2. The meanings and data are products of the past.

3. Every situation confronted in the present is a product of the past; hypotheses for future action must, then, take careful account of past experience, since the present is only intelligible in terms of the past.

4. Thus, any and every inquiry must be based upon disciplined, methodical historical study and upon thorough knowledge of conclusions of scientific inquiry having a bearing upon the problem at hand.

It is the present situation, however, which gets our concern. The past is to be used by us; it is not to master us. Inquiry is to be directed to present problems; our concern is with the use and meaning of experience. Despite their differences, all the progressives have agreed that the real purpose of education is to enable the young to cope with the problems of the present and future. The traditional school is to be criticized, not because of its stress on subject matter, but because of its too-frequent failure to relate subject matter to present and future problems.

Traditionalists in education have insisted that what has been useful in the past must be useful in the future. Accordingly, they have set up school studies to perpetuate, preserve, and extend a fixed body of traditional lore. On the other hand, the child-centered progressivists, in their absorption with the growth and development of individual children, have tended to ignore the social past and to discount the importance of systematic knowledge. The latter may well be closer to realization of important educational values for a free society than the former. It must be recognized, however, that the tools we have for coping with problems of life adjustment in the present are those which the past has provided.[77]

[77] Dewey, *Experience and Education*, pp. 92–93.

The choice, then, is not to revert to the "eternal values" of the traditionalists in setting up educational standards. Nor will the choice be to romanticize the art experience and advocate that a bureaucracy of artists be set up to exercise social control through a unique and mystical method of "creative thought." In full recognition of contingencies in life, painstaking gathering of data, searching of the past for the origins of problems, and projecting of hypotheses for future action when pertinent meanings have been surveyed will be guiding educational principles. The formulation of plans and the testing of their effects are activities in which all may share, for the method of intelligence demands full publicity and open testing by all comers.

Teachers are advised to stress the problematic, contingent, changing nature of reality and to encourage boys and girls to come to terms with a dynamic, ever-changing universe. At the same time, in this view, they will teach that thorough acquaintance with fundamental data and meanings, and knowledge of tested results of previous inquiry, are prerequisite to problem solving. They will see to it that the young are provided with necessary intellectual means for problem solving as problems are presented. They will be forever on guard against careless, unscientific, irresponsible thinking not grounded in mastery of data, meanings, and knowledge pertinent to the problems at hand. There must be an unbending insistence on the supreme value of the intellectual method. This means full, open, public criticism of all matters of common human concern. It is difficult to see how the American public school could become a confessional school and remain public. It is in the faith in free intelligence that secular educators see common ground for public education in a free society.

A feature of the open society is its toleration of many different ideologies and points of view. In other words, in a democratic society, people who in varying degrees advocate undemocratic ways are accepted as members of the community. Children of these people attend the schools, and in the school dedicated to the method of intelligence, the values, commitments, and beliefs on the basis of which various social groups are currently attacking problems should be studied. The young should be made aware of values and commitments that influence the behavior of various groups within the society, whether or not these values and commitments are themselves critically established. To put it another way, education intended to foster critical intelligence ought to include teaching the young about uncritical, nonscientific, nonrational forces operating within the society.

Thus, in school, teachers must see to it that the young people grow up fully aware of traditions, folkways, and mores of their society. Such knowledge and acquaintance is demanded by an educational practice that views command of meanings as instrumentally important in arriving at critically valid conclusions. This way, young people will be taught in school to view traditions, folkways, religious doctrines and liturgies, works of art, and literature as instruments rather than finally established ends. The school as defined here is the institution which makes loyalty to and faith in criticism, experiment, public inspection, and group deliberation the highest loyalty and the deepest faith. Ideas are seen as instruments for resolving difficulties. By their use, problematic situations are transformed so that difficulties which gave rise to inquiry in the first place are removed. All sorts of problems or difficulties gives rise to inquiry. The inquiring that goes on, involving ideas as instruments, is an experience that mediates among other experiences (the latter being experiences which constitute a problem). The aim is to resolve the difficulty; resolution of the difficulty means that a new immediate experience of enjoyment or satisfaction has emerged. The reason why it is maintained that the end of educational endeavor is development of intelligence is that consummations cannot be established and securely held aside from persisting concern about the means that produce consummations and fulfillments. Thus, intelligent living is rich in enjoyment and fulfillment because intelligent living is alert to the conditions by which joys of living are established and extended.

Teachers in their professional capacities must be dedicated to this cause. It is in this sense, then, that teachers cannot be neutral. They are obligated to take positions, in the name of free inquiry, so that their insights and their conclusions may be subjected to the wide-open critical investigation for which the school stands. The orthodoxy which the school represents is the unequivocal dedication to the free human mind. Such a dedication demands that teachers, in their professional capacities as teachers, must stand firm against pressures to modify or relinquish their critical function. In other words, the school is open to all views, but with the all-important qualification that all views must be subjected to unrestrained critical examination.

Again, the canons of the critical method are specific, definable moral values. These canons, plus the results of inquiry in human-social fields having values for man, comprise ethical generalizations and make up the moral code. The items of this code are authoritative, and the young are to be nurtured in respect for their authority. They have authority because they are essential contributory means to intelligence.

III

The Structure of the Disciplines Movement

THE *Structure of the Disciplines Movement* in American education arose after World War II as part of an emphasis on competence, proficiency, power, and excellence stressed by political, military, and business leaders, and by scholars—particularly in the natural and technical sciences. A central notion in this theory was that teaching should stress the underlying concepts and processes characteristic of each field of scholarly inquiry, such as mathematics, language, physics, chemistry, biology, history. Hence, reference was sometimes made to *Process Objectives* or *Process Teaching*. Or, inasmuch as the processes characteristic of scholarly investigation in a field were governed by the fundamental organizing concepts of the field, there was sometimes reference to *Concept Teaching* or *Concept Learning*. Effective inquiry was the objective of such teaching; hence the terms *Inquiry* and even *Inquiry Teaching* appeared, and it was explained that the purpose of such teaching is to engender *Intellectual Power* in students. Inasmuch as the objective was to bring about understanding of basic concepts, subject matter and information of the more conventional sort was used as means, not end—that is, as means for illustrating how data

136

are handled and how explanatory principles are put to work. Thus, a curriculum or course of study constructed with these objectives in mind was sometimes referred to as a *Spiral Curriculum*. Favorite exemplars of teaching method emphasized *Induction* (i.e., of principles from data) and *Intuition* (i.e., of the rule from a series of examples).

In the main this movement was an analytical one, involving neither a social philosophy nor ethical norms as such. To some considerable extent, however, it was inspired by international affairs affecting the United States in the 1950s and 1960s.

CHRONOLOGY

A shift from preoccupation with individual to corporate values, and from personal attitudes to intellectual and social skills in the larger society, affected educational thought after World War II. After 1950 schooling was evaluated more and more according to its contribution to national needs and national policies. The nation supplanted the individual as the center of concern. The immediate or potential contribution of a given educational activity to political and military usefulness was what made it worthwhile and provided the standard by which its effectiveness was judged.

In this way, intellectual competence and power demonstrated by mastery of basic disciplines at work in the technologies of production, distribution, and communication receive greatest emphasis. That is, the human being as *student* comes to be the concern of school people, the school's function being seen as that of imparting intellectual skills and content rather than serving primarily to refine and enrich the total nurture of the person.

In this perspective, talk about individual differences and individuation means something somewhat different than it did before 1950. The concern is with individual differences in intellectual capacity and mode. Programs are "individualized" as the peculiar intellectual competence represented by each person is related to the division of labor prevailing in the larger society. Concern for efficient performance of organizational roles motivates the talk about individual differences.

Obviously, with such shifts in emphasis, the traditional notion of teachers as themselves at home in the intellectual disciplines was strongly reinforced. Thus the specifically intellectual functions of teachers were emphasized more while the role of the teacher as counselor, guide, parent-surrogate was relatively de-emphasized.

As the Democratic Party came back into power after the Eisenhower interregnum, education received increasing attention in Washington. In the person of President John F. Kennedy, but even more in the coterie of expert intellectuals with whom he staffed federal government positions, there was dramatic exemplification of the emphasis upon expertise. At the same time there was unquestionable commitment to intervention by the government to improve the quality of life of the masses to ends identified by the experts and by means they deemed most effective.

Dr. Sterling McMurrin, an academic philosopher of repute, was appointed United States Commissioner of Education. McMurrin, in cleanly argued statements published during his tenure in the commissionership, argued for a rigorous intellectual emphasis in the schools. The schools were to serve all the people, but the job of the schools was to cultivate disciplined excellence in intellectual domains. Larger functions of socialization were minimized while the school was identified as the institution uniquely fitted to perform the function of development of intellectual power. As John Gardner, later to accept appointment as Secretary of Health, Education, and Welfare, put it, the center of concern was with ". . . the difficult, puzzling, delicate and important business of toning up a whole society . . ." [1] To maintain and advance her position in the world, it was argued, America must draw on all her talent, developing the abilities of every citizen to the fullest so that the nation could remain ahead in world competition for leadership.

With genuine competence as the criterion, hereditary privilege can have no place. Nepotism in business and government, legacy systems in social organizations, social snobbism, cannot be tolerated. Performance alone must be the criterion of excellence. American education must be dedicated to the search for, and development of, talent from whatever human source. "Excellence" rather than "equality" or "self-fulfillment" must become the new watchword of our society and our education.

Inasmuch as a primary purpose was to make education work for national ends, education received more and more federal money. The National Science Foundation and the United States Office of Education came to have increasing influence on local schools throughout the country. A major objective was to beat the Soviet Union to the moon and halt the expansion of Soviet and Chinese spheres of influence in Africa and Asia. Since both the space race and the military race depended mainly on advanced technology, greatest emphasis was on the sciences. Moreover, interest shifted from science as a part of general education to production of scientifically competent researchers and technicians. Thus, specialists in science moved into major curriculum-planning roles.

As eminent specialists in the disciplines of human knowledge were called upon to formulate school courses of study, intensive induction into the various subject fields received more and more emphasis in the preparation of teachers,

---

[1] John W. Gardner, *Excellence* (New York: Harper & Row, Publishers, 1961), p. xiii.

relatively less attention in teacher-training programs being given to human growth and development. Even in elementary education this trend was strong, with some schools for small children organized to make possible the moving of seven-, nine-, and eleven-year-olds from station to station whereby they were exposed to a long series of teacher-specialists, each of whom exhibited expertise in a field of disciplined inquiry.

This way, specifically, each candidate for teaching in elementary school was to develop a solid academic concentration in one established academic field, and general elementary teachers were supposed to pass into professional limbo along with general practitioners in medicine. Gains and losses may be analogical. Both medicine and teaching lose with the disappearance of the general practitioner. It is difficult to establish empirically the advantage of human encounter in learning and in healing. But it can be established empirically that people yearn to be known, understood, and loved by others. These qualities are not lost but they suffer marked erosion as general practice gives way to specialization in elementary schools. The slogan of the 1920s and 1930s that "teachers teach children not subjects" may have been maudlin; however that may be, subject-matter specialists rather than professors of child development began to have more influence in teacher training after mid-century; it apparently became more important to know the subject than to know Johnny.

CONTEXT

The little book by John Gardner to which reference has already been made expressed most clearly and impressively the rationale that was to guide in shaping educational policy during the 1960s. Gardner, in arguments strongly reminiscent of Plato's review of the kinds of excellence in the first four books of the *Republic*, holds that such an emphasis does not deny a concern for individual differences. Since people differ, individual differences constitute many kinds of talent and we must value diversity if we truly mean to make the best use of human material. Thus Gardner proposes the question, "In a society such as ours, can we be both equal and excellent?"

We shall have to be exceedingly clear about these matters if we are to develop a more mature view of democracy itself. No democracy can function effectively until it has gone a long way toward dissolving systems of hereditary stratification. This is presumably true of any democracy, but overwhelmingly true of the urbanized, industrial democracy with which we are familiar. On the other hand, no democracy can give itself over to extreme emphasis on individual performance and still remain a democracy —or to extreme equalitarianism and still retain its vitality.

If democracy is to hold these contesting philosophies in balance, the citizens of democracy must understand the implications of each. We have never been willing to explore those implications candidly and incisively.[2]

The good society is, indeed, the one in which the most gifted and capable are at the top,[3] but it is also, and by virtue of this very accomplishment, one in which each man's talent has been identified and nurtured to the full.

We strive, then, toward a mode of equalitarianism in that every individual is given the opportunity to develop his natural capacities fully. We also stimulate rather than stifle individualism and competitiveness by allowing gifted youngsters to achieve as far as possible.

Thus Francis S. Chase wrote in 1964 that the term "excellence" is replacing "equality of opportunity" as the focus of attention in American education.[4] Yet, we must realize

[2] Ibid., pp. 28–29.
[3] Ibid., p. 114.
[4] Francis S. Chase, "Can both Excellence and Quality Be Honored?" *Education Digest* 30 (October, 1964): 27.

that we are far short of the goal of equality. For it is not enough to speak of equality, but of "openness of access." It is not enough that equalities exist; to achieve total equality we must make certain that no one is barred from effective participation in any aspect of life for any reason other than his own inherent inability or indisposition to take part.[5] According to Chase, the connection between excellence and equality is that each person have the opportunity to be and to do his best. "To each his own kind of excellence—this is the brand of equality we must nurture." [6]

Gardner, in pursuit of policy to accommodate both equality and excellence, would restrict higher education to the more capable, work against the widely held notion that everybody should have a chance at college, and use standardized tests to identify types and levels of competence.

The broad conception of excellence we have outlined must be built on two foundation stones—and both of them exist in our society.

1. *A pluralistic approach to values.* American society has always leaned toward such pluralism. We need only be true to our deepest inclinations to honor the many facets and depths and dimensions of human experience and to seek the many kinds of excellence of which the human spirit is capable.

2. *A universally honored philosophy of individual fulfillment.* We have such a philosophy, deeply embedded in our tradition. Whether we have given it the prominence it deserves is the question which we must now explore.[7]

Thus, although not all youngsters are to be encouraged to go to college, the alternative is not narrow trade or industrial training. There are four steps that need to be taken to

[5] Ibid., p. 1.
[6] Ibid., p. 27.
[7] Gardner, *Excellence,* p. 134.

compensate those who naturally would not benefit from a college education:

1. We must make available to young people far more information than they now have on post-high school opportunities other than college.
2. Parents, teachers, and high school counselors must recognize that if the youngster who is not going to college is to continue his growth in learning, he must receive as much sagacious help and counsel as a college-bound student.
3. We must do what we can to alter the negative attitude toward education held by many youngsters who fail to go on to college. They must understand that they have been exposed to only one kind of learning experience and that the failures and frustrations encountered in school are not necessarily predictive of failure in every other kind of learning.
4. We must enable the young person to understand that his stature as an individual and his value as a member of society depend upon continued learning—not just for four years or a decade but throughout life.[8]

Gardner holds that, even if all environmental deficiencies had been compensated for, a significant residuum of individual difference among men would remain. He recognizes that not only demonstrated ability but motivation and eagerness to learn are dependent to a considerable degree upon social environment. Schools are to work systematically to counter these negative influences. Yet he also holds that the ultimate responsibility for learning and growth rests with the individual. He speaks of what he calls the "principle of multiple chances," holding that "human dignity and worth should be assessed only in terms of those qualities of mind and spirit that are within the reach of every human being." [9]

[8] Ibid., pp. 90–91.
[9] Ibid., p. 81.

That is, there is an excellence appropriate to each man. The schools are to make every effort to locate and cultivate this excellence. Despite the advocacy of a plurality of values, "multiple chances," and compensation by educational institutions for environmental disadvantage, the objective is a hierarchial society.

> . . . a society in which the most gifted and most capable people are at the top. This is what we have always thought of as an ideal society. And it is the only kind of society that can hold its own in today's world.[10]

The standards used in the processes of guidance and selection are assumed by Dr. Gardner to have been set. There is an ubiquitous "we" used throughout *Excellence*, the referent never made clear. "We would educate some youngsters by sending them on to college." [11] Who is "we"? Is it society at large, the leaders of the society, the government? Again, "We would educate others in other ways." [12] Apparently, it is the intellectuals who are to make such decisions and set such standards. Plato meets the issue by advocating the royal lie. Dr. Gardner does not do this. Nevertheless, it is not proposed to delegate freely and without qualification to the masses of men—unselected—the prerogative of setting the standards. Despite the effort to argue that we can be both excellent and equal, this doctrine of equality is proportional.

As for the institutional implementation of the sorting advocated, two social workers have pointed out hazards of school policy grounded in strong emphases on selection.

Whatever their differences, however, school record systems appeared alike in the retention of information that documented mal-

[10] Ibid., p. 114.
[11] Ibid., p. 82.
[12] Ibid.

performance. Disciplinary actions, contacts with parents about critical situations, notices of probationary status, suspensions, and class absences were among the kinds of facts most often recorded in student files. These files followed students from grade to grade and from school to school . . . it is much easier for pupils to acquire negative than positive formal reputations since, except for grades and at the upper high school level, "good" events are less often recorded (e.g., special classroom duties). Second, it is hard for the pupil to "live down" his past, especially when the record follows him to another school. . . . Serious questions must be raised about the emphasis on "early identification" when for so many youngsters it results not in service, but in the assignment of negative reputations that cannot be easily surmounted, even if subsequent behavior is acceptable.[13]

To be sure, Gardner would deplore such practice out of hand, just as, at another level, he affirms the democratic political process. But institutionalized practices to implement the recommendations are all too likely to vitiate the generalized affirmations. Plato's ideal society was totalitarian, not democratic, and the philosopher-kings told the royal lie to put it across.

SOURCES

The writings of Jerome Bruner constitute primary sources in discussion of the movement under consideration here. It is now generally considered that a conference of scientists and psychologists held at Woods Hole, Massachusetts, in 1960 brought focus to the movement. Bruner, a Harvard psychologist, reported this conference in the small book—now a contemporary classic—entitled *The Process of Education*.[14]

[13] Robert Vinter and Rosemary Sarri: "Malperformance in the Public School: A Group Work Approach," *Social Work* 10, no. 1 (January 1965): 9–10.

[14] Jerome Bruner, *The Process of Education* (Cambridge, Mass.: Harvard University Press, 1960).

Other works in which Bruner developed themes of this initial statement were *On Knowing* (1964), *Toward a Theory of Instruction* (1966), and, with Rose Oliver and Patricia Greenfield, *Studies in Cognitive Growth* (1966).

Second only to Bruner as a spokesman was the biologist-educator Joseph Schwab, active as a lecturer and author of numerous papers dealing with the teaching of science as inquiry, the structure of the natural sciences, and the concept of the structure of a discipline.

Philip H. Phenix in *Realms of Meaning* provides a philosophical rationale for the movement and a synoptic analysis of the conceptual structures of the various sciences and humanistic studies, while anthologies of importance are *The Structure of Knowledge and the Curriculum*, edited by G. W. Ford and Lawrence Pugno, *New Curricula*, edited by Robert W. Heath, and the Phi Delta Kappa Symposium edited by Stanley Elam, entitled *Education and the Structure of Knowledge*.

Examples of school courses of study constructed on principles advocated by Bruner, Schwab, *et al.* came from the National Science Foundation (NSF), the Physical Science Study Committee (PSSC), the Biological Sciences Curriculum Study (BSCS), Chemical Education Materials Study (CHEMS), School Mathematics Study Group (SMSG), and the Elementary School Science Project (ESS).

THEORY

Some apparent disagreement has arisen among critics whether the structure of the disciplines movement and Bruner's theory in particular is in the heritage of Dewey's experimentalism, a variant of the Platonic tradition, or even a sort of modified Herbartianism. As a matter of fact, grasping the theory of knowledge advanced by Bruner and Schwab is an important condition for understanding the pedagogy.

In the first place, there is no suggestion that knowledge is of some unchanging external reality. This is not a metaphysical realism. Rather, what we have that gives rise to the quest for knowledge is certain regularities of "experience" or "events." A subject matter is made up of data recording such regularities among events. Structure is not discovered within but, rather, is "imposed upon" the data. The data are raw material shaped, formed, "structured" by man. But we do the structuring. The data are not found structured; we construct something of them. Thus Bruner states:

The issue of subject matter in education can be resolved only by reference to one's view of the nature of knowledge. Knowledge is a model we construct to give meaning and structure to regularities in experience. The organizing ideas of any body of knowledge are inventions for rendering experience economical and connected. We invent concepts such as force in physics, motives in psychology, style in literature as means to the end of comprehension.[15]

This way, the end-point in inquiry is not a conclusion, as if somehow something had been found out about reality per se, but rather an act of interpretation. Schwab puts it:

Let us . . . describe the last step of a short-term enquiry, not as the drawing of a conclusion, but as an *interpretation of data.* . . .

The improbability of obtaining definitive proof or disproof suggests that it might be wise, for purposes of teaching, to treat science not as a process of proof or verification at all but rather as a process of discovery, a process of disclosing events in nature and of discovering ways of relating these events to one another

[15] Jerome Bruner, *On Knowing, Essays for the Left Hand* (Cambridge, Mass.: Harvard University Press, 1962), p. 120.

in such as fashion that our understanding is enhanced. In any case, we cannot avoid the realization that science is a process of *constructing* bodies of *tentative* knowledge, of discovering *different* ways of making data coherent, and "telling" about a given subject matter.[16]

There is a sense in which inquiry always precedes and adjudicates among data. For what one seeks and the meaning one assigns to what he finds are functions of inquiry and belong to the side of the inquirer, influenced by his decisions.

The scientific knowledge of any given time rests not on *the* facts but on *selected* facts—and the selection rests on the conceptual principles of the inquiry.[17]

Knowledge, then, is knowledge of the conceptions which are taken to explain experienced regularities or events, these presumed to possess some sort of objective existence, but this presumption itself a human construct. Inasmuch as attention and concern are living, dynamic, growing activities, knowledge keeps changing as experience itself changes. Thus, scientific knowledge is somewhat fragile, always remaining at all points subject to modification. Each field is constantly setting new goals and different procedures or patterns by which to reach them. Each field continues to ask vastly difference questions in its inquiries. There is constant seeking of novel hypotheses and continual establishment of new formulae.

Natural phenomena as now conceived by the sciences must be understood as a dynamic, a drama. The drama unfolds as the

[16] Joseph Schwab, "The Structure of the Natural Sciences," in *Education and the Structure of Knowledge*, ed. G. W. Ford and Lawrence Pugno (Chicago: Rand McNally & Co., 1964), pp. 34–35.

[17] Joseph Schwab, "The Concept of the Strucure of a Discipline," *Educational Record* 43 (July 1962): 199.

outcome of many interacting roles. Therefore, the relation of each role to others must be understood. Second, each role may be played by more than one actor; different "actors," despite their apparent diversities, must be recognized as potential players of the same role. Third, each potential player of a role modifies somewhat the role he plays and, through this effect, also modifies the roles played by other actors. Hence, the unfolding, the climax, and outcome of the drama are flexible, not one rigid pattern, but variations on a theme.[18]

It is assumed that there exists a body of underlying principles (structure) for each field of knowledge (discipline). Teaching will be most effective when its content is this structure and the peculiar method of inquiry characterizing the discipline. The development of the best curriculum for each subject is the keystone of this movement. Joseph Schwab defines structure as including ". . . the body of imposed conceptions which define the investigated subject matter of that discipline and control its inquiries." [19] The structure of the discipline is the concepts, principles, and methods that constitute the discipline. In other words, every academic discipline has its particular ends or goals of knowledge and the means which it contrives to reach these goals make up the structure of the discipline. Hence, a physicist makes use of the means of his discipline to solve problems which will reveal to him a larger glimpse of the goal of physics, an understanding of the universe of matter and energy around us.

Since every discipline has its basic concepts or "representative ideas," [20] content should be chosen so as to exemplify the representative ideas of the discipline. The ideas themselves are too abstract for beginners.

[18] Ibid., p. 202.
[19] Ibid., p. 199.
[20] See Philip H. Phenix, *Realms of Meaning* (New York: McGraw-Hill Book Co., 1964).

The most fundamental ideas are usually not appropriate as explicit content until a fairly advanced stage of understanding has been reached. They are high abstractions that are not meaningful except to persons who possess a considerable fund of knowledge in the subject to which they apply. The less comprehensive ideas are, the more easily they can be understood by the beginning student.[21]

Schwab delineates two components of the structure of a discipline. One is the body of concepts which define the subject matter, but another is the "syntax" of the field—its characteristic procedures and methodologies.[22] These components can, when properly presented and taught, enable the student to grasp the logical structure of the discipline. Conceptualized principles lead to research which uncovers new knowledge, which, in turn, formulates new concepts.

The new knowledge lets us envisage new, more adequate, more telling conceptions of the subject matter. The growth of technique permits us to put the new conceptions into practice as guiding principles of a renewed inquiry.[23]

This, then, is the true purpose of the structure of the discipline approach. The student will gain the capacity to continue learning throughout his life.

By mastering the structure, the student achieves command of the fundamental ideas of a subject, which can then be used as a foundation for recognizing and attacking other problems. "The more fundamental or basic is the idea he has learned, almost by definition, the greater will be its breadth of applicability to new problems."[24]

---

[21] Ibid., p. 327.
[22] Schwab, "Concept of the Structure of a Discipline," p. 203.
[23] Ibid., p. 200.
[24] Bruner, *Process of Education*, p. 18.

It is maintained that the sensitivity to pattern or intellectual form is a characteristic of the modern scientific temper. Older knowledge, it is alleged, tended toward a catalog, while scientific inquiry tends to look for patterns—patterns of change and patterns of relations as their explanatory principles.[25] To have a grasp of the structure of an area of knowledge is to be able to relate other things to it.

EDUCATIONAL APPLICATIONS

After several decades of emphasis on synthesis and co-ordination of specialties in schoolwork, the structure of the disciplines movement, to the contrary, emphasizes the discreteness and integrity of each specialty, as such, in the general curriculum of the school. Rather than fusion, emphasis is on the unique organizing concepts of biology, chemistry, physics; history, geography, and economics; literature, composition, grammar. With university specialists doing the planning in each field, the task of the school is to impart to the young the intellectual skills exemplified in the activities of the specialists. School students are to be inducted into the habits of thought of biologists, chemists, physicists, historians, geographers, economists.

It was assumed that understanding these elements (rather than merely possessing facts) would give the student intellectual power —power to grasp *intuitively* the relationship of new phenomena already experienced. Therefore, ability to think inductively became a built-in goal and teachers were encouraged to let students discover meanings for themselves. The word "discovery" popped up everywhere in articles describing new curriculum projects, authors frequently failing to distinguish discovery as an act of

---

[25] Schwab, "Concept of the Structure of a Discipline," p. 201.

inductive behavior to be sought in learners and discovery as a process of attaining or teaching for such behavior.[26]

The structure of the disciplines movement brought together to an unusual degree scholars in primary fields of human knowledge, professional educators, and school pupils. It attempted to establish common meeting ground between scholar and educator to aid students in their quest for knowledge and understanding. Bruner held that ". . . the curriculum of a subject should be determined by the most fundamental understanding that can be achieved of the underlying principles that give structure to that subject." [27]

This way highly specialized experts must participate fully in designing courses and writing textbooks and instructional programs.

Designing curricula in a way that reflects the basic structure of a field of knowledge requires the most fundamental understanding of that field. It is a task that cannot be carried out without the active participation of the ablest scholars and scientists.[28]

At the same time, Bruner held that "any subject can be taught effectively in some intellectually honest form to any child at any stage of development." [29] He said that what is necessary is that the material be presented in terms the child can understand. Thus basic notions of physics and geometry are accessible to young children when they are expressed in

[26] John I. Goodlad, "The Curriculum," in *The Changing American School,* ed. John I. Goodlad. The Sixty-Fifth Yearbook of the National Society for the Study of Education (Chicago: University of Chicago Press, 1966), p. 39.

[27] Bruner, *Process of Education,* p. 31.

[28] Ibid., p. 32.

[29] Ibid., p. 33.

simple ordinary language through materials with which the child is familiar. This means that the normal child is always "ready" for learning, provided that the learning is scaled to his level of understanding. The new mathematics curricula in which set theory is presented in elementary schools exemplifies this.

The basic ideas of a science can be presented, then, at any and all ages in varying degrees of complexity. Thus, concepts can be further developed in each succeeding year, so that the student will finally achieve a relatively deep understanding of a discipline. (This has been referred to as the "spiral curriculum.") The problem of how these basic ideas can be presented in a manner both effective and interesting remains, however.

Bruner has many notions about how knowledge can be made effective. He says that if we would develop in children knowledge that is powerful and productive—and therefore transferable—we should try first to lead the child to grasp a structure by induction. To do this, he should be provided with many particular instances until he can recognize the underlying regularity. Also, he should be given practice at both "leaping and plodding"—he should go by small steps, and then be allowed to make huge guesses.[30] Bruner holds that the best way to make a subject interesting is to make it worth knowing, which means ". . . to make the knowledge gained usable in one's thinking beyond the situation in which the learning has occurred." [31] This involves somehow teaching the student to think intuitively; that is, to be able to go from a known idea to a good guess at something related to it. Therefore, attempts are made in the new curricula to

[30] Jerome Bruner, "Needed: A Theory of Instruction," *Educational Leadership* 20 (May 1963): 531.

[31] Bruner, *Process of Education,* p. 31.

dwell less on purely factual material and more on major concepts, in the hope that students will grasp the subject as a whole, and gain an "intuitive" understanding of its structure. Then, having mastered general basic ideas, a student should be able quickly to fit a new example into the scheme. Also, because he has labored on basic ideas rather than on bits and pieces of information, he should be more able to change when the specific content changes. He will have become familiar with the overall picture.

Terms like "discovery" and "intuition" are taken to designate the competence developed in young learners to apply basic rules to new problems as they gain familiarity in the ways of thought prevailing in various fields of scholarship. Scholars emphasized that to try to impart all the essential facts in any field is futile. Moreover, the total mass of such facts is increasing so rapidly that in the encyclopedic sense no one man, however eminent, can actually *know* a field. Then what can be known? What is it that the specialist has if the encyclopedic ideal is untenable? He knows the methods, the processes, the basic assumptions of the field. He is at home in the dynamics of an area of inquiry. This way, conventional meanings of the term "structure" perhaps made its choice as a label unfortunate. Really it is not the "structure" of the discipline, but its processes, its dynamic controls, its rules of procedure and evidence that the specialist knows. Not biology but the method of biology is to be taught, not physics but the principles of physical inquiry are to be taught, not grammar but linguistics, not mathematics but mathematical thinking.

The very concept of fact was changing from that of a verifiable certainty to that of an observation taking its relevance from the theoretical construct in which it is used and by which it is described. Facts become facts only within the perspective of the viewer and are communicable as facts only within the communicated content of his perspective.[32]

Now, how do you succeed in inducting young people into a complicated game so that they can begin to play it on their own? How do you teach bridge, poker, or chess to produce the autonomous player? The plays and moves are not somehow natural; they are really quite arbitrary, but in order to play any one of these games you have to learn the rules of the game. This is an intriguing intellectual challenge to which considerable attention has been given from time to time in the history of education. In this instance, however, work of Jean Piaget was drawn upon. Moreover, interest in programming for instruction by mechanical devices supported an effort to set up the process of induction into the methods of a field so that progressive growth in competence could be programmed. Pedagogy, or methods of teaching in the nineteenth-century sense of didactics, was given serious attention by the scholars. The thrust in this effort is to impart to the young methods and skills perfected by specialists. This type of instruction is designed to construct learning situations so that responses called forth are those predetermined to be correct. Its aim is to teach youngsters to do chemistry, physics, biology, literature, composition, grammar the way competent scholars had determined it should be done.

But if this be treason as assessed against the educational ideology of the 1920s and 1930s it must be asked by what authority the immature may claim the option of disregarding the decrees of scholars. After all, in intellectual matters, may the incompetent and immature challenge the hierarchy? The scholars maintain that that part of a field of study or a branch of human knowledge that remains relatively stable while

[32] Goodlad, "The Curriculum," p. 37.

products of investigation in the field multiply and change is the mode of investigating, the way of approaching phenomena, the methodology. All branches of knowledge have at least two major characteristics, their own fund of information and their own method of inquiry (substance and syntax). The content of a discipline may be divided into (a) fundamental facts, (b) basic ideas, (c) concepts, and (d) thought systems. Each science has its own logical language, its own canons of facts and symbols, and its own (sometimes conflicting) ways of relating facts and principles to each other. Each discipline offers something distinctive, and each subject involves a specific mode of thinking.

It would seem, therefore, that the idea of building from the most simple concepts, exemplified by concrete examples, to more and more abstract concepts is implicit in the structure of the disciplines approach. Sequential development is an integral part of the procedure. The emphasis is on unifying concepts, principles, and methods of inquiry with each successive topic designed to develop a central theme or element. "As the scope of a set of principles enlarges, so does the coherence of the body of knowledge which develops from it, the interdependence of its component statements. . . ." [33] Because of this coherence and interdependence, Schwab warns against separation of the bits and pieces of knowledge: ". . . their removal from the structure of other statements which confer on them their meaning, alters or curtails that meaning." [34]

Curriculum Building

The theory of the structure of the disciplines movement makes cognition fundamental in learning. Thus, specific content is primarily important to the extent that it is under-

---

[33] Schwab, "Concept of the Structure of a Discipline," p. 202.
[34] Ibid.

stood as part of a meaningful context. If understanding and perception are the basis of knowing, then unrelated information and skills cannot best contribute to learning. If learning of specifics is important to the extent that they feed the formation of ideas, and if it is the discovery and use of the organizing principles that makes for good education, educators must organize content so that these overriding principles are experienced.

The effect of the movement, then, has been "a fundamental reexamination of the content of many of the subject fields with particular emphasis upon the structure of knowledge in each field and its method of inquiry." [35] Philip Phenix uses the term "representative ideas." They are representative in that they disclose the essence of a discipline. They stand for elements in or parts of the whole of the discipline. Representative ideas express the pattern of a discipline. "Representative ideas are the organizing principles of the discipline." [36]

Bruner says, ". . . for any body of knowledge there is a minimal set of propositions, or statements, or images from which one can best generate the rest of what exists within that field . . ." [37] Three qualities are associated with proper structuring of knowledge. They are economy, productiveness, and power. Economy is the power to simplify the diversity of information within a discipline. Productiveness is the ability to generate new propositions, to discover new knowledge. Power comes from the increased manipulability of mastered knowledge. Bruner says that when a curriculum is developed one must take the student as he is and provide him with a structure that is economical, productive, and powerful for him.

[35] George W. Denemark, "Concept Learning: Some Implications for Teaching," *Liberal Education* 51, no. 1 (March 1965): 54.

[36] Phenix, *Realms of Meaning*, p. 323.

[37] Bruner, "Needed, A Theory of Instruction," p. 525.

In *The Process of Education* Bruner gives four reasons why teaching the fundamental structure of a subject is sound: (1) an understanding of the fundamentals makes the subject more comprehensible; (2) it is easier to remember facts which fit into a pattern than to remember miscellaneous facts; (3) understanding of basic ideas is essential for transfer; and (4) stressing fundamentals makes teachers reexamine them and keep up-to-date.[38]

Once scholars have developed a structure for their discipline, the structure can be translated into a curriculum. At this point the question of the relationship between curriculum and structure arises. The structure is not memorized as a set of principles. Rather, content is selected to exemplify the basic structure or concepts. Each particular illustrates a concept. During his years in school it is expected that a child will be exposed to the structure of different disciplines several times. At each level the content will be more complex, building on his previously acquired knowledge. In this way the student will deepen his understanding of ideas. He will be prepared to handle more complicated forms as he progresses.

Upon completion of each course, the student should find it possible to answer the following:

1. What kinds of questions does this subject seek to answer?
2. What kinds of methods does it use to study these questions?
3. What concepts are basic in this subject to give order and meaning to its specific data?
4. What generalizations are being obtained and what are illustrations of the specific items to which these generalizations apply?
5. How can this subject be used in my daily life?[39]

[38] Bruner, *Process of Education*, pp. 23–25.
[39] R. W. Tyler, "The Knowledge Explosion: Implications for Secondary Education," *The Educational Forum* 29, no. 2 (January 1965): 150.

Such understanding of the basic fundamentals of a field makes mastery of the subject easier for those who come to specialize in it. Thorough knowledge of concepts is to ". . . ensure that memory loss will not mean total loss, that what remains will permit us to reconstruct the details when needed. A good theory is the vehicle not only for understanding a phenomenon now but also for remembering it tomorrow." [40]

To identify the disciplines that constitute knowledge of the world is to identify the subject matter of education. To locate the relation of these disciplines to one another is to determine what may be joined together for purposes of instruction and what should be held apart. These relations also determine decisions about the sequence of instruction.

Teaching and Learning

In this point of view, much emphasis is placed on "intuition" or "discovery." Intuitive thinking is unlike analytical thinking, in that it is not characterized by a step-by-step procedure. Rather, solutions are arrived at by a process that arises out of implicit perception of the total situation. If the student is to develop this capacity for "intuition," he must be nurtured in the basic ideas of the field and must be at home with its methods.

If education applies the two principles of emphasis on basic ideas and stress on intuitive thinking, then indeed ". . . any subject can be taught to any child." Bruner states that it is not necessary to wait until the child reaches a certain age or shows a desire to learn a subject. For a function of a good school environment will be to bring about conditions for learning. The learning of basic principles of a subject, such as physics, can be begun by a seven-year-old if the teacher illustrates the principles by materials familiar to the child.

[40] Bruner, *Process of Education*, p. 25.

Students should learn how to learn. All educators know that learning continues after a student leaves the formality of the classroom. School, if effective, prepares one to cope with problems outside school. Knowing how to learn is a decided asset in today's world. Schwab states:

In the dogmatic classroom, the role of the teacher was to explain what the book left unclear and to test the student's grasp of what he was told. Now, his role is to teach the student how to learn.[41]

The subjects should be taught as modes of inquiry. Schwab explains it this way:

The phrase "the teaching of science as enquiry" . . . . means, first, a process of teaching and learning which is, itself, an enquiry, "*teaching* as enquiry." It means, second, instruction in which science is seen as a process of enquiry, "*science* as enquiry." [42]

Dr. Jerome Metzner, a scientist and science teacher, has the following to say about inquiry in science:

Inquiry is the *modus operandi* of science. It is a departure from authoritarianism, dogmatism and status quoism. It thrives on uncertainty. Today's fact may be tomorrow's fiction. It rejects complacency, conjecture, assertions unsupported by evidence, heresay and superstition.[43]

The role of the teacher is to initiate learning, not stifle it. He should encourage his students in their inquiry rather than appear to be the guardian of infallible truths and therefore

[41] Joseph J. Schwab, "The Teaching of Science as Enquiry," in *The Teaching of Science* (Cambridge, Mass.: Harvard University Press, 1962), p. 67.

[42] Ibid., p. 65.

[43] Jerome Metzner, "Identifying the Problems in Science," address delivered at the NSTA Eastern Regional Conference, Pittsburgh, Pa., October 27, 1966, p. 18.

infallible himself. Classroom procedure should include a "substantial component of doubt, . . . the honest statement of ignorance, uncertainty, and dubiety where these conditions are, in fact, the conditions of knowledge." [44] In short, the attitudes within the classroom should teach the student how to learn and promote this learning.

Insofar as possible a method of instruction should have the objective of leading the child to discover for himself. Telling children and then testing them on what they have been told inevitably has the effect of producing bench-bound learners whose motivation for learning is likely to be extrinsic to the task—pleasing the teacher, getting into college, artificially maintaining self-esteem. The virtues of encouraging discovery are of two kinds . . . the child will make what he learns his own . . . and the sense of confidence it [discovery] provides is the proper reward for learning. It is a reward that, moreover, strengthens the very process that is at the heart of education—disciplined enquiry. [45]

The child, then, must be led to inquire and to discover the generalizations that lie behind specific instances.

Two facts and a relation joining them is and should be an invitation to generalize, to extrapolate, to make a tentative intuitive leap, even to build a tentative theory. [46]

To be sure, the emphasis in all this is on intellectual structures and processes. What about the child himself? Although less attention is given to general growth and development than by the progressive followers of Dewey, considerable interest in the intellectual development of children is shown. An important source for such thinking is the

[44] Schwab, "Teaching of Science as Enquiry," p. 60.
[45] Bruner, *On Knowing, Essays for the Left Hand*, pp. 123–124.
[46] Ibid., p. 124.

work of Piaget, who identified different stages in the intellectual development of the child. The first stage is that of the preschool child. His chief concern is manipulation of the world through action. The child is not able to separate his own goals from the means for achieving them. That is, he arrives at his answer by the trial-and-error method rather than as the result of thought. This stage is primarily active. A second stage of development is the stage of concrete operations. The child is now in school. He is now capable of covert trial and error. An example of this is a child working with groups of objects. When the group is subdivided the child comes to understand that the original objects can be restored, and can perform the restoration implicitly (i.e., conceptually), without manipulating them physically. Nevertheless, concept learning, it is held, can and does take place at all age levels, beginning in preschool years. Even before children could be expected to state a proof in anything approaching respectable form, they can grasp the idea and work with it.

. . . we were privileged to see a demonstration of teaching in which fifth-grade children very rapidly grasped central ideas from the theory of functions, although had the teacher attempted to explain to them what the theory of functions was, he would have drawn a blank.[47]

Bruner distinguished between theory of learning and theory of instruction. Learning theory deals with how learning takes place and what happens after learning occurs. Instruction theory is prescriptive; it is "before the fact" of learning. In order to solve problems a child must have the courage and skill to explore alternative methods of attack. This can be encouraged in school, but may also be power-

[47] Bruner, *Process of Education*, p. 38.

fully nourished by home and other out-of-school influences. Involved are social skills, intellectual skills, linguistic skills, and certain manipulative skills. Awareness of these can help a teacher create the best possible atmosphere to encourage, guide, and strengthen such skills once the child begins school.

In the actual learning of concepts, practice is of little or no importance. Again, while *learning* is a continuous process not limited to the educational situation, it remains mainly passive in contrast to *thinking*, which is active. What is desired in instruction is that children "leap the barrier" from learning to thinking. Thinking is, then, "active learning," leading to new insight through discovery, reorganization, and transformation. The learning act consists of gaining new information, manipulating this to fit new tasks, and evaluating. Some of the steps in problem solving are involved: recognizing and defining; formulating hypotheses; gathering, interpreting, and organizing data in terms of hypotheses; formulating and applying conclusions.

SPECIFIC CURRICULUM PROJECTS— SOME EXAMPLES

Projects of curriculum revision for the schools began even before the Woods Hole conference, and centered in physics and mathematics. Some projects in the social sciences were also undertaken. Large sums of money were provided in the 1960s. The National Science Foundation contributed more than $30 million to science curricula alone. The United States Office of Education provided money for projects in social studies.

The National Science Foundation in 1959 provided a grant to the Physical Science Study Committee headed by Jerrold Zacharias of Massachusetts Institute of Technology. This committee, composed of physicists, teachers, educators

and school administrators, worked intensively to build a new
high school physics course, alleging that books and curriculum guides generally in use in basic high school physics
courses had not changed fundamentally since 1910. Complete renovation of physics was followed by similar projects
in mathematics and science. Work was done on a second
approach to physics, and several new approaches in high
school chemistry, biology, and mathematics. In all these
courses of study, the primacy of certain guiding principles,
and the importance of building on these principles is stressed.
The memorizing of isolated facts as was supposely required
by older catalog-type textbooks is constantly criticized.

John Moore, author of the "yellow version" of the BSCS
biology text, said: "There remain today widely known biology textbooks that are little more than accumulations of
biological data. They have served a useful purpose and
could be excused in times when biology was without a very
clear conceptual structure. But times have changed." [48]

Describing a new mathematics text, the authors asserted:
"From early on, youngsters are taught the essential structure of mathematics—the 'why' rather than the 'how'—through
plane geometry, elementary algebra. . . ." [49]

In the first chapter of *Modern Mathematics: Algebra One*
it is stated: "Nowhere in this book is *algebra* defined. . . .
Instead of a definition, the year's work will begin with an
exploration of the fundamental ideas of algebra." [50]

Physics

Professor Jerrold Zacharias proposed as early as 1956

[48] John Moore, *Biological Science, an Inquiry into Life*. The Biological
Sciences Curriculum Study (New York: Harcourt, Brace, and World, Inc.,
1963), p. 1.

[49] David B. Bergamini and the Editors of *Life, Mathematics* (New
York: Time, Inc., 1963), p. 194.

[50] Myron F. Rosskopf, Robert L. Morton, et al., *Modern Mathematics:
Algebra One* (Chicago: Silver Burdett Co., 1962), p. 1.

revision of texts, and adaptation of visual aids, problem books, and question-and-answer cards to present the structure and quality of the most advanced thinking in physics. Under his leadership there ensued formation of the Physical Science Study Committee composed of influential scientists, high school teachers, and college professors. They concluded that the high school physics course should be rigorous.

It should present physics as the contemporary physicist sees it—as the gradual unfolding of the nature of the universe by a continual process of inquiry, exploration, and discovery, and, as such, one of the most admirable achievements of the human mind and an indispensable part of Western thought and culture. The course should be designed to lead the student to this conception by letting him learn, insofar as possible, by exploring and experimenting as the scientist does.[51]

Subsequent years found physicists incorporating the design of the new physics in texts, laboratory manuals, teacher guides, special laboratory apparatus, written tests, and films. They tested, revised, and tested again the experiments they wished to use to develop the key concepts. Their approach was different from the conventional method, which made use of experiments in which students followed directions and ran perfect laboratory tests to get predetermined "correct" results. The old method, for example, had had students memorize Newton's three laws of motion, while the new approach allowed the student to conduct experiments to discover the laws himself.

The laboratory guides for the PSSC courses contained only minimal directions. These called attention to the important points in an experiment by raising questions. Then the student was left to decide what to do; including the

---

[51] James R. Killian, Jr., "The Return to Learning," in *New Curricula*, ed. Robert W. Heath (New York: Harper & Row, Publishers, 1964), p. 255.

decision whether experimentation is necessary or whether the question can be answered on the basis of concepts already at hand. PSSC physics concentrated on fundamental concepts of classical and modern physics de-emphasizing technological applications. As a result, more atomic and nuclear physics could be presented in the high school course.

Mathematics

In 1952 the University of Illinois Committee on School Mathematics first used its new textbooks in mathematics instruction in the University High School. Course I, which supplanted the traditional first-year high school algebra course, included topics on properties of real numbers, the language of algebra, operations and inverses, deductive organization, order and sets. In developing understanding of the real-number system, the structural concepts stressed were commutative, associative, and distributive laws. The manipulative rules presented by traditional textbooks were developed as applications of the laws combined in varieties of ways.

The UICSM courses did not give rules; instead, materials were organized in such a way that learners were given opportunities to work on simple problems, solutions to which required only experiences they already had. What was practiced in these exploration exercises was not applying a given computing rule to specific problems but finding the underlying properties that apply to all the computing rules. Therefore, a discovery process was embedded in the content of the course. Familiarity with the properties and the student's experience in combining the properties enabled him to design his own computing rules when necessary. Teaching the structural ideas was intended to enable the learner eventually to solve problems on his own initiative.

The UICSM courses were supposed to be taught by the

discovery method. The following description illustrates the intent:

The effective use of this method requires teaching skill of the highest order. The teacher must be an expert interrogator, secure in his knowledge of mathematics, patient when pupils are slow to discover the obvious, capable of following some unexpected pupil suggestions, and considerate in rejecting others. He must know how to capitalize on the occasional explosions of understanding which characterize pupil reaction to this method, and he must avoid the too early verbalization of a principle that has been discovered.[52]

The notion was that discovery in mathematics is a by-product of making things simpler. Starting from manipulation of objects or primitive ideas, a next step is to define them in terms of actions. Then the effort is to provide a representation by a unifying concept which can speak for the actions. The concept remains abstract but can be characterized by its properties. Manipulation and representation are elements in discovery. Intuition is employed when one tries to grasp the meaning and significance of a concept before he can describe it step by step. Intuition may yield a quick hypothesis to be tested, but must be formulated in symbols to achieve transmission of understanding of the structure to others.

Again, in the Suppes Arithmetic Project, begun in 1959, the major emphasis was on concepts, laws, and skills. "Sets" were the common element. The objectives were to introduce various arithmetic concepts before the introduction of corresponding operations on numbers and to use concrete materials and familiar ideas to move via a series of small

[52] National Council of Teachers of Mathematics, *Revolution in School Mathematics* (Washington, D.C.: National Council of Teachers of Mathematics, 1961), p. 79.

related steps toward abstractions and new ideas. In the Hawley-Suppes *Geometry for Primary Grades* the geometric notions and constructions are taught in the first grade. Materials are designed to stimulate reasoning and to develop the ability to read and comprehend mathematical material.

In the Greater Cleveland Mathematics Project stress was on the logic of mathematical thinking, and mathematics was treated in its logical aspect. Learning of mathematical concepts and ideas rather than mere skill in performing operations received emphasis. Reasoning, thinking, and understanding were stressed; concepts were to be formed before routine performance. The Cleveland Project attempted a K-through-12 curriculum making considerable use of visual and manipulative aids.

The group of major importance in the movement for a new approach to mathematics—clearly influenced by, and following in the train of, the pioneering University of Illinois Committee on School Mathematics—was the School Mathematics Study Group, set up by the National Science Foundation and using a report of the late 1950s by the Commission on Mathematics of the College Entrance Examination Board as a base. SMSG produced books for elementary schools in the form of short units, rather than attempting to move the total curriculum down from high school. SMSG and the University of Illinois Commission on School Mathematics worked out a new presentation of high school algebra. Algebra was presented as a study of numbers rather than the art of manipulating letters. New programs in algebra stress the deductive structure more than conventional ones. They retain "discovery exercises," but use deduction with basic laws.

The view was that mathematics should be taught as an active, live, growing subject. Theorems become obsolete as new ones are discovered. In the twentieth century there have been remarkable advances in the field. Related and applied areas have also seen rapid developments. For example, probability and statistics are applied in physical, engineering, biological and social sciences.

Automation has indeed had something to do with changes in mathematics instruction in the schools. Automation involves the introduction of machines that control machines. Examples are long-distance telephone dialing, guided missiles, and automatic airplane pilots. Automation has made possible construction and operation of machines of enormous size, complexity, and cost, and has created a necessity for the design and development of such machines.

The automatic digital computer has made it possible for mathematical theory to be teamed with the computing machine to produce answers required by physicists, engineers, and others. Computations that were formerly impossible can now be made quickly and efficiently. For example, in the launching of a guided missile, the computing machine receives information from radar about the missile's flight. It makes necessary calculations and sets the control of the missile. No human computers could do this in the brief time required for this operation.

Chemists and physicists have found new uses for mathematics; biologists apply mathematics to the study of genetics; businessmen use mathematics for scheduling production and distribution; sociologists need mathematics for complicated statistical analyses. In view of the increasingly wide range of application of mathematical techniques, young people need to understand basic principles of properties common to mathematical systems. With set theory at the core, and with notions of intersection, union, and complementation of sets as corollaries, the various new curricula in mathematics

endeavored the teaching of mathematics as a way of thinking—as systems of concepts at work.

Biology

Schwab, to whom numerous references have been made
in preceding pages as a theoretician of the structure of the
disciplines movement, was the leading spirit in curriculum
revision in high school biology.

The Biological Sciences Curriculum Study (BSCS) was
organized at Boulder, Colorado, in a meeting led by Professor Schwab. The scientists participating in the meeting
concluded that biology as it had been taught emphasized
conclusions, these too often separated from supporting data
and conceptual context. Curriculum revision in the train
of this meeting has defined biology as the science which
considers the living world encompassing zoology, botany,
microbiology, ecology, and genetics. If a student is to find
relationships among these diverse studies he must grasp
fundamental concepts such as evolution and homeostasis.
These are themes that form the foundations of unity in the
life sciences.

It is also important that the student understand how the
scientist discovers and verifies his knowledge. The structure
of science is the scientific mode of inquiry and the fundamental concepts which act as basis and a guide for that
inquiry.[53]

. . . in order for a person to be able to recognize the applicability or inapplicability of an idea to a new situation and to
broaden his learning thereby, he must have clearly in mind the
general nature of the phenomenon with which he is dealing. The

---

[53] Joseph J. Schwab, "The Structure of the Sciences," in *The Structure
of Knowledge and the Curriculum,* ed. G. W. Ford and Lawrence Pugno
(Chicago: Rand McNally & Co., 1964), p. 31.

more fundamental or basic is the idea he has learned, the greater will be its breadth of applicability to new problems.[54]

There are several important reasons why instruction should focus on fundamental concepts. The learning of fundamental principles makes biology more comprehensible, increases the chances for the development of intuitive thinking, decreases the gap between "advanced" knowledge and "elementary" knowledge, increases joy and excitement in learning, and facilities transfer of training.[55]

Notions such as these have been carefully embodied in widely used textbooks produced by BSCS. These have been known as the yellow, blue, and green versions, the cues provided by the textbook covers. The theme of the blue version is human biology, that of the yellow version molecular biology, while the green emphasizes ecology starting with communities proceeding to analysis of interrelationships among individual organisms within the community. While the blue, yellow, and green versions differ in emphasis, common themes appear in each.

Laboratory work has been organized into "laboratory blocks," each of which permitted a student to study a subject in depth, plan an experiment under supervision, gather data and form conclusions arising from critical assessment of the outcomes. For example, the block in embryology provided for initial watching of the development of a chick embryo. Comparisons were then made with the frog or the human embryo.

English

The College Entrance Examination Board established the Commission on English in September of 1959. National

[54] Bruner, *Process of Education*, p. 18.
[55] Ibid., pp. 23–26.

institutes enrolling selected classroom teachers offered courses in language, literature, and composition, and intensive workshops. The announced goal was to propose standards of achievement for college preparatory students in the secondary schools in order to improve the total program of English instruction.

English teachers at the institutes, who had approached grammar in the traditional manner with the idea of persuading students to gain control over the prestige dialect through memorizing rules and doing exercises, were directed to study structural grammar to the end that a student who understood the structure of his language would be able to operate within it successfully on any level. Although some attention was given to the teaching of literature (with historical types of organizations giving way to organization around themes or types), the greatest changes occurred in linguistics.

It is difficult to say exactly when structural linguistics was born, but many people consider the publication of *Language* by Leonard Bloomfield in 1933 an acceptable birth date. In any case, the first big debate between linguists and schoolmen came in the 1930s and centered on the problem of usage. This debate resulted in some modification of traditional prescriptive rules.

The second debate began in the 1940s when linguistic scientists insisted that the schoolroom grammarians were wrong in their whole approach to language. The two books that had the most profound effect on the schools were *An Outline of English Structure* by George L. Trager and Henry Lee Smith, Jr., and *The Structure of English*, by Charles Carpenter Fries, both published in the early 1950s. These books strongly influenced Paul Roberts, whose *English Sentences*, published in 1962, was the first transformational grammar for high school students.

Structural grammarians recognized the fundamental importance of sound, and the distinction between speech and writing. The sounds of a language, linguists insist, *are* the language; writing is merely a set of rules used to symbolize sounds. Traditional grammarians often ignored this distinction between writing and speaking and paid little or no attention to the important effects of such phenomena as pitch, stress, and juncture on the grammar of the language. Again, linguists believe that every language has a grammar peculiar to it, a grammar that differs in many important respects from the grammar of other languages. Finally, linguists agree that the study of language is—or can be—exciting and rewarding *in itself,* apart from whether it will help students to become better writers or speakers.

Basically the linguist divides the sentence into four parts: Class 1 words are nouns; Class 2 words are verbs; Class 3 words are adjectives; Class 4 words are adverbs. The rest of the words that make up sentences are called *intensifiers, auxiliaries,* and *noun determiners.* Emphasis is on sentence patterns. The objective is to impart to students insight into, and familiarity with, a basic structure and pattern characterizing sentences.

COMMENT

Perhaps the major potential pitfall of the emphasis on the structure of disciplines is the assumption that learning the structure or connectedness of knowledge increases the student's ability to think, either intuitively or analytically. While it may increase the latter, its contribution to intuitive thinking, despite the generous use of the term "intuition" by Bruner and others, seems more dubious.

Another assumption stems from the origin of the structure of the disciplines idea in the evolution of the new physics and the postwar knowledge explosion. Both, of course, are concerned with the sciences, and the structure of the disciplines approach, together with curriculum reform centered on it, were first applied in the sciences and in mathematics. But are these emphases, perhaps appropriate for the sciences, equally relevant in the humanities and social sciences? It is possible that the sciences possess a conceptual structure that is inherently sequential. But is this true of history, for example, where concepts do not exist in the form of a technical jargon or in the form of categorized classifications and in which research and interpretations borrow from the concepts of other disciplines? Schwab seems to have this in mind when he states that the subject matter of each discipline is far more complex than any limited model or structure of thought can describe. Of course, bodies of structured knowledge can have defensible and valuable meaning if learned, not dogmatically, but in a context of the conceptions and data that determine their limited meaning and confer their limited validity. To which it might be added—a task even graduate students might find difficult, much less novices on the public school level.

One other question needs asking: What are the assumed values behind the structure of the discipline approach? Is this theory designed to allow the individual to fit comfortably in his world by making decisions of his own in regard to it (as the theory seems to imply) or is it in reality designed to make the individual useful to society in the ways in which society wishes him to be useful? The stress on sequential development in the structure of the discipline approach suggests the programming of learning. Perhaps one assumption is that if we can program computers, why not try to program the human mind? Perhaps we can, but if this were achieved, who would program the computers?

Dubious in the extreme is the ascription of discovery and intuitive insight to instructional procedures thus conceived.

For certainly the so-called disciplines are postulate systems constructed by men and subject to the conventionalism and limitations of time and perspective of all human productions. The "discovery" or "intuitive" understanding comes only as the product of some deliberate indoctrination in the terms, propositions, and hypothesized relationships by making up a field of academic specialization. Such experiences by immature novitiates are inductive only in the sense that they have been induced in the young as a result of deliberate nurture in the presuppositions imposed by men on the continuities and contingencies of a range of characteristic human experiences. The "disciplines" have been made by men; they are not written in the heavens.

IV

Neo-Behaviorism—Teaching Machines and Programmed Instruction

THERE IS nothing radically new about programmed instruction. As teaching is instruction, so teaching is a deliberate or planned or "programmed" endeavor to bring about learning. What is new about teaching machines is the notion that a nonliving device can be constructed to perform the instruction. What is new is the application of automation to instruction. Even this, however, has ties into past practice; for example, a book corrects and prompts as we turn back the page to reconsider. Again, with the book we progress frame by frame as we turn the pages forward. Drill books, workbooks and "home-study" textbooks have also been around for a long time.

Thus, a teaching machine is not a new device, but a mechanical refinement of rather old instructional techniques embodied in books, textbooks, drill books, workbooks, and manuals. The main refinement has been the manner in which there has been built into the machine constraints to make cheating difficult if not impossible.

In addition, the very precision of the machine as a piece

of technical equipment demands a more careful and precise ordering of the material to be taught. A book can "ramble"; the form of print on paper bound into a packet is not so precise as the intervals of space and time constituting the frames of a teaching machine. Teaching machines set material or formal constraints both on the programmer (the "real" teacher) and the pupil. Thus we hear the claim that the machine, once effectively programmed, can do a better job than the human teacher because, by its very nature, it cannot make an error or "cheat" or "get lazy."

The machine is not perfect, but just because it is a machine it can approximate perfection more closely than a human agent. It cannot be in error, nor can it expose the possibility of error to the learner unless it is deliberately programmed to provide for alternative responses (i.e., "branching" rather than "linear" programming).

CHRONOLOGY

Professor Sidney L. Pressey of Ohio State University has generally been credited with devising and using the first teaching machine. Pressey's device was about the size of a portable typewriter. A series of multiple-choice questions were presented to the user; by pressing one of four keys the user indicated the answer he thought correct. Pressey's first papers on the subject were presented in 1924 at the meeting of the American Psychological Association. He claimed to have devised a "simple apparatus which gives and scores tests —and teaches." [1]

Some thirty years later, Harvard's experimental psychologist B. F. Skinner published the paper that has now become

---

[1] Reported in A. A. Lumsdaine and Robert Glaser, *Teaching Machines and Programed Learning* (Washington, D.C.: National Education Association, 1960), p. 23.

a latter-day classic, "The Science of Learning and the Art of Teaching." [2] Skinner, reacting against the ambiguities and circularity of conventional classroom instruction as he had observed it, was horrified by the lack of frequent, direct, and precise reinforcement in standard instructional procedure. How much better, he reasoned, if every child could proceed at his own rate, in small steps, and know immediately if he was correct. Skinner first devised a machine for the teaching of arithmetic. It was housed in a box about the size of a record player, with a window on the top surface through which a series of problems or questions could be presented. By 1958 he had perfected it and was using programs as part of the psychology course he taught at Harvard. By 1963 devices applying Skinner's techniques had been widely publicized, and it was estimated in that year that 80 percent of the programs in use were based on Skinnerian principles. [3]

Basically, Skinner is a behaviorist, and it is possible that he would not object to the boast of John B. Watson, founder of Behaviorism, that given ". . . a dozen healthy infants, well-formed, and my own specified world to bring them up in and I'll guarantee to take anyone at random and train him to become any type of specialist I might select—doctor, lawyer, artist, merchant-chief and, yes, even beggerman and thief, regardless of his talents, penchants, tendencies, abilities, vocations, and race of his ancestors." [4]

Skinner's basic laboratory procedure for studying the control of behavior has been to put an animal in a situation in which it will perform a likely operation. When the animal

---

[2] B. F. Skinner, "The Science of Learning and the Art of Teaching," *Harvard Educational Review* 24, no. 2 (Spring, 1954): 86–97.

[3] Herbert A. Thelen, "Programed Instruction: Insight vs. Conditioning," *Education* 83 (March 1963): 417.

[4] John B. Watson, *Behaviorism* (New York: W. W. Norton & Co., Inc., 1924), p. 82.

takes this step, it is presented with a reward or "reinforcer." For example, a rat is placed in a box with a lever at one end. If the rat depresses this lever, he is rewarded with a small pellet of food. Thus, the rat is reinforced for producing the desired behavior. This process is known as *operant conditioning;* the organism emits a desired response and is reinforced for it. The rat "learns" this reinforced behavior. He will keep emitting this response as long as he is reinforced. If reinforcement is stopped, the response drops off and soon becomes extinguished. Since behavior is controlled through the use of reinforcers, the pattern or schedule of reinforcement is effective in controlling the response rate, so that reinforcement need not be given every time a response is emitted.

From this type of experimentation, Skinner derived five basic principles: (1) operant conditioning, (2) reinforcement, (3) immediacy of reinforcement, (4) extinction, (5) shaping.[5] These principles can be illustrated by a reference to Skinner's original (1953) machine. With this device, a printed question appeared in a small window. Next to this window, another window exposed a blank section of paper on which the learner wrote an answer to this question. As soon as he had composed his answer, he released a lever which carried his answer under a third window, where he could see both his response and the correct response. If his answer was correct, he moved on to the next step. If his answer was incorrect, the question would appear again. The student was immediately reinforced by knowledge of the correctness of his answer. Here we see the five principles at work. The learner emits a response and is immediately reinforced. Incorrect answers are extinguished because not reinforced. The material is divided into many small steps that

[5] See B. R. Bugelski, *The Psychology of Learning Applied to Teaching* (New York: The Bobbs-Merrill Co., 1964), pp. 210–211.

lead, through shaping, to more complex behavior.[6] According to Skinner, if material is correctly programmed, there will not be "mistakes" on the part of the learner. "Each step must be so small that it can always be taken, yet in taking it the student moves somewhat closer to fully competent behavior." [7]

CONTEXT

Programmed instruction and teaching machines express the reach of contemporary technology into an area until recently not so much affected by it. If teaching is, indeed, to become increasingly technological, undoubtedly the substance of educational endeavor will be to some extent transformed thereby. C. Northcote Parkinson, somewhat antedating the widespread use of mechanical searchers, punched cards, and computers, argued that when people are appointed to positions, and provided with desks and typewriters, they soon devise activities to keep themselves, their helpers, the desks and typewriters busy.[8] More recently Marshall McLuhan applied Parkinson's notion to devices not requiring a constant human agent as tender.[9] Both Parkinson and McLuhan hold that an agent (living or mechanical) appointed to a position with tasks unspecified or vaguely specified draws to itself from its surroundings tasks to fill its capacity. Many years ago, George Kingsley Zipf developed a calculus of human behavior based on what he called the "prin-

[6] B. F. Skinner, "Why We Need Teaching Machines," *Harvard Educational Review* 31 (Fall 1961): 379.

[7] Ibid., p. 385.

[8] C. Northcote Parkinson, *Parkinson's Law, and other Studies in Administration* (Boston: Houghton Mifflin Co., 1957).

[9] H. Marshall McLuhan, *Understanding Media* (New York: McGraw-Hill Book Co., 1964).

ciple of least effort." His thesis was that effort always flows toward a "vacuum" or toward a lowest existing vacant level, and that the direction in which effort will be exerted by men can better be identified this way than by tabulation or assessment of ostensible purposes.[10]

Parkinson, McLuhan, and Zipf suggest that ideologies to justify, explain, or defend the use of the extra secretary or extra machine are generated after the fact. Although the Zipf work had no popular audience, the public response first to Parkinson and more recently to McLuhan has been enthusiastic and somewhat hilarious. For it does, indeed, provoke our sense of the ridiculous to consider that a major portion of human effort is to devise ways to use the outrageous contraptions that are dropped off in our front yards minus directions, and the assistants that the increased birth rate delivers to offices minus job descriptions. Yet there is plausibility to the analysis, even as it provokes our sense of the ridiculous. Elemental human needs are simple indeed. The inordinate complexity of industrial civilization is not necessary; it less ministers to than artificially creates wants, many of which we should be happier without.

That continuing emphasis of the humanistic tradition which remains despite ever-changing and radically controversial proposals as to means is insistence on man as criterion. Not man as someone says he is, or as someone arbitrarily selects spokesmen, but *man* as ordinary people, man as *men*. Educational argument during the first half of the twentieth century was based squarely upon this criterion. The arguments were over means. In this sense, partisans to arguments about education before World War II were all humanists—Thorndike, Judd, Dewey, Rugg, Hutchins, Adler,

---

[10] George Kingsley Zipf, *Human Behavior and the Principle of Least Effort* (Cambridge, Mass.: Addison-Wesley Press, 1949).

Whitehead. They all held the human criterion squarely in focus; they argued only about means.

Sometime after World War II, overwhelmed by the monstrosities of mechanical ingenuity that technology continued to turn off its assembly lines, and fearful lest we lose our national identity in technological competition, the criterion was lost. Educational theory was dominated for a time by mechanics and engineers—organizational and public relations manipulators of the Parkinsonian sort, and hardware technicians manipulating the gadgets commented upon by McLuhan.

Television, computers, and sophisticated electronic data processing devices have come since World War II. Shifts in educational practice have occurred to fit the machines that have been invented, some purely conceptual (e.g., simulation and game theory), others embodied in material objects (e.g., a computer or an overhead projector). As simulation and game theory are intriguing inventions claiming use in instruction, so is the language laboratory playback technique and other versions of immediate recording and playback by means of tape. Others are blow-up, slow motion, and speed-up of sounds and movements.

KWIC ("Key Word in Context") retrieval of recorded information promises not only changes in libraries but also changes in instructional method. In this technique an index of key words is developed analytically to cover the range of important topics contained in a massive printed text (e.g., the Bible or a collection of legal statutes). The text is transcribed in toto on electronic tape. Immediate electronic retrieval of passages containing a "key word" becomes possible. One of the purposes of *Educom*, an organization to which some forty major American universities belong, is to extend this system, the end in view being immediate retrieval of a desired comment in text from any library in the world.

Omar K. Moore's talking typewriter is a miniature version of the worldwide retrieval network forwarded by *Educom*. In a day when all recorded knowledge has been indexed, a talking typewriter fully plugged in could, it might be supposed, answer any question to which the mind of man has ever published a response.

SOURCES

The primary source of ideas discussed in this chapter is Professor B. F. Skinner of Harvard University. The work that most clearly and impressively states the theoretical position underlying his work is *Science and Human Behavior* (New York: Macmillan, 1953). However, his most-discussed volume is an intriguing utopian story, *Walden Two* (New York: Macmillan, 1948, 1962). An article considered to have sounded a keynote for the programming effort in American education in the 1950s and 1960s is "The Science of Learning and the Art of Teaching," *Harvard Educational Review* 24 (Spring, 1954). Other writings in which Skinner's basic notions are expressed are *The Analysis of Behavior: A Program for Self-Instruction* (New York: McGraw-Hill, 1961), and *The Technology of Teaching* (New York: Appleton-Century-Crofts, 1968).

Skinner is in the tradition of E. L. Thorndike and John B. Watson, who pioneered in the development of a scientific, behavioristic, mechanistic psychology in the earlier years of the century. More recently, educators and psychologists who have contributed to the "new behaviorism" are Robert Glaser and A. A. Lumsdaine, who edited two volumes for the National Education Association on *Teaching Machines and Programed Learning*, Robert M. Gagné, and Francis Mechner.

An interesting critique of Skinner's ideas appears in

James McClellan's *Toward an Effective Critique of American Education* (Philadelphia: Lippincott, 1968).

THEORY

Skinner and his disciples insist that a phenomenon they call *operant conditioning,* differing in important respects from classical conditioning, occurs in learning. Classical conditioning is based on the contiguity of response and stimulus; no reward is necessary. Operant conditioning, however, is based on the law of effect (reinforcement) and the reward is essential for conditioning. The further distinction may be made that classical conditioning evokes involuntary responses dependent on emotional conditioning in which the autonomic nervous system is involved. Operant conditioning evokes an overt voluntary response which involves the higher mental processes and the central nervous system.

In a laboratory situation, reinforcement is provided to strengthen the likelihood of recurrence of a desired response immediately after the occurrence of the desired response. Reinforcement is withheld after any other response. In the classroom situation Dr. Skinner believes that material to be learned may itself provide automatic reinforcement, since any not unpleasant change in the environment may per se constitute reinforcement.[11] If this "natural" reinforcement is inadequate, other possibilities in a classroom are appropriate for external reinforcement.

In some learning situations, the subject does not make the correct response on the first or successive tries. In such situations, behavior that conforms most closely to the correct response is reinforced until the correct response is evoked.

[11] Cf. Skinner, "Science of Learning and the Art of Teaching."

This technique is called *shaping*. Skinner tells us that the individual is a "functionally unified system of responses." [12] The purpose of teaching, then, is to bring about desired responses by a pupil. Thus, we place a pupil before a teaching machine; when the desired response is elicited we immediately reward him and reinforce the response until it becomes a part of his repertoire of overt behavior. Immediate reinforcement of desired responses is a necessary condition to learning the desired response. If the student displays unwanted responses, reinforcement is withheld.

All of this procedure is explicitly directed to the controlling of behavior and the shaping of conduct. It is recognized by Skinner himself, if not by all proponents of psychological behaviorism, that such procedure is in conflict with the traditional view of man.

The traditional view of human nature in Western culture is well known. The conception of a free, responsible individual is embedded in our language and pervades our practices, codes and beliefs. Given an example of human behavior, most people can describe it immediately in terms of such a conception. The practice is so natural that it is seldom examined. A scientific formulation, on the other hand, is new and strange. Very few people have any notion of the extent to which a science of human behavior is indeed possible. In what way can the behavior of the individual or of groups of individuals be predicted and controlled? What are the laws of behavior like? [13]

In this Skinnerian version of the behavioral scientific view, man has neither free will nor the capacity for taking spontaneous action; there is really no such thing as conscious-

[12] B. F. Skinner, *Science and Human Behavior* (New York: The Macmillan Co., 1953), p. 285.
[13] Ibid., pp. 9–10.

ness or mind; human behavior can, in principle, be predicted and controlled as certainly as the progress of a chemical reaction. Application of the scientific method to study of human behavior has rendered man predictable and thus controllable. We see that in natural evolutionary process reflexes and other innate patterns of behavior evolve because they increase the chances of survival of the species. Likewise, operants grow strong because they are followed by important consequences in the life of the individual. Teaching may thus become the deliberate selection of operants to be reinforced or extinguished by means of deliberate granting or withholding of reward to implement such selection.

It is to be noted that, in contrast to older auto-instructional procedure such as that of Pressey, teaching not preceded by any sort of venture by students is now proposed. Older devices assumed that the student would first do some reading or perform a laboratory exercise. The student first made some effort to deal with an assigned task, after which the "teaching machine" functioned as an adjunct to point up important issues and clear up difficulty. The Skinnerian approach, to the contrary, begins with preselected material presented in precisely the manner and order decided on by the programmer. The method, then, is more didactic and authoritarian than older methods. Again, great emphasis is placed upon error avoidance; the learner should not see incorrect answers, let alone be subjected to questions sufficiently difficult to make it likely for him to make a mistake. In other words, the objective is to provide programming of such rigor that the subject will be unaware of possible alternatives; the steps to appear necessary and inescapable. Sidney Pressey, in criticizing this procedure, has suggested that the effort of the writer of such a program will be to ". . . seek artfully to shape the student's responses so that, without his quite knowing what is happening, he is cued, reinforced, and faded into his learning . . ." [14]

EDUCATIONAL APPLICATIONS

Skinner has argued that learning is a science while teaching is an art. The former assumption involves the notion that certain unequivocal standards can be applied to learning, and to the degree that these established procedures are applied, results will be fruitful. Learning is governed by laws of man's action upon and reaction to various media. The learning process follows a regular pattern of step-by-step sequence, each stage providing the basis for the next. Teaching on the other hand is seen as an art—that of bringing the student and the program together. Since learning as a personal achievement comes from the interaction between a learner and the scientifically constructed program, the teacher functions as an overseer or intermediary. It is the direct relationship between student and machine that will bring about learning; through a teacher's artistry this relationship is set up and sustained.

By programed instruction, I mean the kind of learning experience in which a "program" takes the place of a tutor for the student, and leads him through a set of specified behaviors designed and sequenced to make it more probable that he will behave in a given desired way in the future—in other words, that he will learn what the program is designed to teach him.[15]

Advocates of programming have claimed to be in the heritage of Socrates and Descartes. The Cartesian method

[14] Sidney L. Pressey, "Basic Unresolved Teaching-Machine Problems," *Theory into Practice* 1, no. 1 (February 1962): 84.
[15] Wilbur Schramm, *Programed Instruction; Today and Tomorrow* (New York: Fund for the Advancement of Education, 1962), p. 1.

provided for clarity, distinctness, and rigorous inference. Descartes was a mathematician; his arguments did indeed exhibit beautiful clarity and precision. Comparison with the Socratic method, however, would appear much more dubious, for the Socrates of Plato's dialogues examined all branching alternatives in the course of argument. To the contrary, here we have a theory of learning by stimulus and response effected by reinforcement of correct responses and careful, logical arrangement of the learning material.

Instrumentation

The program of instructional materials can be placed in a teaching machine or in a programmed textbook. The program may consist of pictorial, printed, or even auditory material. For example, the student may read a sentence and supply a missing word or listen to a spoken question and respond appropriately. The student can record his response in one of several ways. He may respond by pushing a key on a typewriter keyboard, by writing on a strip of paper exposed in a machine, or by indicating a choice from an array of words or visual patterns. Immediately after the student has responded, the correct response is revealed.

Thus the teaching machine, over a period of time, leads the student through a carefully prepared program. The program consists of hundreds or thousands of steps arranged so that the student can proceed, without encountering undue frustration, from items of little difficulty to items requiring greater skill of analysis and comprehension. In summary, these are the essential items of programmed instruction.

1. an ordered sequence of stimulus items,
2. to each of which a student responds in some specified way,
3. his responses being reinforced by immediate knowledge of results,

4. so that he moves by small steps,
5. therefore making few errors and practicing mostly correct responses,
6. from what he knows, by a process of successively closer approximation, toward what he is supposed to learn from the program.[16]

A. A. Lumsdaine points out the following similarities between teaching machines and a private tutor:

1. There is constant interchange between program and students. Unlike lectures . . . the machine induces sustained activity. The student is always alert and busy.
2. Like a good tutor the machine insists that a given point be thoroughly understood . . . before the student moves on.
3. Like a good tutor the machine presents just the material for which the student is ready.
4. Like a skillful tutor the machine helps the student to come up with the right answer. It does this in part through the orderly construction of the program and in part with techniques of hinting, prompting, and suggesting . . .
5. Lastly . . . the machine, like the private tutor, reinforces the student for every correct response, using this immediate feedback not only to shape his behavior most efficiently but to maintain it in strength in a manner . . . as holding the student's interest.[17]

Thus, teaching machines, it is characteristically argued, provide for individualized instruction and evaluation and consequently work toward the enhancement of human freedom.[18]

---

[16] Ibid., p. 2.
[17] Lumsdaine and Glaser, *Teaching Machines and Programed Learning*, p. 143.
[18] Ibid., *passim;* this claim is also one frequently made by Skinner.

A teaching machine works by presentation of a fact or a relationship in a simple setting called a *frame*. The student makes an active response, a write-in answer most often, or a multiple-choice response if only recognition is required. He then moves the material to the next frame, by pushing a lever or button if using a teaching machine, by turning the page or sliding a marker down if using a book-type program. In the margin next to the second frame he now finds the correct answer, thus reinforcing his correct association. In the so-called scrambled texts the student, upon incorrect response, is referred to another section where reteaching steps are presented. In most programs, however, each frame is so simple and so strongly supported by previous steps that errors are at a minimum. The pupil proceeds through the program learning at his own rate of speed. Motivation is promoted by ensuring the constant success of the learner, confirming his success immediately after each response, allowing him freedom to pace his own learning, and by coaching him through clues incorporated in the frames.

Active responding, immediate feedback, measurable objectives, and material presented in a logical sequence of small steps are characteristics which identify programmed instruction whether the device which controls the presentation of the program is mechanical or in more conventional book form.

Sounds, words, and pictures are used in some machines. Frequently, the visual portion of a program is imprinted upon paper sheets, cards, discs, paper roll, on slides, film strips, motion picture film, or computer tapes. The program may be a book; it may be in the form of tapes or strips of paper; it may be a series of microfilmed slides; it may be auditory material to be used with a tape recorder.

It is important that the sequence of steps from frame to frame is effective. If the steps are too great the student will make mistakes; if they are too small he will respond correctly, but his learning will be unnecessarily tedious. If a response is correct, the learner is immediately reinforced. Incorrect responses become extinct inasmuch as they are not reinforced. Finally, the sequence of the questions results in the shaping of the learner.[19]

A physics program which was rather widely used before 1965 divided pages into panels or frames. There were five panels per page and several hundred pages. Some relatively simple devices made of paper have been inexpensive, ranging in price from three dollars to thirty-five dollars. The Air Force used a "Subject Matter Trainer," a push-button matching machine, which was relatively expensive. One elementary mathematics machine used four plungers to record a response. If the response was the preferred one, the machine exhibited the next frame; if not, it remained the same. In another paper device, the answer to each question was given on a following page. This machine was inexpensive but not cheatproof, inasmuch as there was nothing to prevent the learner from looking ahead. It is alleged, however, that this does not affect achievement adversely unless the cheating greatly reduces covert response. A machine for map tracing has been developed. Another makes use of a sound motion picture. In a so-called "scrambled book," the page to which the student is directed depends on his answer.

In 1959 three companies were involved in commercial manufacture of auto-instructional devices. In 1960 there were seventeen. The total jumped to sixty-three in 1961; growth continued until the late 1960s, when there was some slackening of interest in programmed instruction. By 1967 Xerox, General Electric, IBM, Raytheon, RCA, Minnesota Mining and Manufacturing, and Sylvania had joined with publishers

---

[19] See Bugelski, *Psychology of Learning Applied to Teaching*, p. 212.

and manufacturers of educational materials looking toward long-term collaboration in production of instructional devices.

One of the most fascinating machines was Omar Khayyam Moore's "talking typewriter." The talking typewriter was a standard-size typewriter with colored keys, a small speaker, an exhibitor frame on which printed material could be displayed, a projector which resembled a miniature television screen, and dictation equipment. It was placed in a sound-proof room. Only the keyboard was accessible to the child—nothing else was in the room to distract his attention. The child, when he saw this instrument, naturally began to play with it. When the child's interest in the machine began to wane, a teacher who watched through a one-way mirror switched a control dial which lifted a curtain from over the exhibitor frame, and a red arrow pointed to a single letter. The machine's voice named it at the same time. The child tried to press a key, but found that none except the correct one could be pushed down. This printed the letter and the voice named it again. A new letter then popped up and the child again hunted for it. As the child advanced, he found that the exhibitor frame showed him a series of letters instead of just one. Eventually, the child realized that these letters he was printing on the typewriter were words familiar to him.

Programming

The activity of programming begins as programmers estimate a reasonable starting point, including what they think the child should know and excluding what they think he already knows. After writing the subject matter in an orderly way, in small sequential steps, the programmers test it on a small representative group.

Programmers use three main types of frames: (1) terminal response only, e.g., "A low hanging cloud is called ———"; (2) prompted; (3) copy. The copying frame requires two sentences; one to introduce the term and one to get the student to repeat it. Copying frames characteristically involve oversimplification and do not yield understanding. In principle a terminal item should include no prompts, neither formal, that is, resting upon form or structure, nor thematic, that is, involving substantive meaning. A thematic prompt may indicate the general category of a response, state an opposite, provide an equivalent word or phrase, or provide an association. An example of this would be: "Like a bird, Pegasus had two ———." Of course, the sequence prompt would operate in any program made up of segments as logical sequences. The strength of each prompt, or the probability that it will control the response is calculated according to: (1) logical strength—calculated by how many responses in the responder's repertoire would make sense; and (2) psychological strength—calculated from empirical measurement of actual response. Prompting or coaching cues of varying degrees of subtlety and indirectness keep the learner responding correctly and keep the motivation up by ensuring continuing response.

We have noted the distinction between the program which, scientifically constructed, brings about the learning, and the teacher, by whose artistry program and child are brought together and supported in relationship. Thus, the teacher does not himself do the programming. Then, who does? There is, clearly, a disjunction between teacher and programmer or "instructional designer" similar to the distinction between the teacher and the textbook on which he bases his course in conventional instruction. However, there is an organization collaboration in "instructional designing" which suggests more the engineering laboratory than the relationship of scholar, textbook writer, editor, publisher, printer, and manufacturer more characteristic of conventional book production. In the engineering approach to programming the start is with the conceptual network stipulated by scholars as the "structure of the discipline." Analysts working at the next stage identify behavioral responses that manifest familiarity with the concepts. Attention then turns to the anticipated clientele and a systematic assessment is made of the behavioral repertoires supposedly already possessed by the clientele. Next the steps or stages by which desired behaviors may be induced are determined. Finally, tests to determine degree of success in moving from preinstructional to specified terminal behavior are constructed. These are intended to determine levels or degrees to which, as a matter of fact, desired terminal behavior is called forth in response to predetermined cues.

This engineering approach to learning seeks behavioral analysis of subject matter, inasmuch as only behavioral marks of learning allow for quantification in assessment of results. That is, the assumption is that only a change in overt behavior which can be identified and measured counts as learning. Thus, the analysis of subject matter according to logical or conceptual relationships must yield to breaking it down into steps susceptible to some sort of overt behavioral distinguishing marks.

Component repertoire refers to a behavioral analysis. . . .

From the point of view of instruction, the practical requirement for component-repertoire analysis is to identify the kind of behavior involved so that the learner can be provided with instructional procedures and environmental conditions which best facilitate the learning of that kind of behavior. The underlying assumption is that the learning of various kinds of component repertoires requires different kinds of teaching procedures, and a research task is to identify the learning processes and appropriate instructional procedures associated with different component repertoires.[20]

This point of view is interpreted to reinforce the emphasis on process objectives commented on earlier in discussion of the structure of the disciplines movement. Behavioral objectives come to be thought of as process objectives. Processes to be taught are response differentiation, association, multiple discrimination, behavior chains, class concepts, principles, and strategies.[21] Or again, effort is to bring students to mastery of processes such as observation, classification, prediction, inference, generating hypotheses, selecting fruitful hypotheses, testing hypotheses and deciding upon experiments, or even such general traits as perseverence and curiosity. The term *process* is used somewhat ambiguously, however, as psychological behaviorists have in mind behaviors or specific ways of doing things which can be observed and measured, while scholars using the term in the same context mean methodologies or dispositions making up the procedural manual in a discipline. Again, teachers may have in mind pedagogic processes and methods such as the so-called discovery method intended to bring about change in behavior, and lasting habits of mind.

In this fuzziness of meaning of "process" is exhibited a fundamental problem which must plague especially those who would hope to make teaching so rigorous that the steps

[20] Robert Glaser, "The Design of Instruction," in *The Changing American School,* ed. John I. Goodlad. The Sixty-Fifth Yearbook of the National Society for the Study of Education, Part II (Chicago: University of Chicago Press, 1966, p. 219).

[21] Ibid., with credit to Robert M. Gagné.

can be machine-programmed. What exactly is the objective insofar as changed behavior is concerned? What can the student DO at the end that he could not do at the beginning? "Understanding," "appreciating," "admiring," "favoring," "opposing," "questioning" are not manifested by DOINGS which can be marked and counted.

But what the student can DO after he has been taught will, of course, be in part a function of what he could do before he underwent instruction. Thus, it is important to assess pre-instructional variables. Has the student mastered necessary motor skills to begin? Does he know enough? Has he mastered necessary intellectual skills? Does he have the ability to make the discriminations necessitated by the new material? Since children must be taken from where they are in school —with whatever repertoire of maturity, learnings, and abilities their natural endowment, previous teachers, home and neighborhood nurture have given them—programming must somehow allow for a plurality of stations of entering behavior

. . . the assessment of preinstructional behavior is considered to be the determination of an entering behavioral repertoire which the instructional process is designed to guide and modify.[22]

The first two considerations in programming, then, are: (1) Where do you want to go? (2) Where are these children now? The answer to the first question must be stated in a series of descriptions of things they can do (spell *cat;* look up *tree, muscle,* and *spasm* in the dictionary and use the words properly in a sentence; locate *Nigeria, Switzerland, Greece* on a globe). Answers to the second question must also be specific so that you can know where to start (Does the child know his letters? Can he hold a pencil? Can he make the

[22] Ibid., p. 225.

letters or must he be taught how to do that first? Can he spell *tree? muscle? spasm?* Does he know how a dictionary is ordered? Can he write? Can he write a sentence? Does he command a large enough vocabulary to provide a reasonable context for the words? Can he read a map? Can he read and discriminate the names of these countries as labels?). Now this is a terribly big order. Each child will bring a different competence to the task. The individual diagnoses demanded will be trying and time-consuming. Nevertheless, if the essential structures ("processes") are clearly identified, and if programs start back far enough, it should be possible to discover where a child is vis-à-vis certain instructional objectives and then write a prescription of learning activities to bring him to the desired objective. This, in fact, is the procedure followed in the so-called Individually Prescribed Instruction (IPI) pioneered by the University of Pittsburgh Learning Research and Development Center at Oakleaf School in Baldwin-Whitehall.

Another solution, however, might be provided if more of the child's early life could be strictly controlled. One of the projects pushed by Chancellor Litchfield during the last year or two of his tenure at the University of Pittsburgh was for a "Responsive Educational Continuum." The notion was to establish an integrated educational system from about age three through university, with the full course continuously planned so as to do away with discontinuities. Skinner has apparently advocated seriously bringing up little children in a strictly controlled, psychologically antiseptic environment (i.e., the "Skinner box").

So the reasoning goes. In order to program we must know the entering or preinstructional behavior. We can know this by making individual diagnoses of each child and then setting up an individually prescribed program for each. Or we can try to standardize entry experience so as to achieve uniformity of competence among children of a given age at a given time and place. Some of the theory surrounding the Head Start program is derived from the supposed argument for the Skinner box. If the entry experiences could be controlled, school programs would be much more effective.

These knotty considerations only set the stage for planning the instructional process.

Once the content and component repertoires involved in terminal behavior objectives and subobjectives are described, and once the entering behavior of the student also is described, a precise instructional process can be implemented.[23]

To get from here to there, you need to decide: (1) What do you want him to do next? and next? and next? (2) How do you get him to do it each time? (3) How do you make sure he continues to do it this way and doesn't slip back? The three considerations are interrelated, for the ideal sequencing is one in which one step leads into the next such that success in completion of one (reinforcement) quite literally invites or impels into the next step, and the whole chain is self-sustaining and reinforcing from step to step as progress toward a goal is experienced and enjoyed by the learner.

One theory is that each step should be so small and so easy that you cannot make a mistake, while carrying you along well enough so that, on completion of a few steps, you know you have progressed. This is small-step linear programming of the sort advocated by Dr. Skinner. Another view is that the initial steps should be gross generalizations and that the steps should exhibit progressive refinement of the subject matter. A third view is one that provides for

[23] Ibid., p. 226.

detours and even blind alleys, error being allowed but the branches always leading back to the preferred main track (the "correct" line of answers).

Setting up the steps leading from *entering* or *preinstructional* behavior to *terminal* or *objective* behavior is called *sequencing*. A particular step in the sequence as prepared for a line in a programmed text or a display in a teaching machine is called a *frame*. This sometimes *sequencing* is called *framing* if the reference is to the specific technology at work.

Mathematics and the so-called exact sciences, such as physics, seem to lend themselves more readily to sequencing than such subjects as political science and literature. Although most of the interest has been in such fields and—with little children—in the teaching of reading, the new educational behaviorists maintain that in teaching any subject decisions finally have to be made about "what is to be learned before what." Programmed reading texts are deliberately organized to develop certain linguistic regularities, with vocabulary and structure quite deliberately controlled. For example, in the beginning letters which are easily discriminated because radically different in form are introduced, and additional letters are not introduced until a vocabulary of words spelled with these letters has been mastered.

Another important feature of instruction it is claimed machines can do better than a teacher working with a large group is to provide immediate report whether a response is "right" or "correct." In conventional teaching a child has this experience when he "recites." However, with thirty-five children in the room his turn comes only infrequently, and much of the report back is delayed several hours. That is, the paper or the workbook section done in class today is frequently not checked and turned back until tomorrow. A machine, on the other hand, reports "correct" or "incorrect" immediately, the way a private tutor or coach would. What the programmers have emphasized—a finding actually embedded in research at least as far back as Thorndike but frequently forgotten—is that unreinforced practice does not do much good and may even do harm.

Most programs available now, whether in book form or in a fashion to be used in machines, are for shorter instructional units rather than entire courses. Linear-type programs were more popular than branching types in the early 1960s. Few teacher-made or "homemade" programs appeared, but teachers showed interest in using commercially produced programs, choosing critically among them.[24] Somewhat unexpectedly, teachers of handicapped children, especially the deaf and the mentally retarded, have found uses for the programmed materials. Business and industrial training programs have made use of programmed books and devices. School dropouts have used programmed instruction. Some evidence shows that children who cannot maintain a personal relationship with the teacher react favorably to the impersonality and nonpunishing context provided by teaching machines.

Experimental analysis of operant behavior of psychotic persons is underway. Such experimental study using programmed instruction suggests that intense forms of behavioral breakdown may be ameliorated through programmed instruction. There is some evidence that mental retardants can be trained by means of programmed devices. International education specialists study possibilities of exporting programmed instruction to newly developed countries to assist in educational endeavors. The military has made

[24] See W. James Popham, "The Changing Face of Programmed Instruction," *California Journal of Education* 31 (November 1962): 112–122.

impressive use of programmed instruction in training programs.

CRITIQUE

At the beginning of this chapter, reference was made to literature suggesting that technological means may draw substance to themselves in such a way that the means, by their very emergence, may shape and control ends. Since 1950 this has, indeed, characterized American education. Technicians and mechanics, having invented various new devices which appear to function as instructional instruments, advance proposals for the deliberate nurture of youngsters to make use of these devices. It has become apparent that these means underlie conceptions of educational ends not always placed in proper perspective to be criticized fully, reshaped, and reformulated in the light of available alternatives.

In response to this misuse of technical devices, complete rejection of instruments of learning other than those provided by direct interaction of biological man with his social and natural environment is one possibility. At the opposite extreme is the option of accepting the new techniques as setting the authentic form for deliberate education in twentieth-century industrial society. Advocates of strict linear programming represent the latter extreme.

Linear Programming

Teaching machines and programmed books following the principles of B. F. Skinner are unacceptable as means of deliberate education in a free society. It is not enough to reinforce effort, according to the linear programmers. This, they allege, is a major weakness in the older theories of the progressivists of the 1920s and 1930s. Not reinforcement of persistence in the task but reinforcement of specific correct responses, and only those, is provided. Given this emphasis on the importance of specificity and immediate feedback, there is argument for the machine, for only in a one-to-one tutorial situation can this be achieved by a human teacher.

But even more, it is alleged, the reinforcement provided by the teacher is all too frequently merely verbal. A linear program, however, blocks the possibility of an alternative. The machine will not turn, the cue will not appear, unless the preferred response is made. In linear programs the response is constructed. The learner's responses are conditioned to those decreed by the programmers. Degrees of freedom of response are reduced so that only proper responses are reinforced.

Briefly, Skinner's theory is that the student can be led to the desired terminal behavior through many successive steps, each reinforced by knowledge of the results. The task for the programmer is to discover the particular sequence of steps that will lead the student to the desired outcomes with a minimum number of errors along the way. This is a basic principle of Skinnerian programming technique. The learning model (stimulus-response) used by the linear theorist is the rewarding of correct responses for desired behavior. This model can be summarized as follows: (1) Small amounts of material are learned; responses to the new material are required. (2) Student errors on a fully developed program are so few that correct responses are assumed to indicate learning. This instructional method based on structuring small bits of information into logical, sequential order will work best for those subjects in which a logical order is most apparent. The physical sciences, the biological sciences, mathematics, and languages are the obvious choices for programming. The limited applicability of programmed instruction is stressed explicitly by some students of the movement. For example, L. B. Resnick states:

By explicit instruction I mean the deliberate modification of other human beings. . . . Programmed instruction is applicable only where we do in fact want to change behavior in a given direction. There are cases where for political or ethical reasons we do not want to. . . . When we honestly do not wish to change behavior, neither programmed instruction nor any other kind of instruction is appropriate. "Exposure" is the most we should attempt.[25]

Resnick continues by saying that there are "intangibles" or "unmeasurables" believed desirable in the student's repertoire and recommends that substantial attention be devoted to "analyzing precisely those skills that have always seemed somehow undefinable." [26]

The parameters of appropriate subject matter for linear programming are so closely delimited that there has been a tendency to circumscribe knowledge within those narrow boundaries.[27] Identification of educational aims becomes rationalization forced by the nature of programmed instruction itself. Riesman a number of years ago suggested that social studies be abandoned in the public schools since they could not be taught with "rigor" or "candor." [28] His attitude later changed when he realized that, "were social studies abandoned," those students not going on to college "would get no

[25] L. B. Resnick, "Programmed Instruction and the Teaching of Complex Intellectual Skills," *Harvard Educational Review* 33, no. 4 (1963): 467.
[26] Ibid., p. 468.
[27] Ibid., *passim.* Resnick's thesis is that the domain of knowledge must not be restricted arbitrarily to what can be quantified.
[28] David Riesman, *Constraint and Variety in American Education* (New York, Doubleday & Co., 1958), p. 128.

formal orientation in a confusing world." [29] Riesman also suggests that the social studies constitute an area filled with values but short on facts. Yet it is important that students be actively and wholeheartedly engaged in studies concerned with the individual's relationship to the world around him. How can the individual make intelligent use of science and technology unless he has given sober thought to where he is and how he got there?

Although it has been assumed by many that programmed instruction is most useful when considered an adjunct to conventional education—an aid rather than a substitute for the teacher—this viewpoint is not universal: "In fact, it is conceivable that teachers, in attempting to interact with pupils using currently designed programs, might have a negative effect on the learning process." [30] There is no question but that some of the more enthusiastic supporters of programming have considered the teacher expendable. The description of a completely automated school resembles a description of libraries of the future in which information retrieval will depend upon man-computer interaction made possible through use of devices similar to the Rand tablet. The scientist is pictured working in a small room filled with equipment through which he can tap a computer that has stored all the knowledge of his field.

In schools where teaching machines have been used, difficulties such as the following have been reported:

1. Relatively high initial cost.
2. A large capital expenditure required to equip even one classroom.

[29] Ibid.

[30] Fred Guggenheim, "Curriculum Implications and Applications of Programmed Instruction," *The School Review* 73, no. 1 (Spring 1965), p. 60.

3. Possibility of equipment breakdowns and consequent interruption of learning.
4. Students deliberately jamming and breaking machines.
5. Students occasionally complain of boredom.
6. Some students cheat, look ahead in their books, skip over the hard questions, and appear indifferent.
7. Some students are not able to work independently.

At whatever cost, it may be questioned whether the machine can instill a love of truth, justice, or freedom. It is possible to make a film or to turn out literary materials containing the appropriate sentiments. And perhaps a photogenic professor with a gift for the theatrical can, with the help of a foundation grant, turn out a spectacular that will arouse students to action. This type of teaching can tap emotion and incite action. It does not, however, institute a relation between the teacher and pupil such that the meanings of truth and justice and freedom are sharpened by dialectic and inspired by conversation. One must find it possible to talk back to Socrates. Great and wonderful is the institution that attracts to its faculty a variety of personalities who exemplify the diverse patterns of the good life and who, by teaching, conduct their pupils on their own individually guided tour in the wisdom of the race. In such an institution each classroom is a new perspective from which the world looks new and fresh and revelatory.

Admiral Rickover, who has not always been right about American education did, nevertheless, speak effectively in the following:

Teaching is an intensely human activity that can, in the nature of things, be only marginally affected by technological process, as when typewriters are used instead of pen and ink or better mechanical means are invented to find and record documentary records: tapes and films can be used as aids in certain learning processes—acquiring a good accent in a foreign language would be an example of the value of tape recording. But essentially education consists of one knowledgeable human being giving out of himself knowledge and insight he has acquired, and by his skill— art would be a better word—inducing another human being an ignorant pupil, to absorb this knowledge and to learn how to use his mind to best advantage. In education, the "newest" does not necessarily make for the "best" education.[31]

Branching Programming

Sidney Pressey, who, as we have noted, is given credit for early pioneering in programmed instruction, provided alternatives among which the pupil was to discriminate. Advocates of linear programming have claimed that to have branches (i.e., a multiple-choice situation in which a response deemed incorrect by the programmer can be chosen) is to teach error. It is better, they hold, not to introduce incorrect alternatives into the field.

An alternative to linear programming, and one which provides in its construction for incorrect responses, is a branching program. This type of programming has been used in the construction of "scrambled books." It attempts to adjust the speed of intake to the student's capacity by sending him to alternate branches of the program depending upon whether he made (or selected) the called for response or one of the (usually) several inappropriate responses. A different path is provided for each response. If the student progresses without error, he remains in the primary path and completes the program in the minimum amount of time.

Although both of these techniques may be considered tutorial, the branching method can conform more closely

[31] H. G. Rickover, *American Education, A National Failure* (New York: E. P. Dutton & Co., Inc., 1963), p. 70.

to the student's needs because it is possible to use alternate routes through the program, depending upon the individual's rate of absorption. Although both are based on breaking complex units of knowledge into small bits for easier consumption, and on instant feedback of the correctness or incorrectness of a response to reinforce the student, linear programming involves more rigorous manipulation of the material to implant selected terminal behavior and provides little opportunity for individual vagary.

For the linear programmer, the materials follow a specific model. The intrinsic programmer, to the contrary, exploits a particular technique which permits inanimate materials to assume some of the educational functions that previously required a live instructor. He depends on the development of new techniques that allow established ideas about teaching to be more effectively and efficiently implemented. Intrinsic programmers do not impose assumptions about the nature of the learning process upon their work. It is the "structural" or "intrinsic" feature of including diagnostic questions throughout the exposition and providing remedial material for those who fail the questions which produces learning. The intrinsic programmer is not interested in how the student learns but whether he learns. The techniques used include written materials developed to accommodate a range of educational purposes, expository text, questions, answer choices, and remedial materials for each wrong answer. Suggestions following the text serve diagnostic purposes leading the learner to prompt remedial action through additional explanation in a supplementary text.

The intrinsic model is more easily adapted to the individual learner since he covers only what he needs in order to learn the material. The intrinsic program makes provisions for the slower student but challenges and allows for the faster student. The student is expected to give the right answer because he has understood the material he has read on the point in question, not because he has given a certain response more often than another.

Branching programs set up to follow initial reading and discussion, followed in turn by identification of difficulties, errors, misunderstandings, differences in point of view, and reasons supporting alternative and preferred views, are not morally objectionable. According to available evidence regarding their effectiveness, there is no reason why such aids to learning may not be used and criticized by teachers and pupils. They may take their place alongside books, maps, dictionaries, encyclopedias, models, and charts as aids to learning.

Computers

Computer-based instruction is, of course, subject to the criticisms which may be made of linear programming when it is used to bank such programs. Increasingly, however, new uses of computers for analysis, recordkeeping, and other administrative and time studies have come to light. Complete records of individual accomplishment can serve as instrumentalities of respect for individual differences. Computers can record results of student work and store them. They are unbiased and can render objective reports of individual performance on tasks which are susceptible to precise measurement. Computers can aid teachers by relieving the clerical load of recordkeeping. They can simplify payroll and scheduling.

As the computer is used not for teaching but for research, analysis, and problem solving, for storage and information retrieval, it holds promise as powerful instrument for the advancing of humane education. Again, one of the more promising services rendered in recent years by the combination of computers and refined analytical-statistical techniques is in determination of appropriate standards of competence. Measures of achievement should be based on appropriate objective criteria. The criterion in spelling should be spelling words correctly. In arithmetic the appropriate standard is not determined by a measure of standard error. Performance of students should be judged not by norms but by assessment of competence demanded to perform tasks. Norm measures of accidents in driving a car, using a band saw or a forge, or compound fractures on the playing field are not appropriate in assessing competence. Not the norm but the criterion of effective objective performance should guide judgment. Statistical analysis supported by the computer can do much to clarify our norm-confused educational standards. Our goals in education need to be set according to reliable knowledge of what men need to know and do to live competently. This is to say that the computer can render a service in identification of educational goals. It should not be used to teach; it may be pressed into service in the ongoing task of determining by continuing analysis of human predicaments in our intractable world what educational standards mark competence in human endeavor.

School Buildings

Recalling again the popular Parkinson-McLuhan inversion, it must be granted that the way schoolhouses have been built has influenced the form and content of instruction. Since American parents living in the North Temperate Zone have insisted that their children be as carefully shielded from the weather at school as at home, schools have been built with mighty solid walls and partitions. Then it becomes necessary to use teaching methods which fit the way the building, the rooms, and the furniture have been arranged. With few exceptions, such as the monitorial system of

Lancaster and Bell which made use of a large gymnasium-like hall, schools throughout the modern era have been built to accommodate instructional groups of twenty-five to fifty. Furniture arrangements have been formal, presupposing the students facing the teacher. Desks, tables, or counters to accommodate books and papers is a relatively recent innovation. Prior to the nineteenth century stand-up writing stations were built around the walls, the central floor space of the room being occupied by the benches.

Equipment in schoolrooms has not been complicated. The idea has been that of a meeting hall to accommodate not more than fifty people engaged in listening, speaking, reading, and writing in the room under one permanent chairman. The physical relationship has been that of audience to speaker; schoolrooms have been like churches in organization of space and station relationships, and a large conventional school building containing many rooms has been described as a "ceramic egg crate of uniform boxes."

The traditional schoolroom expressed the assumption that whatever education is, it centers in the dispensing of information. The room was built on the assumption that information is dispensed by word of mouth and by printed or written word. To whatever degree tape, disc, slide or movie projector, radio, or television dispense information, to that degree different organization of space and furniture might be suggested. To whatever degree there may be incorporated in the school activities demanding performance with apparatus other than pencil, paper, crayon, again changes in room and furniture organization are suggested (e.g., the home economics suite, wood, metal, automobile and print shops, art and music rooms, speech and dramatic rooms, along with extensive and complicated equipment).

Although acoustical problems have yet to be fully solved, movable partitions have been developed that are sufficiently soundproof so that many newer schools provide flexible partitioning. If this technology could be fully perfected so that partitions could be shifted in a variety of combinations to accommodate groups of from six to six hundred on one floor space, inventive teachers with no prompting whatever from advocates of fads such as "team teaching" would find all sorts of ways to combine and recombine their efforts. Of all educational technologies, the one that could make the most difference would be workable, completely adaptable, absolutely soundproof movable partitions. If this technology could be mastered, teachers would cooperate in a whole range of ways not even dreamed of by the formal advocates of flexible grouping.

Another area where the results of recent technology have been somewhat disappointing is ventilation, lighting and lighting control, temperature and temperature control. Far too many new schools have been too hot or too cold, with awkward lighting controls presenting obstacles to smooth adjustments of rooms for use of projection devices.

Adaptation of school buildings to available space with realistic assessment of land values is gradually being achieved. The one- or two-story building set in spacious grounds or the campus-type construction have been used in areas where land is relatively plentiful and cheap. On the other hand, it is finally being recognized that high-rise, multistoried structures with roof-garden exercise and play areas can make sense in big cities.

Again, there are some signs of realistic recognition of the school building as not only a place for instruction of children from nine A.M. to four P.M. but as a lively community center open to various age groups fifteen hours a day. The possibility of the school library, perhaps deliberately located on a street exit, functioning as a neighborhood library for all has been exploited here and there. Opening gymnasiums, shops, auditoriums, playing fields to the entire community after four P.M. is occasionally achieved.

The way we build buildings that serve as educational media can, indeed, mightily affect the message we communicate in our endeavors as educators.

V

Humanistic Psychology

SUPERFICIALLY, THE concern expressed by counselors for special feelings of individuals may appear to challenge the retreat from humane education embodied in the intellectualization and mechanization of schooling since 1950. Yet the point of view and the practical techniques of contemporary professional counseling are susceptible to manipulation for institutional ends. Behavioral scientific evidence supports the strategy of placing people at tasks that support, and are supported by, their unique sets of preferences, avoidances, likes and dislikes, affirmations and denials. The institutional machinery will run more smoothly, we have learned, if people can be placed in functions within the organizational structure where they feel at ease, in which they find themselves "at home." This is increasingly important when organization jobs become technical but at the same time sensitively cooperative, with all variations of a particular function affecting all others. Fitting the person to the job means fitting all aspects of the person to all aspects of the job in a situation in which all functions are delicately related to all others in the network. Persons must be "opened up" so that their inner workings may be appropriately coordinated to synchronize with other subsystems in the institution.

This way, school guidance and counseling can be put to

the service of national ends and cultivation of intellectual expertise in an intensive effort to enable an individual to become aware of himself so that all dimensions of his person may be appropriately integrated into the power system. This may have had something to do with the massive support of school guidance programs and the subsidization of graduate study in counseling. Guidance services have increased in every state, and most school districts have added personnel and increased the budget for support of guidance and counseling activities in junior and senior high schools. A present trend is to introduce specialized counselors into elementary schools to make possible an even earlier start on the comprehensive inventory of personal traits that may be drawn upon in staffing national institutions.

Within local communities, pressure for such services has come at the extreme ends of the socioeconomic spectrum. Ambitious, prosperous people wish to have their children slotted into the most prestigious colleges. Children and youth of the poor and dispossessed contribute to urban unrest and add to the expense of social disorganization as they are not placed either in continuing education or the labor market. At both ends of the scale the questions are: What manner of children are these? What hidden strengths are beneath the surface?

CHRONOLOGY

Despite the tendency of contemporary guidance and counseling specialists to denigrate the vocational-placement orientation of early pioneers in the guidance movement, they still work with the notion of distributing people to appropriate roles. Vocational counseling in the beginning was identified with occupational choices, which in turn were thought to be the foundation of useful and happy lives. Frank Parsons, a significant figure in the history of American educational reform, believed that people suited to their jobs would tend to be active in the creation of a more efficient and humane industrial system. Gradually, this concept broadened to include general counseling programs that would aid youngsters in their choice of studies. By the early 1930s leaders in the guidance movement such as Professor John Brewer of Harvard were arguing that school guidance counselors should concern themselves with all life activities of pupils.[1]

With the popularity of intelligence and aptitude tests, counselors came to regard these tools as a scientific way to predict vocational and educational success. Some guidance people began to see a larger framework for the theory and to interpret their work as an entirely new philosophical structure for education. These workers were concerned with broader concepts than merely vocational choices or curriculum planning. They became involved in a reference of total life-style planning. The counselor was seen as the person not only instrumental in helping the student choose his eventual vocation but also in the whole process of selection of personal models after whom he patterned himself.

Guidance thus became an integral part of education, and was seen to play an important role in helping young people meet the challenge of change and develop a positive view of self. The notion was to help them become persons who, as Arthur Combs said, are ". . . liked, wanted, acceptable, able, and worthy . . . persons of dignity and integrity . . ."[2] They were also to have a realistic awareness of their weaknesses

[1] See John M. Brewer, *Education as Guidance* (New York: The Macmillan Co., 1932).

[2] Arthur Combs and Donald Snygg, *Individual Behavior*, rev. ed. (New York: Harper & Row, Publishers, 1959), p. 240.

and inadequacies, but Combs describes them as "adequate persons" inasmuch as they have achieved positive regard for their worth. Hence, an honest appraisal of inadequacies cannot destroy the whole personality. One reason is that fully functioning persons are flexible, cultivating as a life style the discipline of self-assessment. The person himself must understand the situational and personal determiners involved in his experience so that he can proceed to choose wisely in the future. The ideal is a self-realizing, self-developing person who guides his choices by apprehension of substantive rather than artificial delimiting factors.

CONTEXT

The range of choices open to young people is generally considered to have been vastly extended in recent decades. This may be questioned, however, inasmuch as peculiar intellectual, social, and emotional demands of various positions have been identified. Thus, although the range of vocational possibilities has been broadened, the range of reasonable choices, given knowledge of all relevant personal and contextual variables, has been increasingly refined if not absolutely narrowed.

However this may be, contemporary theory of counseling and guidance places enormous emphasis upon the self, self-knowledge, choice, and autonomy, and insists that the aim of guidance in education is ". . . to promote maximum self-development by enhancing the individual's power to choose for and direct himself." [3]

---

[3] Norman A. Sprinthall and David V. Tiedeman, "Guidance and the Pupil," in *The Changing American School*, ed. John I. Goodlad. The Sixty-Fifth Yearbook of the National Society for the Study of Education, Part II (Chicago: University of Chicago Press, 1966), p. 65.

The intellectual tools for this enterprise are drawn from ego-psychology, to some extent from psychoanalysis. Detailed professional knowledge of the school as an institution and of the complicated and demanding world of business and industry outside the school are not overly stressed. The counselor's training need not always include teaching experience, and teaching is not to be a part of his responsibility when he is assigned to a school. Fifty percent or more of the counselor's time is to be devoted to individual counseling. The school counselor is to adopt the role of clinical specialist and healer of souls. He is a specialist consultant representing the interests of the individual against the awkward regimentation of the school, or, perhaps at best, serving as an intermediary.

The newer theory of counseling is one emphasizing personality, with emphasis on therapeutic cleansing at this level more than mastery of critical experimental or logical methods. In contrast, counselors and school guidance workers of an earlier generation characteristically assumed that information and intellectual discipline were the tools, so that the function of guidance was much more that of inventory of overt skills commanded by pupils actually or potentially, survey of job and further education possibilities provided by the society, and advice to students and parents built out of such inventories. The procedure, thus, was "directive."

In the newer, more "nondirective" approach is a tendency to denigrate information, it having been suggested that a certain conflict exists between the imparting of information and education.

The imparting of information as the theoretical role for guidance is as disjunctive to the goals of guidance as is the presenting of information by the classroom teacher to the goals of teaching.

Both activities deny major educative goals—carrying forward disciplined inquiry in the case of the classroom, and learning to make one's own personal decisions in the case of counseling.[4]

The view extends, then, to the notion that imparting information interferes with disciplined inquiry and that information is not always the central factor in making one's personal decisions. There remains a strong apparent antipathy toward making descriptive knowledge of the social, economic, and political facts of life essential considerations in counseling. The knowledge admitted, in other words, is knowledge of human growth, development, and personality dynamics, with less emphasis upon knowledge of an objective social or material world. The claim is, nevertheless, that this shift in emphasis brings counseling closer to teaching and reinstates it as a complementary function to teaching. Even so, argument and empirical evidence are produced to denigrate information, even in specific reference to vocational choice.

Super's studies of career pattern are most noteworthy. His research indicates that vocational maturity is a planning orientation within the individual and is *not* related to the amount of specific information or content that an individual knows concerning a vocation.[5]

Thus, the growing emphasis upon "rational powers," "cognitive problem-solving," and "planning orientation" in counseling really stresses the function which reasonable assessment of the self, including emotions, feelings, hopes, fears, and aspirations can serve. Indeed, to think critically about

[4] Ibid., p. 71.
[5] Ibid., p. 77, with footnote calling attention to Donald E. Super and Phoebe L. Overstreet, *The Vocational Maturity of Ninth-Grade Boys* (New York: Bureau of Publications, Teachers College, Columbia University, 1960).

one's self is surely to be preferred over the mere search for feeling; but there is question whether such concentration upon the self without comparable attention to the objective context is, indeed, "rational." For how can the student achieve mastery of his own destiny except as he is highly knowledgeable about the actual complexities, frustrations, controls, and specific opportunities provided in contemporary industrial society?

SOURCES

Based on a composite of the notions of Arthur Combs, Earl Kelley, Abraham Maslow, Gordon Allport, and Carl Rogers, humanistic psychologists in education concentrate on unique development of each individual. It is their belief that wisdom, truth, and beauty do not exist as absolutes outside the mind of man. Meanings are personal concepts of the individual, who, when allowed freedom to perceive and behave, develops self-understanding, tolerance, and respect for others. The truly becoming individual works out a set of values remarkably like other self-actualizing individuals, yet each man retains an individuality unique to himself. It is the duty of the counselor to concentrate on helping each of his counselees formulate a set of unique beliefs and a way of practicing them, rather than emphasizing "right" values. The differences should be valued. All learning should be aimed at formulating the aspirations and desires of the unique individual, so that he can understand himself, and through this, build personal regard for others.

Such counseling theory takes a dynamic view of personality. Each human being, starting with what he has by heredity, should continue to change and grow through experiences during his entire lifetime. Seen in this light, the teacher and the administrator are also changing and growing as they guide the pupil in his discovery of self. Just as the student becomes, so do educators and administrators.

Knowledge is not a static goal to be sought for its own sake. Through enlightened teachers who respect the uniqueness of the individual, each child must feel free to develop to his fullest potential, using and assimilating knowledge with joy and enthusiasm. Each new situation helps to change and mold his personality as he approaches understanding and self-actualization—the state of being that facilitates the continuation of growth and change. Learning in order to be effective must have personal meaning, so that the individual will act on his knowledge and understanding when the time and place arises. The adequate person must be well informed about himself and the world in order to set realistic goals for himself. In this way he can achieve success, which, in turn, reinforces his sense of adequacy. This theory provides no place for the concept that it is man's nature to be belligerent and lazy. This way, no one can be unmotivated. Through lack of understanding of self, one may, however, be motivated toward the wrong thing—toward that which interferes with continuing growth, change, and self-realization.

Rogers and Client-Centered Therapy

For more than a quarter of a century Carl R. Rogers has emphasized the supreme importance of the individual in counseling. The terms *client-centered* and *nondirective* refer to him and his influence. His notions were formulated before and during World War II as he worked with juvenile delinquents in Rochester, New York. He crystallized his emphasis on therapy as experience and clients as persons rather than objects to be manipulated or directed as he served on the faculties of the Ohio State University, the University of Chicago, and the University of Wisconsin. Rogers did not dwell on the client's past; no attempt was made to interpret or explain past feelings and environment in professional jargon. No program for reeducation or rehabilitation was prescribed.

The goal of his client-centered therapy was to provide a climate that would free the client to become himself. He is invited to discuss any subject he wishes, a resemblance to Freudian free-association, but no attempt is made to seek out unpleasant childhood experiences or cause-and-effect relationships between the past and the present. No attempt is made to solve any of the client's problems; the aim is the client's increasing self-acceptance and the integration of all aspects of his personality into a totality the client can understand and perfect. "Satisfying living consists, not in a life without problems, but in a life with a unified purpose and a basic self-confidence which gives satisfaction in the continual attack upon problems." [6]

To provide this climate the therapist must be trustworthy, dependable, and consistent in his relations with the client. He must feel empathy with the client, entering into the private world of the other and accepting his attitudes and emotions. He can do this because he feels that the client is a true person whose views, however inadequate at the present, are valid to *him*.

The therapist's attitude toward his client must be positive. He must not condemn in any way any feelings revealed to him. He must act with sensitivity and absence of threat. This is of utmost importance. It is the client who must see relationships, who must face his own reality and be responsible for himself and his actions. This is what the therapist must teach him. Therefore, the therapist can make no decision for the client, draw no parallels for him, solve no problems, and

[6] Carl R. Rogers, *Counseling and Psychotherapy* (Boston: Houghton Mifflin Co., 1942), pp. 217–218.

assume no responsibility or authority over him, however much the client may desire this. The therapist must refrain from advice and from premature interpretations and insights into attitudes the client has not yet fully accepted. Nevertheless, there are and must be limits to the empathy of the relationship. The therapist must maintain his own identity, emphasizing the individuality of the client. Each interview is carefully limited as to time. Time becomes a great reality the client must work against.

The following are the steps in Rogers' therapeutic process: An individual comes for help. This in itself is a responsible decision, and the client must see it as such and approve it. The helping situation of client and therapist is defined. The client is told that he can work out his own solution to his problems. This, too, increases the stature of his self-image. The therapist encourages free expression by the client, accepting, recognizing, and clarifying (not interpreting) the client's negative feelings. After the negative feelings have run their course, there is usually a tentative expression of positive impulses by the client, quickly drowned in a new sea of complaints. The therapist makes no attempt now to underline the positive feelings, although he accepts and recognizes them. This process may continue for many sessions. Slowly, insight by the client is gained—a perception of new meaning in his own experiences. He sees new causal relationships and begins to understand his behavioral symptoms. The client then may attempt to classify possible decisions and courses of action. Minute but significant positive action is now reported. In further sessions there is bound to be some regression, but gradually a further and more complete insight is gained by the client. His actions become increasingly integrated, positive, and self-directed. He reacts less and chooses more. He comes to rely on the therapist less. He has gained self-confidence and self-acceptance, and becomes less dependent on approval of others. His need for counseling ceases. He is on the way to becoming a true person in the existential sense.[7]

Rogers considers that psychometric tests, as well as intelligence, achievement, and interest tests, when required by the institution, are a hindrance to the counseling process whose purpose it is to release growth forces. The results of testing often cause defensiveness, dependence, and a decreasing sense of responsibility. Such devices should only be used when an individual requests and seeks them.

Client-centered therapy does not approach the counseling situation with a set of chosen techniques based on selected theoretical premises. Freudians, Jungians, and others approach a situation viewing man in a certain light. Their techniques help the person understand his problem in light of the theory held. Client-centered therapy, on the other hand, is one aspect of a movement described as ". . . an attitude toward therapy, not a set of new techniques but a concern with the understanding of the structure of the human being and his experience that must underlie all techniques."[8] A person's experiences are unique to him. The therapist does not interpret; instead, the client is allowed to express his feelings. These feelings are then rephrased in such a manner that the client is able to continue his monologue (really a dialogue) in a more fruitful context. It is not the purpose of the therapist to interpret the actions of the client according to the world view of the therapist. The counselor must try to understand and accept the world view of the client. Rogers says, "The essence of therapy, as I see it carried on by myself and by others, is a meeting of two *persons* in which the therapist is openly and freely himself and evidences this per-

[7] Cf. Ibid., pp. 31–44.
[8] Rollo May, "The Emergence of Existential Psychology," in *Existential Psychology* (New York: Random House, Inc., 1961), pp. 18–19.

haps most fully when he can freely and acceptantly enter into the world of the other." [9]

From the above examples, one sees how the client-centered approach holds a subjective view of human perception. Technique is not adhered to dogmatically because the client may see reality in a way that is not suited to a particular technique. Different techniques are applicable in different situations. When one interprets in the light of a chosen theory, one is imposing one's own world view on the other. The client-centered method redirects in order that the person will be conscious of his own peculiar problems. As he comes to recognize these, the person's reality takes on a new meaning. He becomes aware that every aspect of his personality involves some choice or decision. The amount or degree of decision-making, however, depends on many factors, some of which are determined. The client, after realizing his ability to choose, must accept it. This is most difficult, for defense mechanisms are not easily dropped. It is much easier to rationalize away a bad grade than to accept responsibility for failure. Nevertheless, a goal of client-centered therapy is to have the person take responsibility for his actions.

For Rogers, in any interpersonal relationship such as that which exists in our schools, the aim is to help the individual to be increasingly ". . . open to his experience." [10]

A fully functioning person according to Rogers is

. . . a human being in flow, in process, rather than having achieved some state. . . . A person [who] experiences in the

[9] Carl Rogers, "Two Divergent Trends," in *Existential Psychology,* ed. Rollo May (New York: Random House, Inc., 1961), p. 88.

[10] Carl R. Rogers, "Toward Becoming a Fully Functioning Person," in *Perceiving, Behaving, Becoming: A New Focus for Education,* Yearbook of the Association for Supervision and Curriculum Development (Washington, D.C.: National Education Association, 1962), p. 23.

present with immediacy . . . is trustingly able to permit his total organism to function freely in all its complexity in selecting, from the multitude of possibilities that behavior which in this moment of time will be most generally and genuinely satisfying. . . . Such a person is a creative person . . . [and is a person who] lives a life which involves a wider range, a greater richness, than the constricted living in which most of us find ourselves.[11]

How can the counselor bring this purpose to fruition? "In a wide variety of professional work involving relationships with people . . . it is the *quality* of the interpersonal encounter with the client which is the most significant element in determining effectiveness." [12] There exists between the counselor and client a certain psychological climate which is unique.

The conditions which constitute this climate do not consist of knowledge, intellectual training, orientation in some school of thought or techniques. They are feelings or attitudes which must be experienced by the counselor and perceived by the client if they are to be effective. . . . Essential are: a realness, genuineness, or congruence in the therapist; a sensitive, empathetic understanding of the client's feelings and personal meanings; a warm, acceptant prizing of the client; and an unconditionality in this positive regard.[13]

This suggests that the foundation of this movement is the worth of the individual. The teacher and the pupil or the counselor and the client—all are individuals. This is a two-

[11] Ibid., pp. 31–32.
[12] Carl R. Rogers, "The Interpersonal Relationship: The Core of Guidance," in *Guidance: An Examination,* ed. Ralph L. Mosher, Richard F. Carle, and Chris D. Kehas (New York: Harcourt, Brace, and World, 1965), p. 49.
[13] Ibid., p. 57.

way street on which each must be true to himself and to the other. Only on these terms can the purpose of education be realized for both.

This concept of self is the individual's notion of who he is in relation to his environment. It is this self-concept that determines his behavior. This phenomenal self is, for a person himself, reality. The person does not respond to the objective environment but what he perceives it to be, regardless of how distorted or personalized his perception. These subjective realities are tentative hypotheses that a person entertains about environmental situations.[14]

Self-concepts are complex and variable and they determine how persons will react to and deal with a wide variety of situations. These conceptions of who and what one is not only comprise central valves and belief systems, but also include images of oneself as physically strong or weak, attractive or unattractive, popular or unpopular, and so on, based partly on the reflected appraisals of other people with whom one has had contact. This self-concept determines our behavior. Most behavior is organized around efforts to preserve and enhance this phenomenal self.

Allport on "Becoming"

Gordon W. Allport consistently defines personality as transitive process and not a finished product. Personality has some stable features, but it is at the same time continually undergoing change. Personality is becoming an individual person. It is defined here more as a verb and not as a noun because personality is not a static thing, but a moving, growing one. The process of becoming is governed not only by stimuli from one's environment, but also by a disposition in

[14] See Carl R. Rogers, *On Becoming a Person* (Boston: Houghton Mifflin Co., 1961), pp. 107–124.

each of us to realize all of our possibilities, "to become characteristically human at all stages of development." [15] We become ourselves as we live our lives. As infants we are beings, but we are not socialized beings in any sense of the word. We become socialized as we grow in an environment of other people. There are stages of development in the process of becoming, and earlier stages are incorporated into later stages. In becoming an individual, the person depends a great deal on loving relationships with significant persons in his environment. As we relate to others we attain a self-concept or a personal identity, and we also arrive at a point when we have a personal conscience. A mature person is, therefore, one who has successfully incorporated earlier stages of his development in the present. He is a free individual. Even though he remains incomplete—he is still becoming— he now has the ability to accept himself and others; he is one who can take responsibility for his own actions; and he is capable of directing his life in good relationships with others.

It is knowledge of our own uniqueness that supplies the first, and probably the best hints for acquiring orderly knowledge of others. Each individual is functionally autonomous. That is, a given activity or form of behavior may become an end or goal in itself, although it was originally engaged in for some other reason. This way, teachers can serve to guide children in the here and now toward the future with the full assurance that as the child moves toward maturity the activities and behaviors will continue as autonomous functions of the individual. This is not to say that an old dog cannot learn new tricks, that the mature individual will act only as he did when a child, for the mature individual will possess an extension of self which will enable him to

[15] Gordon W. Allport, *Becoming* (New Haven: Yale University Press, 1955), p. 28.

participate in and enjoy a wide variety of different activities. But we can guide the direction these activities will take. We can stimulate ability knowing that it will become intense, autonomous interest. Herein lies the control, the organization which was lacking from early progressive education. Control is not seen as teacher authority, but as teacher guidance of the individual's unique adjustments to his environment. Organization comes from the individual as he chooses how to define his situation and selects the perceptions that constitute his reality. Allport maintains:

> Mental health and happiness, it seems, does not depend upon the satisfaction of this drive or that drive, it depends rather upon the person finding some area of success somewhere. The ego must be satisfied, not the hunger drive, nor the sex drive, nor the maternal drive, however temporarily insistent these segmental tensions may be.[16]

In this sense man is unique. No other animal but ". . . man alone has the capacity to vary his biological needs extensively and to add to them countless psychogenic needs reflecting in part his culture and in part his life-style." [17] There are many aspects of self and personality; these are known as the proprium or all the regions of our life which we regard as peculiarly ours.[18] Included are the bodily me, self-identity, ego-enhancement (selfishness and pride), ego extension (a high regard for possessions, lived objects, ideal causes, and loyalties), the rational agent (the ego), the self-image (ideal and real), propriate striving (ego-involved), and the knower (that which transcends all other functions of the proprium and holds them in view). "From birth to death the mainten-

[16] Gordon W. Allport, *The Nature of Personality: Selected Papers* (Cambridge, Mass.: Addison-Wesley Press, 1950), pp. 128–129.

[17] Allport, *Becoming*, p. 22.

[18] Ibid., p. 40.

ance of the phenomenal self is the most pressing, the most crucial, if not the only task of existence." [19]

Man, then, by his very nature transcends culture; the personality of a human being is never to be understood as merely the product of cultural influences.

Obviously, a man's culture is one of the sets of circumstances from which he draws his style of life. It is never correct, however, to say that personality is merely the "subjected side of culture." This view is tempting to anthropologists and sociologists whose attention is preoccupied with the sociocultural conditions of becoming. [20]

Allport does not provide metaphysical arguments to support his assertion of man's uniqueness and his transcendence. He simply affirms it, but affirms it without qualification. He apparently views man as a creation of natural, not supernatural forces, nevertheless finding man above nature in his unique characteristics as man.

The outstanding characteristic of man is his individuality. He is a unique creation of the forces of nature. Separated spatially from all other men he behaves throughout his own particular span of life in his own distinctive fashion. It is not upon the cell nor upon the single organ, nor upon the group, nor upon the species that nature has centered her most lavish concern, but rather upon the integral organization of life processes into the amazingly stable and self-contained system of the individual living creature. [21]

Maslow and Self-Actualization

Abraham Maslow refers to the process of becoming as *self-actualization*. For Maslow, the self-actualizing person is

[19] Combs and Snygg, *Individual Behavior*, p. 45.
[20] Allport, *Becoming*, pp. 81–82.
[21] Gordon W. Allport, *Personality: a Psychological Interpretation* (New York: Henry Holt & Co., 1937), p. 3.

one who is also growing, moving. This is the person who is creative, no matter what he does. He is "open to experiences" because his personality has not reached a standstill—he has not closed himself. The healthy person is a "fully functioning" one. He can express himself without fear of strangulation and without fear of ridicule. He is spontaneous and natural in his behavior.[22] Like Allport, Maslow stresses the natural uniqueness of man. Man is not on the same continuum as animals for he is capable of creating purposes for behavior and of projecting himself into the future.

Successful adjustment to reality is the achievement of self-actualization. But since one's potentialities are real, then successful adjustment to reality includes successful expression of the highest potentialities of which a person is capable. The individual is not a passive accommodator to social forces that press on him, but an active seeker after mastery over these social forces and the expression of his highest intellectual and aesthetic potentialities. Mental health or good adjustment is a matter of positive striving and continual growth.[23] If man is given the opportunity, he will express his nature. When he does not do so, it is because the social conditions of life prevent the realization of his potential. Self-actualization instincts are inborn qualities whose expression depends not on thwarting but on favorable life circumstances.

The self-actualizing, fully functioning person is one who has a positive view of his self, the self being, as Maslow puts it, ". . . an essential inner nature which is intrinsic, given, 'natural' and usually, very resistant to change." [24] In this self,

[22] Abraham H. Maslow, *Toward a Psychology of Being* (New York: D. Van Nostrand Co., Inc., 1962), p. 129.

[23] See Ibid., pp. 177–200.

[24] A. H. Maslow, "Some Basic Propositions of a Growth and Self-Actualization Psychology," in *Perceiving, Behaving, Becoming; A New Focus for Education* (Washington, D.C.: National Education Association, 1962), p. 35.

or inner nature, Maslow includes man's ". . . instinctoid needs, capacities, talents, anatomical equipment, physiological balances, prenatal and natal injuries, and traumata to the neonatus." [25] He states that he would include man's ". . . defense and coping mechanisms, 'style of life,' and other characterological traits, all shaped in the first few years of life." [26] This inner nature of man is found only after all of his layers of defenses have been peeled off, after he has realized his superficial roles in contrast to what he really is. Man must then like his inner nature, what he really is.

The self-actualizing individual must be completely open to experience and must be able to accept what he perceives. In this way he will be more capable of dealing with the problems that confront him, whether they be external problems or those which arise within himself. The more secure the individual's self, the less he will feel threatened by events and the more open he can be in relating to the world about him. Openness to experience and acceptance, it thus appears, are related to the individual's freedom from threat, and this freedom in turn is a product of a positive self and identification. [27] Because the individual thinks well of himself and trusts himself, he finds others trustworthy. He comes to build an interdependent relationship with others, thus developing values related to the welfare of other human beings. The self-actualizing, fully functioning individual, therefore, develops and holds human values. This individual, because he respects himself and because he values others, will not become authoritarian. He will accept and adapt to changes—not only those concerning himself, but those concerning others. This individual will become, through healthy growth, a continually changing process, a self-actualizing, fully functioning person.

[25] Ibid.
[26] Ibid.
[27] Ibid., pp. 37 ff.

This person would be mature. He would be able to "transcend deficiency-needs." He would be in a "state of Being, rather than striving, . . . an 'authentic' person, being fully human." This process of growth is the process of becoming a person.

Maslow suggests that the need of man for truth is like the human need for food—inherent in the inner nature of man.

The needs for knowledge, for understanding, for a life philosophy, for a theoretical frame of reference, for a value system, these are themselves conative, a part of our primitive and animal nature (we are very special animals).[28]

The movement toward maturity is never-ending. For the very process of growth which is life is the process of becoming a person. Thus one can always become more than he is at any given moment. One can always grow and become more of a human being. By the decisions one makes he builds his life. Whether made consciously or subconsciously, they are the stuff by which growth occurs. Man must always strive to become more than he is. He must learn to understand himself and he must take responsibility for the choices he makes. A man is his decisions. One must accept himself for what he is, not underestimating what he can become.

Maslow proposes a hierarchy of needs with self-actualization as the final goal.[29] In one sense this might appear to be in conflict with Allport's conceptions of functional autonomy and propriate striving. But this is misleading. For "the most important thing about man is his existence, the fact of his being and becoming. . . . It is not the physical self each of

---

[28] Abraham H. Maslow, *Motivation and Personality* (New York, Harper & Row, Publishers, Inc., 1954), p. 151.
[29] Ibid., especially Chaps. 5 and 12.

us seeks to maintain, however. It is the self of which we are aware, our *self-concepts,* we seek fulfillment for." [30]

Hence, both Allport and Maslow are speaking of the adult and his mature style of life. But implied by both is the necessity of satisfaction of earlier needs in order later to attain the final stage of propriate striving or self-actualization. Early life history is of less significance than the living existential present. Most important is the individual in the present. His goals for the here and now and for the future provide information enough toward understanding him.

THEORY

In what has gone before there has been little or no reference to traditional metaphysics. How could there be a body of theory about education not somehow related to notions about the universe in which man resides, the nature of humanity, and the special characteristics of the nonhuman realm of material and living things within which man makes his abode? But yet, this is just the point. Theories with little reference to the great, perennial, ultimate considerations have been guiding ones in education since 1950. A plethora of ideas, some of them supported by empirical evidence, are available. But educational practices have not been related to fundamental metaphysical and ontological considerations. Instead, we have been overwhelmed by the Frankenstein of our own technology, scared stiff of the Russians, and frantically preoccupied with the race with our neighbors for status. Consequently, much thinking about schooling has rested upon proximate criteria of national strength and socioeconomic power.

[30] Arthur W. Combs, *The Profesisonal Education of Teachers* (Boston: Allyn and Bacon, Inc., 1965), p. 16.

Do we have embedded in recent counseling and guidance theory a return to fundamentals in educational thought? Do we find here a resurgent humanism? Shall we get our bearings, after all, from the counseling and guidance people who concentrate on the *person*? It is the purpose of this section to examine these questions.

According to Rollo May, the existential approach in psychology and psychiatry was practically unknown in the United States until about 1958.[31] It is from the psychological and psychiatric interpretations of existential thought that the counseling and guidance people get much of their intellectual grounding; although they occasionally mention Husserl, Sartre, Kierkegaard, and Camus, their sources are not at this philosophical level but in the interpretations advanced by psychologists such as Carl Rogers, Abraham Maslow, Gordon Allport, as discussed in the preceding section.

A fundamental point is that what is worth identifying, concentrating on, defining, studying about is the immediate presentations of experience to us. This is what is important— *phenomena*, not necessarily what is considered to "be behind" them; *existence*, not some hypothesized essence. This, in a way, seems like a return to familiar doctrines of American philosophers like William James and John Dewey who had so much to say about "experience." And it appears to be a needed emphasis—that is, the emphasis on human beings struggling, suffering, doing, undergoing—on what is *immediate*, what is *present*, what is here and now with us—with immediate experiencing."

Now, James and Dewey were clearly and explicity in revolt against nineteenth-century Idealism. This philosophy had its source in Hegel, and was being forwarded by T. H.

[31] Rollo May, "Foreword," in *Existential Psychology* (New York: Random House, Inc., 1961), p. 7.

Green and Bernard Bosanquet in England, Josiah Royce and William Ernest Hocking in America, while James and Dewey were at the height of their careers. Idealism insisted that it is not the immediate experiences that are important, rather the meanings behind them. Idealists held that all finite events are to be understood not immediately, in and of themselves, but against a background of permanent, ordered principles which themselves remain unseen, unchanging, but yet order all existence. Pragmatism rejected this view and argued for experience as the center of concern. But pragmatism was a thoroughly social philosophy, especially in its Deweyan version; it was optimistic; it was taken by its proponents to be democratic.

Existentialism continues the pragmatist emphasis on experience but qualifies the social, democratic, and optimistic parts of pragmatism. The modern philosopher taken to be the main source of existentialism is Sören Kierkegaard of Denmark (1813–1855). Kierkegaard himself was a profoundly religious man—a Christian—holding that man must accept the existence of God by faith even though it is difficult if not impossible to support this affirmation by reason. Later thinkers, however, built upon Kierkegaard's emphasis on the necessity for choice, or affirmation, but found no basis for arguing that man must choose Christianity, or any other religion for that matter. Thus Jean Paul Sartre (1905—), a French philosopher, playwright, novelist, and journalist, has forwarded a thoroughly atheistic existentialism carrying on Kierkegaard's emphasis on choice but denying any necessity for choosing a religious outlook, and arguing that human life has no purpose. His view is that existence is ultimate ("existence precedes essence") and that we must choose, while by choosing we make ourselves ("We are our choices").

Rogers has made explicit his sense of affinity with existentialism.

There are in Kierkegaard . . . deep insights and convictions which beautifully express views I have held but have never been able to formulate. Though Kierkegaard lived one hundred years ago, I cannot help but regard him as a sensitive and highly perceptive friend.[32]

The meaning of human existence is that it is man's nature to exist—"to stand out into reality, to participate in being, to be present to all that is." [33]

Man *is* existence. Existence is projection; it "becomes." "Man is always what he is yet to be." The center of man's existence is the individual himself and not society. But man is not alone in the world. He is connected to other men; he communicates with others; therefore, he cannot live in a state of anarchy. Life is seen as a gift which is, in part, a mystery. The person, therefore, must be committed inwardly to life— this is his way of participating in life. Man is free to choose his commitments in life. In his choices he becomes himself. He is the product of his choices. He is, therefore, an individual who is different from all other persons. He may have many likenesses to others and he may belong to and live in a group; but even in a group he remains an individual, an authentic self.

All of this says that man's existence is more important than his essence. In other words, the real, living person is more important than any abstract statement we can make about him.

The philosophy of existentialism stresses meaning; only through the development of meaning in his life can man become, can man make something of the absurdity which

[32] Rogers, *On Becoming a Person*, p. 199.

[33] Adrian Van Kaam, *Religion and Personality* (Englewood Cliffs, N.J.: Prentice-Hall, Inc., 1964), p. 1.

surrounds him. This puts a new emphasis on the purpose of instruction. Man cannot be "taught" what the world is about; he must create this for himself. Reality must become personal meaning for each individual. What do these ideas mean for education?

Existentialism propounds the belief that man cannot accept the ready-made concepts of existence which have been forced upon him. When man is born into this world he exists, but as what? This question leads to the belief that man himself must answer this question. Thereby man creates his essence; he creates that which he is to be. This is a new image of man, a man who consciously assimilates and utilizes his experiences to become a MAN.[34] Sartre has defined this new man through his perception of himself: "I conceive myself both as totally free and as unable to prevent the fact that the meaning of the world comes to it from myself." [35] This implies the idea that reality is that which man perceives. Brée and Guiton have said that the French novelists writing in existentialist spirit have conceived the novel hero as being ". . . a free agent capable of shaping his own life and choosing his own destiny." [36] The novel hero is in the reflection of an artist's conception of MAN in his age. We cannot treat people as machines, first pulling one lever then another, and expect predictable results. Therefore, we cannot say that the stimulus-response principle is a sufficient description of man's behavior.[37] It is also necessary to communicate experience to enhance cultural concern.

[34] Germaine Brée and Margaret Guiton, *An Age of Fiction; the French Novel from Gide to Camus* (London: Chatto and Windus, 1958), p. 4.

[35] Sartre, as quoted in Ibid., p. 5.

[36] Ibid., p. 8.

[37] See Abraham H. Maslow, "Eusychia—The Good Society," *Journal of Humanistic Psychology* 1 and 2 (Spring 1961): 1–7.

Human emotions are viewed in a new light. In the past we have tended to curb emotional growth because it was rather untidy for adults.[38] But "to fail to feel when feeling is appropriate is emotional deficiency as truly as color blindness is perceptual deficiency; to feel emotions when they are inappropriate is emotional illusion as truly as it is perceptual illusion to see a straight stick thrust into water as bent." [39]

We see this new view of man offering hope because he is considered as one who is striving for a constantly growing self. This quality is inborn. But like other parts of us it can be destroyed, distorted, or forced into some wrong direction. Such effects flow from man's inhumanity to man, for a maladjusted person is synonymous with a threatened one. Humanistic existentialists are anti-deterministic in that they see the person transcending both himself and his culture. The center of existence is man, rather than truth, laws and principles, or essence. Man is characterized by decisions, will, and choice. Skinner can be considered to represent man as manipulated and controlled, while Sartre might represent the other end of the continuum which sees man as supreme, answerable only to himself, responsible for his own actions. Not that culture determines a person's fate but that man is the maker, and therefore the master, of culture. It is man who imposes meaning on his universe, although that universe may function quite well without him. There is no room for Plato's self-existent Ideas nor for an ultimate truth which lies waiting beyond the immediate grasp of man.

An individual human is a part of the biological, evolutionary continuum. His reality is partially dependent on the characteristics of his genetic heritage. He is further affected

[38] See Adrian Van Kaam, "Humanistic Psychology and Culture," *Journal of Humanistic Psychology* 1 and 2 (Spring 1961): 94–100; also Horace B. English, "Education of the Emotions," *Journal of Humanistic Psychology* 1 and 2 (Spring 1961): 101–109.

[39] English, "Education of the Emotions," p. 103.

by forces outside himself, such as the time and place in which he spends his life, his family background and position in society, his early training and experiences, his culture, and his interaction with the persons and things of his environment throughout his life. Man is an animal subject to the same external forces as are other beasts. He is also a product of internal drives of need-fulfillment, as are other living beings. He has basic union with the entire earth and its inhabitants, and has no reality apart from his environment. Yet as the most highly developed living organism, he finds himself, in turn, acting as a force of change and evolution on the rest of reality. He can rearrange the landscape, control life, and produce new forms of it. He can influence his own future generations through the effect of culture, which both automatically and deliberately renews itself and carries on its ever modifying traditions, becoming a force in itself above its individual members.

Nevertheless, positivistic science alone cannot discover the intrinsic nature of man as he exists as a being in the world. The scientific method, concentrating on verifiable, measurable facts and quantities, cannot reach a certain aspect of man which lies above his externally determined nature. Man's world has no meaning to him outside his relationship and attitude toward it. And since, even on a biological scale, each man is a bit different from all others, having a slightly different genetic and environmental heritage, there are as many realities as there are men. Since each man is a bit different from one moment to the next as a result of shifting external forces, his point of view is constantly modified. There is continuous interaction between man and his environment. Thus, no statement of reality can be made without considering how man as an individual feels and sees his world. The importance lies in how man *perceives* time and space, the reason of his existence, and his goals.

Man must be aware of the limitations of experimental scientific knowledge. He must also be vitally aware of the way he is determined by forces outside himself, in other words, how unfree he is. He must realize that since no one else can be in his skin, seeing as he sees, he is ultimately alienated from others and alone in the face of life and death. The initial reaction brings despair. Yet in this realization of his lack of freedom, of his morality, and his aloneness, man achieves freedom because he has accepted and internalized this reality. Upon second glance he realizes that there is a part of him which seems beyond the reach of the sensed objective world. In part this is the world of his mind which is not merely a complex reaction to stimuli, but which can recombine past experiences and reactions, and bring to them something which is distinctly personal. This is known as insight—the perception of relationships and unity. Man can be conscious of the forces operating on him, of the possible choices he may make, and he can make a reasoned decision. It is in this way that he rises above the determined world to become ultimately free. To be free is to be human—to choose and to move.

Existence, then, is a restlessness, a hunger beyond Freud's animal drives and Skinner's conditioned responses. This restlessness is called "becoming." It is not just aimless wandering, but is directed by the aims and goals which the individual sets for himself in terms of what he wishes to make of himself (a projected self-image). Replacing old religious and moral absolutes, this provides the individual with a solid formula for living, enabling him to surmount the alienation and suffering which do not cease simply because he has developed his freedom.

Since there are really no absolutes, there is a great amount of risk in every temporary goal man devises. Yet, through reasoning and experience man must commit himself to his goals. Commitment implies not only mental decision but physical action in this world. Man must not stop at contemplation. At the same time, realizing that he himself is a free person, not a completely determinable thing, the individual must be aware of this same quality in others he meets, and in mankind in general.

Thus the individual regards and treats others as persons, not as things. This relationship, termed "I-Thou" by the philosopher Martin Buber, saves the existential point of view from a certain tendency toward subjectivism and anarchy. The individual must realize that others possess, or may possess in the future, the same qualities of dignity, respect, and freedom he himself has. He may not allow others to assume the responsibility of his own decisions, nor may he attempt to run the lives of others.

Because man can perceive no eternal absolutes, he is limited in his action to the reality of the "here and now." He has a responsibility to promote the dignity of all humans. Thus he becomes actively involved with the improvement of his society and the needs of the world.

Phenomenology—Life as Happenings

In order to understand this it is extremely important that we concentrate on the phenomenon as given, attempting to experience the authentic presentation as it comes, without presupposition. Thus, we may say that we consider the *existential* and *phenomenological* aspects of experience to be the most real and the most deserving of attention. Not "Why did it happen?" but "Exactly what did happen?" not merely as observed but as experienced or "lived through." Among philosophers, Edmund Husserl (1859–1938) and Martin Heidegger (1899——) are associated with *phenomenology* .

as a form of academic philosophy, Heidegger having been a teacher of Jean Paul Sartre, and having been influenced both by Husserl and Kierkegaard. The phenomenological stance is especially important at first; later, in order to formulate policy it is necessary to move away from the phenomenal to search for generalizations. But scholarly generalizations will be stronger and more dependable if the phenomenological stance can be cultivated initially. "What really happened?" "How was it, really?" These are important questions.

But perfect objectivity is impossible. To be human is to experience reality from a particular point in space and time. We can, however, cultivate the discipline of first trying to achieve phenomenal objectivity while recognizing the impossibility of perfection, and then working systematically to become aware of our own predispositions. Another thing we can do is guard against unthinking acceptance of the notion that we should always explain the more complex by the more simple. There has been a good deal of this in recent behavioral-scientific methodology but it is no axiom; it is not necessarily so; it is merely a convention. When human consciousness is present, for example, a good many things will need to be explained by the very presence of consciousness. Consciousness becomes a vital causal agent and is not to be reduced to "drives," "tensions," or "conditioned responses."

Man is not a passive recipient of stimuli from outside himself. He is a vital center the source of much shaping, thus a creature of will and decision. Even in situations of extreme compulsion such as torture or solitary confinement in a prison or confinement in a network of obligations, man is never solely the creature of his fate so long as he has some inkling of what is happening to him. That is, to be conscious at all of what is happening is to introduce a force into the situation that changes it. If there is consciousness, then there is a self, and this changes things by the fact of its presence.

My self, or my being (the two at this point are parallel), is to be found at that center at which I know myself as the one responding in these different ways, the center at which I experience myself as the one behaving in the ways described by these varied functions.[40]

In all interpretations of human and social phenomena, then, including education, the experience of identity is looked upon ". . . as a *sine quo non* of human nature and of any philosophy or science of human nature." [41]

Hope and Reality—The World as Man's Home

To be sure man is, or should be, for himself, and those aspects of nature and culture which depress man, obscuring his hopes, are to be worked against. But the existentialist movement, most clearly at work professionally in education in counseling and guidance theory, has sometimes appeared to pit man against his world, setting the individual against culture. Not only romantic critics of society and schooling such as Paul Goodman, Jonathan Kozol, John Holt, and Edgar Friedenberg have set the young against the context which sustains them. Such a position is suggested by Professor Maslow, to whom we are much indebted for glimpses of hope. Maslow, in referring to the point of view designated as existential or humanistic psychology comments:

. . . people who have independently been coming to the

---

[40] May, "Emergence of Existential Psychology," pp. 47–48.
[41] A. H. Maslow, "Existential Psychology—What's in It for Us?" in *Existential Psychology*, ed. Rollo May (Random House, Inc., 1961), p. 53.

same conclusions are all responding to something real outside themselves.

. . . This something real is, I believe, the total collapse of all sources of value outside the individual.[42]

From this essentially negative position there flows the view that the authentic person asserts his authenticity against the established order and thus becomes a rebel. And since it has been stipulated that the individual is the only source of value, it would appear to follow that the individual is always right against society. This somehow seems an impossible position to take—that any eccentric manifestation which is, nevertheless, authentic vis-à-vis one human being has an authority higher than that of the going social custom. Not only does this position seem to be unjustifiedly anarchic and individualistic, but it accentuates man's loneliness in its reinforcement of idiosyncrasy. The hope is that the anarchy and the aloneness can yield to the ongoing dynamic of choice. Here is the possibility to be stressed. In its emphasis on the shaping force of individual persons existential humanism supplies a rationale for creativity within which lies promise for novelty, inventiveness, a better world forever within our grasp if only we choose it.

Not only may there be found here the germ of theory to support social-political action and a vigorous grappling with the social problems of the future. The idea can also be very personal. For instance, although the inevitability of death is recognized, this teaching is that by making appropriate choices a person can indeed, shape the style of his dying. Thus, in contrast to one's birth, over which he has no control, he can, by taking thought and exercising choice, influence the style of his death.

[42] Ibid.

The life of every human being centers on himself, and what has been called self-affirmation, or the courage to be is the commitment to preserve the integrity of self. Moreover, all persons needs to participate in other beings; we never want to live it all out alone. Yet the outward thrusts are always tentative because we risk ourselves in participation. And just as it is possible to turn against and destroy others so the self, aware of self, is capable of self-destruction. This possibility is another dimension of self-consciousness within which lurks the possibility of tragedy—a possibility present only at the human level and open only to one engaged in human participation. Thus human behavior is indeed ". . . in some significant ways, something more than the behavior of our laboratory animals." [43]

In face-to-face relationships, there appears evidence that sharing self-awareness is essential to mutual growth.

I have come to realize that only when I am able to be a transparently real person, and am so perceived by my client, can he discover what is real in him. [44]

Thus a manipulative and impersonal relationship is less likely to bring about personal growth and self-awareness than a genuine experience of interpersonal integrity. Does it make any difference? Rogers reports astonishing empirical evidence that self-awareness coupled with some realistic knowledge of the environment makes for stronger, more consistent, and more satisfying living. [45]

The more recent versions of positivistic philosophy have not provided a theory of human nature. Adopting a method-

[43] Rogers, "Two Divergent Trends," p. 87.
[44] Ibid., p. 88.
[45] Ibid., pp. 91–92.

ological stance generally suggested by experimental science, attention has been devoted to modes of human behavior but not to a theory of man. Here in the existentialist concepts we may have the makings of a contemporary theory of mankind. When such a theory of mankind is joined with a responsibly formulated world view and lived by, it becomes a fundamental part of the personalities of men. It then becomes fallacious to separate therapy or counseling from the age-old task of wrestling intellectually and morally with objective reality. There is continuity between selves and their world, and sharp disjunctions between subject and object become fallacious. Thus might existentialism lead back to certain endeavors ordinarily associated with traditional philosophy. Thus might counseling theory, however eccentric some of its current manifestations, lead to some vigorously intellectual humanistic philosophy of education.

EDUCATIONAL APPLICATIONS

Inasmuch as the self is achieved, wrought out, or learned, school should provide an atmosphere where selves can develop in a healthy way. Children thrive better, so we are told, when relieved from intense competition, harsh discipline, fear of failure. Thus can each child grow to understand his own needs and values and take charge of the experiences for changing them. This way, self-evaluation is beginning and end of the learning process; as learning proceeds children become freely growing, nonfearful, understanding individuals. In classrooms characterized by such atmosphere, young people proceed naturally and without fear, it is alleged, to become active, responsible, and trustworthy. There is no undue emphasis on obedience and conformity. Encouragement and acceptance by teachers foster trustworthiness and a sense of security. The protective overlay of defensiveness which too often has characterized relationships between teachers and students is gone.

Democracy, it is said, must be the soil in which the self-actualizing individual grows—not the democracy of the mediocre average but a democracy of unique individuals who value differences and respect one another. Children and young people come to value difference and change, and also to share in mutual respect for the value of work and the creativity of man. Creativity is not the special endowment of a few. Rather it is a process, capacity for which resides in every person. The raw materials of creativity are eagerness, curiosity, imagination, and wonderment. A prime challenge to schools is to release and encourage growth of these capacities. The teacher is in position to foster individual growth. He can facilitate development of originality and creativity by providing a climate as well as basic skills and tools which make exploration possible. Creativity does not grow through restraint and conformity, and authoritarian schooling can but produce conforming, not creative pupils.

Within clasrooms, it is the responsibility of teachers to provide the atmosphere and the opportunity to enable each individual to grow and change. School grades or reward tokens do not foster growth. The aims of school tasks should be to nurture self-discipline and cultivate self-evaluation.

Hence, the fundamental purpose of education is individual growth and self-actualization rather than mastery of knowledge per se. Openness to experiences, imagination, and fantasy are encouraged. Mass testing and mass teaching do not facilitate this kind of growth and development. Learning should never be a competitive endeavor within a climate of anxiety. Primary emphasis must always be on the person as learner, not on the learning program. The schedule must be flexible and open, and the teacher must build positive relationships between himself and his students. Each individual must be taken into consideration. The ungraded school and the discontinuation of assignment to ability groups are suggestions for providing freedom for growth and development. Self-government, pupil participation in planning, the encouragement of a free atmosphere, and abolition of standardized ability tests are proposed.

The educator must know himself in order to provide the setting in which he, his colleagues, and his students live in this atmosphere of self-trust. Students are not to be treated as subordinates. The teacher, committed to the view that all learning is self-learning, believes that human beings want to grow. Hence, challenges are welcomed, not avoided, for it is recognized that only by overcoming difficulties can there develop the enjoyment in struggle that displaces fear.

Since man is inherently good, under the guidance of the educator he will perceive, behave, and become through the process of choosing values suitable to him. Moral judgments are made not according to traditional standards but according to fitness to individuals. All behavior is thus viewed contextually as a function of the person at the instant of action. An individual's behavior is a function of how he perceives himself and his world. The individual is continuously engaged in striving toward self-actualization or self-realization. Thus, a "fully functioning" or "adequate" person is characterized by his openness to all experience and his full acceptance of himself.

Perceiving, Behaving, Becoming

Notions such as those reviewed in the preceding section were explicitly applied to teaching, school curriculum, and organization of instruction in a yearbook published in 1962 by the Association for Supervision and Curriculum Development.[46] *Perceiving, Behaving, Becoming* was edited by Arthur W. Combs of the University of Florida, Chairman of the 1962 Yearbook Committee. Combs, along with Earl C. Kelley of Wayne State University and Donald Snygg, who had collaborated with Combs in authoring a widely used professional textbook,[47] have been leaders among educationists pressing for the application of the point of view to all phases of schoolwork.

The professional theme running throughout the Yearbook is the importance of a deep, honest, straightforward relationship between teachers and students—a relationship in which knowledge and wisdom are achieved through the mutual interaction of living beings, the genuine sharing of life. The book advocates heterogeneous grouping and limitation of class size to twenty. Grades and the grading system are to be abolished.

Behavior has a direct relationship to how a person perceives; hence, to understand a person's behavior we have to understand his perceptual field.[48] A positive self-concept is fundamental to learning; this is built out of experience, more caught than taught in interrelationships among people.[49] One learns that he is liked and accepted not so much from being told so but by the actual experience of being liked and accepted. Teachers need to convince each child of his importance. Teachers should be careful in applying labels to children ("lazy," "poor reader," etc.) for individuals may indeed come to think of themselves this way. Children need positive evaluation, not labels. Good self-concepts issue in worthwhile behavior. Man is a social animal but not a collective one; in the anonymity of collectivism he loses meaning

[46] NEA, *Perceiving, Behaving, Becoming.*
[47] Combs and Snygg, *Individual Behavior.*
[48] NEA, *Perceiving, Behaving, Becoming,* p. 65.
[49] Ibid., p. 84.

and individuality. The tendency in contemporary society toward collective institutionalization in many phases of life is a hazard. Schools must resist taking on this characteristic feature of twentieth-century culture. Mechanization and impersonality must be counteracted with concern and respect for the needs of individuals and their right to be different.

The Purposes of Education

If education is the process of forming fundamental dispositions, intellectual and moral, toward nature and fellow men, then the point of view examined in this chapter can indeed be taken as a general theory of education. This theory, then, insists without compromise that explanations of human action as the result of conditioning are completely unacceptable for they leave out the person. This theory holds that what the person does is, after all, always a function of the person, and that when you try to explain him by drives or operant conditioning your explanations are faulty because you are leaving *him* out. So, applied in a practical way to teaching, this view is that you must never explain away your students as people—by grades, rank in class, IQ scores, or achievement-test marks. It is the other way up. Your students are persons—each one—and these marks are merely little records of movements they have made. The person always transcends any behavioral manifestation of personality.

The horrendous danger in educational techniques of the followers of Skinner and Bruner as discussed in earlier chapters of this book is that man is made over into the image of the techniques by which he is studied. To the contrary, for the humanistic psychologists the person thinking always transcends the structure of the disciplines by which he thinks, and the person transcends his behavior, however induced. Man chooses, then assesses and judges his behavior. The self is immanent in choice, transcendent in reflection and judgment. Man is a living being. Life transcends and judges all manifestations of life. This way, we can always do more than we do. Since we have the power (because we are alive), we live always with the anxiety of deciding how much of the power to use and in what direction to exercise it. Life in any person is greater than any particular manifestation at any time and place of that life. So life is "becoming," and the "becoming" is progressively shaped by the choices exercised in what Kierkegaard called "dreadful freedom."

Education in contemporary industrial society may well be cleansed and strengthened by the emphasis on man for himself embodied in the so-called third force, existentialist, or humanistic psychology. However, the world in which we live remains intractable, and the intellectual tools which men have forged to deal with it are systematically impersonal. Hence, the educational notions stressed by this movement have been severely criticized for being anti-intellectual, romantic, superficial, impractical in an industrial society. One solution to which currency has recently been given is that of institutionalizing a distinction between the counseling and the teaching function in schools. Thus, with teachers taking somewhat larger responsibility for acquainting youth with experimental scientific knowledge of the material, economic, social, and political world in which they reside, counselors endeavor to serve the complementary function of assisting youngsters to know themselves. But this encourages anti-intellectualism in counseling and the dehumanization of teaching.

A better hope for a rapprochement between the humane and the intellectual is in the renaissance of the recognition that self-knowledge may grow around a conception of vocation. Thus may serious study of the vocations of men become a primary means of self-knowledge. Thus might the disjunction between teaching and counseling disappear. One day, then, there might be a return to the notion that men come to know themselves and progressively realize freedom as they become civilized persons. The notions that effective teaching is, after all, the shaping of disposition and character, that the only teacher worth his salt works as a counselor, and that the only counseling that really works is that of a teacher would gain currency.

When this occurs, some recent trends in curriculum and method will be subjected to radical review, for teaching will once again be conceived as an interesting and inescapably personal activity.

Notes

This schema for analysis of American educational theory in the twentieth century identifies two major ideological changes in the larger society to explain and interpret shifts in point of view concerning the work of schools. The first of these is evolution and the rise of the social sciences. It is held that this is the crucial separation between the liberal arts tradition and progressive education. Progressive education, as interpreted here, is what happened to educational thought when educators accepted evolution and then tried to construe the education of the young accordingly. On the other hand, the liberal arts tradition is conceived here as education that treats man as a transcendent being, not to be understood in his essential nature by experimental science.

Popular works that have interpreted education this way are C. P. Snow, *The Two Cultures and the Scientific Revolution* (New York: Cambridge University Press, 1962), Paul Woodring, *A Fourth of a Nation* (New York: McGraw-Hill Book Co., 1957), Mortimer Adler and Milton Mayer, *The Revolution in Education* (Chicago: University of Chicago Press, 1958), and Martin Mayer, *The Schools* (New York: Harper & Row, 1961). More professional works which make much of this distinction are John L. Childs, *Education and the Philosophy of Experimentalism* (New York and London: The Century Co., 1931), *Education and Morals* (New York: Appleton-Century-Crofts, 1950), and *American Pragmatism and Education* (New York: Holt, 1956). Boyd H. Bode's *How*

253

We Learn (Boston: D. C. Heath and Co., 1940) and various writings of John Dewey make reference to the prescientific origins and continuing assumptions of traditional literary education.

The second major ideological shift in the larger society which brought about a crucial change in educational point of view occurred during and after World War II. This was the shift from a conception of education as primarily individual cultivation to the notion of education as capital investment and means of production of industrial, military, and national goods. With all the arguments among traditionalists, essentialists, progressives, or whatever, before World War II there was the steady assumption that making life richer, more satisfying, more meaningful and rewarding for individuals living in their society with their fellow men was the ultimate educational goal. In contrast, some time immediately after mid-century education came to be thought of as an instrument of national policy to shape, and be shaped by, national and corporate concerns. In addition to works cited in the text, see Daniel Bell, *The End of Ideology* (Glencoe, Ill.: The Free Press, 1960), Ronald Berman, *America in the Sixties* (New York: Harper & Row, 1971), Kenneth E. Boulding, *The Meaning of the Twentieth Century* (New York: Harper & Row, 1964), Lawrence A. Cremin, *The Genius of American Education* (New York: Vintage Books, 1965), Amitai Etzioni, *Studies in Social Change* (New York: Holt, Rinehart and Winston, 1966), Francis Keppel, *The Necessary Revolution in American Education* (New York: Harper & Row, 1966), Donald N. Michael, *Cybernation: the Silent Conquest* (Santa Barbara, Calif.: Center for the Study of Democratic Institutions, 1962), and *The Unprepared Society* (New York: Basic Books, 1968). Robert Nisbet's *The Degradation of the Academic Dogma; the University in America, 1945–1970* (New York: Basic Books, 1971) and David Riesman and Christopher Jencks's *The Academic Revolution* (Garden City, N.Y.: Anchor Books, 1969) discuss and criticize changes in higher education. At this writing, tremendous popular as well as professional interest has been generated by Alvin Toffler's *Future Shock* (New York: Random House, 1970).

If but two interpretive works supporting the notion of a major educational shift occurring after World War II were to be studied, the following deserve special recommendation: John I. Goodlad, ed., *The Changing American School* (The Sixty-Fifth Yearbook of the National Society for the Study of Education, Part II [Chicago: University of Chicago Press, 1966]), and the already mentioned *Degradation of the Academic Dogma* by Robert Nisbet. The Goodlad volume discusses the lower schools; Nisbet's book shows how the universities changed after the war.

CHAPTER I. / THE LIBERAL ARTS TRADITION

The liberal arts tradition in education is the Greek tradition. Always threatened by rhetoric, and almost invariably corrupted by the vocational and institutional goals of the institutions with which it has been connected, it has lived through the centuries as an ideal, a norm, or a measure. See Henri Marrou, *A History of Education in Antiquity*, trans. George Lamb (New York: Sheed and Ward, 1956), on this point. Werner Jaeger, *Paideia*, trans. Gilbert Highet (Oxford: B. Blackwell, 1944–1946), is a scholarly analysis without peer of the Greek tradition in education.

It is customary to use the cave myth in Book VII of Plato's *Republic* as an educational allegory. Actually the chariot myth of the *Phaedrus*, followed throughout its appearances and reappearances from beginning to end of the Dialogue, supplies the main doctrines of the Great Tradition in education in metaphysical context. It teaches that man's genius is the buried recollection of the truth, that classes of human excellence bear a relationship to the degree to which the soul once saw truth. It further states that man is of three parts—intellect, will, and appetite—and that the intellect must rule.

To supplement the discussion of the text, a suggestion would be to read Plato's *Phaedrus*, Book VII of the *Republic*, and possibly St. Augustine's *De Magistro*, this latter reference showing how the pagan ideas of Plato were reformulated by an early Christian scholar. Then, to understand and sense the force of the argument for revival of the liberal arts in earlier years of this present century, Mark Van Doren's *Liberal Education* (New York: Henry Holt & Co., 1943) should be studied.

Recent statements of the liberal arts point of view that have given some attention to post-World War II developments in American society and education are Mortimer Adler, *The Difference of Man and the Difference It Makes* (New York: Holt, Rinehart and Winston, 1967), and Robert Maynard Hutchins, *The Learning Society* (New York: Frederick A. Praeger, 1968).

In today's standard educational parlance, the terms "humanistic" and "humanistic education" have been taken over almost entirely by those influenced by existential psychology and movements in education associated with Carl R. Rogers and Abraham Maslow (see Chapter V). This "humanism" is different from the literary humanism of the traditional liberal arts scholars and educational theorists such as Van Doren, Hutchins, and Adler. Their traditional "great books" humanism does indeed appear to have fallen on evil days. At this writing in 1972, the possibility of stirring great enthusiasm in any quarter for an educational program centering in the Great Books and the classical languages would appear to be slim indeed.

For a devastating critique of the liberal arts tradition as the educational correlative of white colonialism, see Frantz Fanon, *The Wretched of the Earth* (New York: Grove Press, 1965).

CHAPTER II. / PROGRESSIVE EDUCATION

There has been considerable resurgence of interest in John Dewey and progressive education since about 1965. For a scholarly reexamination of Dewey's pedagogy see Arthur Wirth, *John Dewey as Educator* (New York: John Wiley & Sons, 1966). Writings of Paul Goodman, e.g., *Compulsory Mis-education* (New York: Horizon Press, 1964), make reference to Dewey and suggest the value of educational progressivism. Charles Silberman's

Crisis in the Classroom (New York: Vintage Books, 1970) likewise treats Dewey sympathetically. Commentaries on Dewey's philosophy and educational theory of earlier date which remain of primary value are Sidney Hook's *John Dewey, an Intellectual Portrait* (New York: John Day Co., 1938) and the writings of John L. Childs and Boyd H. Bode (see Notes to the Introduction).

If one were to attempt an intensive introductory study of John Dewey's educational thought, working with primary materials, a suggestion would be to read *My Pedagogic Creed* and *The School and Society* first, taking account of publication dates. These have been reprinted in Martin Dworkin, ed., *Dewey on Education* (New York: Bureau of Publications, Teachers College, Columbia University, 1959). Careful study of *Democracy and Education* (New York: The Macmillan Co., 1916) and *Experience and Education* (New York: The Macmillan Co., 1938) should follow. Again, it is important to keep in mind that *Experience in Education* was written more than twenty years after *Democracy and Education,* and with a view to what had been going on in schools in the name of "progressive education."

Among recent works interpreting American pragmatism and the pragmatic philosophers in social and historical context are: Milton Konvitz and Gail Kennedy, eds., *The American Pragmatists* (New York: Meridian Books, 1960), an anthology of selected original writings by the major pragmatist philosophers; C. Wright Mills *Sociology and Pragmatism* (New York: Paine-Whitman Publishers, 1964); and *The Sociological Imagination* (New York: Oxford University Press, 1959). Also, Edward G. Moore, *American Pragmatism: Peirce, James, Dewey* (New York: Columbia University Press, 1961), Darnell Rucker, *The Chicago Pragmatists* (Minneapolis: University of Minnesota Press, 1969), and Horace S. Thayer, *Meaning and Action: A Critical History of Pragmatism* (Indianapolis: The Bobbs-Merrill Co., 1968). Paul E. Pfuetze's *Self, Society, and Existence* (New York: Harper Torchbooks, 1961) compares the social philosophy and theory of personality of George H. Mead with that of Martin Buber.

CHAPTER III. / THE STRUCTURE OF THE DISCIPLINES MOVEMENT

Educators have always emphasized the importance of intellectual structure as a characteristic of intellectual maturity. Concepts have been viewed as the end of learning, and conceptual development has been considered to be the course of educational development. In recent American scholarship, philosophers have published works in the long tradition of endeavors to order knowledge more effectively. Long before educators began talking about the work of Jerome Bruner and Joseph Schwab, Professor F. S. C. Northrop published *The Logic of the Sciences and the Humanities* (New York, The Macmillan Co., 1947), and W. Oliver Martin, another philosopher with a lively interest in education, wrote *The Order and Integration of Knowledge* (Ann Arbor: University of Michigan Press, 1957).

Working quite independently of Bruner, David R. Krathwohl, Benjamin S. Bloom, and Bertram B. Masia published *Taxonomy of Educational Objectives, The Classification of Educational Goals, Handbook II: Affective Domain* (New York: The David McKay Co., 1964), following up the earlier *Handbook* which outlined the cognitive domain. Another interesting work emphasizing the importance of intellectual structuring of educational subject matter is Harry S. Broudy, B. Othanel Smith, and Joe R. Burnett, *Democracy and Excellence in American Secondary Education* (Chicago: Rand McNally and Co., 1964). The point to be made is that during the 1960s, and even earlier, a number of philosophers, psychologists, and educationists were studying the conceptual structure of human knowledge and the processes of concept formation. Some, like B. O. Smith, Robert Ennis, and Arno Bellack, studied the language of classroom teaching, the role of logic in teaching, and the logic of teaching. See, for example, Arno A. Bellack, Herbert M. Kiebard, Ronald T. Hyman, and Frank T. Smith, Jr., *The Language of the Classroom* (New York: Teachers College Press, Teachers College, Columbia University,

1966), and Arno A. Bellack, ed., *Theory and Research in Teaching* (New York: Bureau of Publications, Teachers College, Columbia University, 1963). Also, Robert H. Ennis, *Logic in Teaching* Englewood Cliffs, N.J.: Prentice-Hall, Inc., 1969), and *Ordinary Logic* (Englewood Cliffs, N.J.: Prentice-Hall, Inc., 1969).

Some of the scholars, curriculum specialists, and classroom teachers who had been active in the mid-1960s in the new curriculum movements were impressed by difficulties in handling conceptual materials with very young or culturally disadvantaged children, and recently the developmental psychology of learning has been getting more attention. This has taken the form of a strong revival of interest in Jean Piaget's studies of intellectual development of children. See, for example, Irene J. Athey and Duane O. Rubadeau, *Educational Implications of Piaget's Theory* (Waltham, Mass.: Ginn-Blaisdell, 1970), Eleanor Duckworth's translation of Jean Piaget, *Genetic Epistemology* (New York: Columbia University Press, 1970), Bärbel Inhelder and Jean Piaget, *The Early Growth of Logic in the Child*, trans. E. A. Lunzer and D. Papert (New York: W. W. Norton Co., 1969), David Elkind, *Children and Adolescents; Interpretive Essays on Jean Piaget* (New York: Oxford University Press, 1970), and Barry J. Wadsworth, *Piaget's Theory of Cognitive Development* (New York: The David McKay Co., 1971).

A corollary of the interest in concepts and structures in curriculum and teaching has been a move to identify and study the systemic character of schools taken as complex social organizations. Philip Jackson, in *Life in Classrooms* (New York: Holt, Rinehart and Winston, 1968), analyzed the classroom as a social system. Students of educational administration were influenced by the work of Amitai Etzioni, *A Sociological Reader on Complex Organizations* (New York: Holt, Rinehart and Winston, 1969). A systems analysis approach to the study of educational institutions from the point of view of the administrator is represented by Frank William Banghart, *Educational Systems Analysis* (New York: The Macmillan Co., 1969), Daniel E. Griffiths, ed., *Behavioral Science and Educational Administration*, Sixty-Third Yearbook of the National Society for the Study of Education, Part II (Chicago: University of Chicago Press, 1964), and Daniel E. Griffiths, ed., *Developing Taxonomies of Organizational Behavior in Educational Administration* (Chicago: Rand McNally and Co., 1969).

Publications such as these demonstrate lively continuing interest in systems, structures, concepts, and models as analytical tools for enlarging educational wisdom, and also as worthy educational ends. It may be, however, that some are now less optimistic than they were a few years ago that effective pedagogy can at all stages be built upon a structure of the disciplines approach.

CHAPTER IV./NEO-BEHAVIORISM—TEACHING MACHINES AND PROGRAMMED INSTRUCTION

The intense interest in teaching machines and programmed learning which gripped educators in the mid-1960s has all but passed. What remains is a gradual but steadily increasing understanding and acceptance of newer instructional technologies as aids to teaching and learning. The perspective is more historical, with greater awareness on the part of proponents and detractors that teaching is a mediating activity which constantly makes use of human inventions in enlarging man's abilities to interact with his world. See Paul Saettler, *A History of Instructional Technology* (New York: McGraw-Hill Book Co., 1968). Practically all colleges and universities of any size, and many public school systems, now maintain their own computer centers, and gradually a national network to make possible full sharing of such facilities takes form. Scheduling, marking of tests, maintenance and analysis of records is now commonly coputerized. See M. Clemens Johnson, *Educational Uses of the Computer* (Chicago: Rand McNally and Co., 1971), Donald D. Bushnell and Dwight W. Allen, eds., *The Computer in American Education* (New York: John Wiley & Sons, 1967), Alan Ross Anderson, ed., *Minds and Machines* (Englewood Cliffs, N.J.: Prentice-Hall, Inc., 1964), and John W.

Loughery and others, *Man-machine Systems in Education* (New York: Harper & Row, 1966).

B. F. Skinner the man, and what he stands for, remain of interest, and professional psychologists generally continue to acclaim Dr. Skinner as one of the great psychologists of this age. A study of Skinner's views, based on primary sources, might begin with *Walden Two* (New York: The Macmillan Co., 1948), including next *Science and Human Behavior* (New York: The Macmillan Co., 1953), and his latest book *Beyond Freedom and Dignity* (New York: Alfred A. Knopf, 1971). Richard Evans' taped interview with Skinner was published in the interesting little book *B. F. Skinner, the Man and His Ideas* (New York: E. P. Dutton Co., 1968), and James McClellan's discussion of Skinner in *Toward an Effective Critique of American Education* (Philadelphia: J. B. Lippincott, 1968) could be consulted after study of Skinner's own writings. Skinnerian pedagogy might be assessed in the light of G. S. Reynolds, *A Primer of Operant Conditioning* (Glenview, Ill.: Scott, Foresman and Co., 1968).

Despite the passing of excitement concerning teaching machines per se, the application of Skinnerian pedagogy by means of explicit contingency management making use of tokens, money, rewards—perhaps even drugs—continues to stir controversy. The object of this pedagogy is to modify behavior, shaping-in desired responses and extinguishing undesirable behavior. What *works* in "behavior modification," then, is what is important. See Norris G. Haring and E. Lakin Phillips, *Educating Emotionally Disturbed Children* (New York: McGraw-Hill Book Co., 1962), and Leonard P. Ullmann and Leonard Krasner, *Case Studies in Behavior Modification* (New York: Holt, Rinehart and Winston, 1965).

Some institutional policies of great import in American education during 1970 and 1971 appear to be fully consistent with, if not directly derived from, Skinnerian views. According to behavioristic educational theory, instructional objectives are to be stated as behavioral goals. See Robert F. Mager, *Preparing Instructional Objectives* (Palo Alto, Calif.: Fearon Publishers, 1962). These objectives once determined, teachers are to be held accountable for achieving them; they are hired, that is, to induce specified behaviors in the young: that is their job. See John D. McNeil, *Toward Accountable Teachers* (New York: Holt, Rinehart and Winston, 1971). Moreover, it is possible to assess from community to community and from school to school the extent to which the specified goals are met. Thus, a "national assessment" of American education is deemed possible and is, in fact, underway; full results have not yet been published.

The years 1970 and 1971 saw much professional discussion of "accountability" and the "national assessment." See "Accountability," *Kappan* 52, no. 4 (December 1970), a special issue edited by Myron Lieberman. In instances where teachers were unable or unwilling to account for their teaching results, or in situations where assessment showed clearly that production was below par, arrangements were made to contract work out to private instructional corporations. See *Accountability and the Controversial Role of Performance Contractors* (White Plains, N.Y.: Knowledge Industry Publications, 1971). Texarkana (Arkansas), Gary (Indiana), Seattle, and Grand Rapids are among cities entering into performance contracts with knowledge-industry companies. These companies characteristically make use of "pressure cooker" techniques, including "contingency management" and "behavior modification" methods. The Office of Economic Opportunity has in several instances supported a voucher system that would provide educational credits to parents so that they can make direct payment to a company accepting accountability for instructional results in the form of measurable changed behavior by children. The voucher system allows parents to purchase the most efficient educational services available, not necessarily through their local, publically constituted Board of Education. Christopher Jencks publicized this system in several articles in the *New Republic* in 1969–1970.

Within this general climate of "behavioral objectives," "accountability," and "performance contracting," the U.S. Commissioner of Education, Dr. Sidney Marland, spoke strongly in 1971 of the importance of effective job training in high schools. He insisted that it was time the secondary schools became accountable for producing young people actually possessed of marketable job skills. See Grant Venn, *Men, Education, and Manpower* (Washington, D.C.: American Association of School Administrators, 1970).

CHAPTER V. / HUMANISTIC PSYCHOLOGY

In 1970 and 1971, as various government agencies called for accountability, as the U.S. Commissioner of Education called for production of marketable job skills in the high schools, and as Gary and Grand Rapids signed performance contracts, strong waves of individualistic dissent swept through the ranks of professional educators and education-minded citizens. It is tempting to pin educational behaviorism on the Establishment and identify it as the Establishment position, attributing the so-called humanistic revolt to anti-Establishment educational radicals. That would overstate the case, but a plausible case can be made.

As early as 1966 Dr. John Goodlad suggested in his writing in *The Changing American School* (Notes to the Introduction) as well as in his book *The School Curriculum and the Individual* (Waltham, Mass.: Blaisdell Publishing Co., 1966) that a revolt was in the making against an education in the service of corporate society. Despite efforts to bring about a rapprochement in counseling theory between behaviorism and humanistic psychology (see John D. Krumboltz, ed., *Revolution in Counseling* [Boston: Houghton Mifflin Co., 1966]), the humanistic movement became increasingly popular in the late 1960s, influencing curriculum theory very strongly. Note the popularity, for instance, of publications such as Carl Nordstrom, Edgar Friedenberg, and Hilary Gold, *Society's Children: a Study of Ressentiment in the Secondary School* (New York: Random House, 1967), Ryland W. Crary, *Humanizing the School* (New York: Alfred A. Knopf, 1969), Crary and Louis A. Petrone, *Foundations of Modern Education*

(New York: Alfred A. Knopf, 1971), and Melvin L. Silberman, ed., *The Experience of Schooling* (New York: Holt, Rinehart and Winston, 1971). The University of North Dakota's widely discussed New School for Behavioral Studies in Education, although making use of some of the technology of the behaviorists, seems clearly to be oriented more to openness and human encounter. In Philadelphia the notion of the open school is applied in the Parkway secondary school program, and the chairman of the Department of Educational Administration at New York University writes on educational administration drawing from traditional sources in existential philosophy.

Dr. Arthur Combs, having published on *The Professional Education of Teachers* (Boston: Allyn and Bacon, 1965), followed with *Florida Studies in the Helping Professions,* University of Florida Monographs, Social Sciences No. 37 (Gainesville, Fla.: University of Florida Press, 1969). Other publications of the middle and late 1960s representing humanistic, existential, or personalistic approaches to schooling are William R. Coulson and Carl R. Rogers, eds., *Man and the Science of Man* (Columbus, Ohio: Charles E. Merrill Co., 1968), Abraham Maslow, *Toward a Psychology of Being* (Princeton, N.J.: D. Van Nostrand Co., 1968), Rogers, *Freedom to Learn* (Columbus, Ohio: Charles E. Merrill Co., 1969), and Harold O. Soderquist, *The Person and Education* (Columbus, Ohio: Charles E. Merrill Co., 1964). Abraham Maslow's *The Farther Reaches of Human Nature* (New York: The Viking Press, 1971) came out in the year of his death.

All of the publications listed thus far are professional ones, intended for professional readers. They are sober, systematic, careful, scholarly statements that were not designed for a popular audience, but have attracted strong and enthusiastic attention in the university schools of education and among teachers on the job. Of greater influence on the lay public may be a group of publications with political overtones, and ones proposing radical changes in educational institutions. To many, Ivan Illich seems to be calling for the abolition of the school as we know it, in his *Celebration of Awareness: a Call for Institutional Revolution*

(Garden City, N.Y.: Doubleday and Co., 1970). Some see the preoccupation with sensitivity and encounter groups as an extension of an anti-intellectual movement destructive to education in critical thinking. See Terry O'Banion and April O'Connell, *The Shared Journey: an Introduction to Encounter* (Englewood Cliffs, N.J.: Prentice-Hall, 1970). More than this, it is possible to list a number of explicitly radical critics of the schools who imply or state explicitly that their educational proposals are to be conjoined with modifications of political and economic institutions in the larger society. Without exception, they reject behaviorism, opting for the sort of educational climate forwarded by Rogers, Maslow, Combs et al., rather than that of Skinner. Books in this category, written mainly for a lay audience but given some attention by professionals, are Ronald Gross and Beatrice Gross, eds., *Radical School Reform* (New York: Simon and Schuster, 1969), Neil Postman and Charles Weingartner, *Teaching as a Subversive Activity* (New York: Delacorte Press, 1969), George Dennison, *The Lives of Children* (New York: Random House, 1969), James Herndon, *The Way It Spozed to Be* (New York: Simon and Schuster, 1969), Herbert Kohl, *36 Children* (New York: New American Library, 1967), Jonathan Kozol, *Death at an Early Age* (Boston: Houghton Mifflin Co., 1967), Peter Schrag, *Village School Downtown* (Boston: Beacon Press, 1967), and John Holt, *How Children Fail* (New York: Pitman Publishing Corp., 1964).

Index

Abilities, differing, 50–52
Absolutes, 28, 36, 47, 71, 79–80, 83, 115, 121, 123, 219, 240
Action, social, 99–101
Activity, problem-solving, 127–29
Adaptability, 83, 109, 248
Adler, Mortimer, 34, 37n., 40n., 45n., 48n., 49, 52, 67, 181
Aesthetics, 88
Africa, 139
Alienation, 240
Allport, Gordon, 22, 219, 226–29, 234
American Council on Education Psychological Examination, 93
American Psychological Association, 177
Anarchy, 79, 88, 241
Anti-intellectualism, 4, 14
Aquinas, Saint Thomas, 36, 80
Aristotle, 29, 31, 32–33, 36, 74
Artist-planners, 102
Artists, 89–90
Asia, 139
Association for Supervision and Curriculum Development, 248–49
Astronomy, 9
Attendance, compulsory school, 62
Augustine, Saint, 36
Authoritarianism, 4, 7, 83, 87–88, 126, 160, 247

Auto-instructional technique, 186, 191
Automation, 169, 204
Autonomy, functional, 227, 232
Awareness, organic, method of, 90

Babbitt, Irving, 34, 37n., 41n.
Barnard, Henry, 3, 7
Beale, Howard K., 4
Beard, Charles, 9, 81n.
Becker, Carl, 9, 80–81
Becoming, process of, 219, 226–29, 240
Behavior, 39, 75, 77, 199
    reinforced, 179
Behaviorism, 21, 178. See also Neo-behaviorism
Belief, fixing of, 125
Beliefs, public inspection of, 107–10
Bellamy, Edward, 95
Bergamini, David B., 164 n.
Biological Sciences Curriculum Study (BSCS), 146, 164, 170
Biology, 9, 64, 151, 154, 170–71
Bloomfield, Leonard, 172
Bode, Boyd H., 70, 104, 105–106, 118
Bosanquet, Bernard, 235
Botany, 9
Brameld, Theodore, 70, 101, 104
Branching programming, 206–208

267